Sporting Doubles

Sporting Doubles

A Gallery of Great Sportsmen
who Represented their Country
at More than One Sport

Foreword by Lord Cowdrey

Jeremy Malies

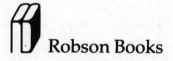

Robson Books

First published in Great Britain in 1998 by Robson Books Ltd,
Bolsover House, 5–6 Clipstone Street, London W1P 8LE

Copyright © 1998 Jeremy Malies
The right of Jeremy Malies to be identified as author of this work has been
asserted by him in accordance with the Copyright, Designs and Patents Act
1988

British Library Cataloguing in Publication Data
A catalogue record for this title is available from the British Library

ISBN 1–86105–230–8

Typeset by David Onyett, Publishing & Production Services, Cheltenham.
Printed in Great Britain.

In memory of
Chris Summers

Contents

FOREWORD   vii

ACKNOWLEDGEMENTS   viii

INTRODUCTION   ix

Chapter 1   SAMUEL WOODS   1

Chapter 2   ERIC LIDDELL   13

Chapter 3   DENIS COMPTON   25

Chapter 4   MILDRED ZAHARIAS   37

Chapter 5   ALBERT HORNBY   47

Chapter 6   REGINALD 'SNOWY' BAKER   61

Chapter 7   CHARLES BURGESS FRY   75

Chapter 8   CHARLOTTE 'LOTTIE' DOD   91

Chapter 9   MAURICE TURNBULL   100

Chapter 10   JOHNNY DOUGLAS   112

Chapter 11   THE HON. ALFRED LYTTELTON   124

Chapter 12   'PATSY' HENDREN   133

Chapter 13   REGINALD SPOONER   141

Chapter 14   KENNETH GANDAR-DOWER   153

Chapter 15   FRANK MITCHELL   164

Chapter 16   ANDREW STODDART   174

Chapter 17   REGINALD FOSTER   185

Foreword by Lord Cowdrey

Denis Compton was everyone's hero – he was certainly mine at the age of 12 towards the end of the war. He was such an outstanding cricketer and footballer, and seemed to enjoy it all so much, giving enormous pleasure to spectators.

I only saw him a few times on the cricket field, and each time I was lucky. But I saw him play a lot of football, on the left wing in wartime matches, and later, of course, with Arsenal.

With a few school friends, I would spend every waking minute outside the classroom playing cricket or football. Understandably the inspiration I received from watching Compton sparked in me the desire to be a double international – cricket and football for England. It proved to be too tough a target, but I was just so lucky to achieve one of my ambitions.

Most young sportsmen with a good eye and a gift of timing soon get a measure of playing all ball games naturally, and to those without such clear gifts, it can all seem rather unfair. But breaking through to the top requires the extra powers of concentration, learning to live with disappointments, keeping a high level of fitness, retaining enthusiasm for the 'rough and tumble' and staying young in heart.

Of the unusual double and multiple internationals here, C. B. Fry was the one who most caught my imagination. Cricket, rugby, soccer and athletics for Oxford University, as well as finding time to equal the world long jump record. Later he was to captain England against Australia at Lord's. He was surely one of the greatest all-round British sportsmen.

When I started playing for Kent, H. A. Pawson was a fine cricketer, supremely fit and fast between the wickets. He had taken Charlton Athletic to a Cup Final at Wembley and had won amateur international caps. Over the last 20 years he has been our top fly fisherman and the world champion – a unique double international.

This is a fascinating subject, as this splendid book demonstrates.

I do hope that our great British sportsmen of the future will be allowed the time and opportunity to excel at more than one sport. They will find a lot more fun out of having a rest from one occasionally. For the others in the team there is the added interest of meeting and playing alongside such talented all-round athletes.

Colin Cowdrey

Acknowledgements

These essays followed a suggestion by Chris Summers and articles by Frank Keating in *Punch*. I have doggedly tracked the biographical footsteps of David Frith who was unstinting in the help he gave me. Special gratitude is due to Fred Inglis whose vision colours everything I write.

For general encouragement, I must mention Rob Boddie, librarian at Sussex CCC, and Norman Epps, statistician (and much more) at the same. Richard de Costobadie was a source of consistent advice and material help. Jim Swanton extended an avuncular wing and was unfailingly kind.

The following have all given support: Harry Carpenter; Alistair Cooke; Douglas Fairbanks Jnr.; Vivian Jenkins; Sir Tim Rice, Lord Cowdrey; Lord Briggs; the Rt Rev. David Sheppard; Barry Norman; Ern Toovey; David Smith; Norris McWhirter; Nigel Coster; Ron Coello; Graham Thorpe; Viv Thompson; Brian O'Gorman; Michael Wolton of the MCC Library, David Guilford of Eton College; John Mitchell of St Peter's School; Rex King of the English RFU; Greig Thomas of the Australian RFU; Jane Frazer of the New Zealand RFU; John Mulford of the New South Wales RFU; Kathi Spinks of the New South Wales State Library; John Parsons of the *Daily Telegraph*; Kevin Mitchell of the *Observer*; Michael Owen-Smith of the *Cape Times* and Andy Brooks of *Sports Illustrated*. David Sampson sent much priceless material from Australia and was patient and consistently charming. Georgina and Olive Turnbull contributed to the chapter on Maurice Turnbull.

Hugh Brodie of Blackheath RFC was hugely supportive. Edward Spooner provided invaluable information about his father. Jack Foster, Virginia Wynn Jones (née Foster), June Fisher (née Foster) and George Chesterton assisted with the chapter on R. E. Foster. Hugh Hornby contributed to the chapter on A. N. Hornby.

Roger Kay, John Deverill, Rob Marshall, Andy Cheesman, Tony Harris and Andrew Briggs also gave support.

Thanks finally to Russell Levinson, an old school friend, and Oliver Andrew, an old schoolmaster. They have both spent hours polishing the manuscript and have made good some spectacular deficiencies.

Introduction

Many of these essays deal with the amateurs of the Golden Age, a period which has been delimited by the early 1890s and the outbreak of the Great War. Despite this core subject matter, I hope to avoid the cheery platitude that the turn of the century saw cricket and other games at a summit from which they have since only descended. It's a myopic stance and one that has undermined so much that has been written about sport ever since. In the 1990s a generation of ex-cricketers-turned-journalists have constructed their own 'Golden Age', and the same kind of spurious nostalgia has emerged in the narcosis of the 'bowled four of them an over in my day' school of radio commentary.

My source materials have covered a bizarre gamut from Arthur Ashe's history of black American athletes to the autobiography of Beatrice Lillie. From these, the list of major double internationals soon topped 400. Naturally my choices are the result of personal prejudice. Any attempt at a comprehensive treatment would be as protracted as Mr Dick's Memorial.

While some of the subjects have been chronicled before, they are still far from being worked-out seams. Most of these athletes have never received so much as an occasional essay. The more familiar figures remain seminal and cannot be excluded. Thus, in the career of C. B. Fry, one detects not only the acme of dilettantism but also the first death-rattle of amateurism.

The sports tend to be cricket with either rugby or soccer. There are, however, some more extravagant combinations, one of the more notable being Charles Wreford-Brown's international appearances as a foot-baller and chess player. Wreford-Brown is the first in a surprising number of links between chess and football. Anybody who can remember the Norwegian football side of the late 1980s might be surprised to learn that its centre forward, Simon Agdestein, went on to become a chess grandmaster. (Agdestein once commented that playing Anatoly Karpov was more intimidating than being marked by Franco Baresi.)

The dearth of present-day double internationals is the result of professionalism, longer seasons, rigorous training and the disappearance of the leisured class. Despite these overwhelming factors, a frequent response may well be: 'Of course they don't make them like that anymore.'

The truth is that they do. While many people are aware that Viv Richards played football for Antigua, it will be an eye opener for them to learn that Graham Thorpe played three schoolboy football internationals in 1987. Had he been playing at the turn of the century, Thorpe might have joined the ranks of senior double internationals. The fact that Jeff Wilson, the All Blacks winger, once played limited-overs cricket for New Zealand has been well publicized. A more obscure detail is that Jonty Rhodes has been close to selection for the South African hockey team and would certainly have won a cap had his allegiance not switched to cricket.

Having conceded that the era of the double international has gone, perhaps we should look for its high noon. This may well have come in 1922 when Leo Price trotted out for the England rugby and hockey teams on successive Saturday afternoons.

From an earlier era, the roster of sporting double internationals includes the imposing figure of Dr. W. G. Grace. Amid the hoopla currently surrounding the 150th anniversary of his birth, few have reflected that in addition to being a superb hurdler and pole vaulter, Grace played lawn bowls for England on six occasions at the turn of the century.

The palm for England dual internationals will always be caps for the full national sides at cricket and football. Fourteen men hold this distinction and three are represented here. Two of the fourteen (Willie Watson and Arthur Milton) have been omitted for the simple and gratifying reason that they are still with us. A recent loss, Denis Compton, did not win a full cap at football but played in wartime internationals. Only a pedant would quibble over his presence here.

J. W. H. T. Douglas found a place on the strength of 23 Test matches for England and an Olympic gold medal for boxing. (His appearance for an England amateur football team in 1913 elevates him to the status of a treble international but was no more than a brief distraction in a hectic life.) Douglas's extraordinary career ended in 1930 when he drowned in a shipping accident so unnecessary and farcical that it beggars belief. His boxing gold in the 1908 Olympics had been gained at the expense of a quadruple international and perhaps the richest character in these essays. A scoundrel of the first chop, Reginald 'Snowy' Baker remains the greatest all-round sportsman produced by Australia.

Albert Hornby and Andrew Stoddart are the only men to have captained England at cricket and rugby and they have both been included. Stoddart blew his brains out with a duelling pistol in 1915 and is a salutary reminder that sporting success can be followed by failure in other walks of life. His end was only marginally more tragic than that of his contemporary, Gregor MacGregor. Having kept wicket for England in eight Test matches and played as a rugby full-back for Scotland thirteen times, MacGregor's descent into alcoholism was excruciating. Another Scottish rugby player, Eric Liddell, is treated in detail and while the chapter hovers between sports history and film criticism, it attempts to redress a spate of indifferent biographies.

There are many tragic figures, none more so than Reginald Foster. He is perhaps the most notable dual international of them all, being the only man to have captained England at cricket and football. Foster died of diabetes at the age of 36. His 287 at Sydney in 1903 remains the highest Test score by an Englishman in Australia.

Major omissions include Wilf Wooller. He is often said to have been desperately unlucky not to have been a Test cricketer and thus a double international. Wooller matched seventeen appearances for Wales at rugby with over 13,000 runs in first-class cricket, many of them in the finest company. His rugby career was cut short by the war (which he spent on the Burma-Siam railway building bridges for the Japanese) but he had in fact won dual honours back in 1938 when he played international squash.

Only two men have won football and rugby caps for England, J. W. Sutcliffe and C. P. Wilson. An engaging pedagogue, Charles Plumpton Wilson turned out as a forward for the England rugby side against Wales in 1881. Three years later he played football at right-back against Scotland and Wales. At Cambridge he found time to win a cricket blue and compete in a 25-mile bicycle race against Oxford. As an innovative schoolmaster, he later took charge of Sandroyd School where his more starry-eyed pupils included Sir Anthony Eden.

There are few conclusions here and the research has thrown up only one frequent attribute, an element of ambidexterity. A search for further unifying factors has proved quite fruitless and is beside the point. The subject of double internationals has simply provided a framework for a book on athletes who have been largely neglected by sports historians.

Some of the anecdotes are hoary old chestnuts but they remain evocative. Occasionally they are being dusted down against my better judgement; they are tendered with apologies to those who find them gratingly familiar. Heroes live longer than history, perhaps they are truer than history. At the height of their careers, most of these athletes were the subject of idolatry that verged on deification. Find somebody old enough to have sporting memories stretching back to before the Second World War. If you ask them to list their heroes, you will get a selection that features some of the personnel here. Anybody who omits them is an amnesiac.

Jeremy Malies
Peacehaven, East Sussex
1997–8

'There are some men, otherwise most respectable, who commit bigamy with sport.'

R. C. Robertson-Glasgow, *Cricket Prints*, 1948

'To say that Waterloo was won on the playing fields of Eton is not to say that Napoleon might have been saved by a crash course in cricket.'

Joan Didion, *Slouching Towards Bethlehem*, 1968

'You see what I'm looking for is not someone to start me thinking, but someone to stop me: someone who, before I know what I'm doing, will have made me clasp my hands together instinctively in an attitude of total worship.'

David Baddiel, *Evening Standard*, April, 1994

1

Samuel Woods

b. 13 April 1867, d. 30 April 1931

*'We restrict the word "integrity" to people either simple or complex,
who have a strong sense of righteousness or, if they are public men, of
self-righteousness. Yet it surely means no more than what it says:
wholeness, being free to be spontaneous, without reck of consistency
or moral appearances. It can be as true of forlorn and bewildered
people as of the disciplined and the solemn.'*

Alistair Cooke, *America Observed*, 1988

The subject is a colossus, a man who as an undergraduate not only
played for Australia versus England at cricket but for England versus
Wales at rugby. Later he would captain England at rugby and play
cricket for England against South Africa. Sam was childlike in his
freshness and simplicity, and there are as many stories concerning
him as there are about W. G. He is a myth-maker's dream. Years after
his death, grown men would swap Sam Woods anecdotes in the way
that children trade cigarette cards or autographs. The treatment here
will become a patchwork of anecdotes but they breathe more life into
the man than a sackful of statistics.

He was born at Ashfield, Sydney, into a family of 13. His father,
John, had emigrated from Ireland and made a fortune freighting
lumber on the burgeoning Australian railways. He was a pioneer of
lawn bowls in New South Wales and a successful and popular Lord
Mayor of Sydney. A benevolent autocrat, Woods senior doted on his
sons, buying all of them cornets. For Sam the music lessons were not
a success and his repertoire never extended beyond *Killarney*.

The family lived on Manly Beach and Sam took the ferry to Sydney
every day. During the journey he would spar with one of the deck-
hands, Peter Jackson. In his autobiography, Sam recalls how in 1892
he was in a London crowd that saw Jackson beat Frank Slavin for the
unofficial heavyweight championship of the world. Jackson became
an intimate of the family, regularly skippering their boat. The Woods

entourage spent Christmas in Fiji where Sam once stole a stone god. On discovering their loss, the natives pursued the family schooner in canoes.

Fijian natives, music masters and cricket opponents alike were relieved when Sam was sent to England in his early teens where he entered Brighton College in the Christmas term of 1884. Walter Parnell-Smith recalls that when Sam arrived he asked if the college had a good cricket team. On receiving a non-committal reply, he responded: 'You'll have a better one next year.' He had been brought up on rugby, and was distraught to find that the college played soccer. Fully grown he would be a shade over six foot in his socks and, with hands like buckets, he turned himself into a first-rate goal-keeper.

After only two weeks of serious competition, Sam played in goal for the college XI against Burgess Hill. (Playing on the left wing for Burgess Hill was a future England Test captain and Hollywood idol, Aubrey Smith.) The college lost 7–1 but its magazine is positive about Sam's performance. 'Woods's services were frequently needed, and, although at times he appeared not to exert himself sufficiently, his goalkeeping was decidedly good.' The end of season review is lavish: 'An immense acquisition to the eleven; his defence is always strong, and often brilliant.' However, Sam found goalkeeping cold and lonely, and he soon switched to full-back. As a schoolboy cricketer he was prodigious, and in 1885 he took 59 wickets at an average of 8.44. In the 1886 Brighton College athletics meeting, he came second in the shot put and the hammer with distances of 31' 8½" and 84' 2". At long-jump he achieved 16' 6".

Sam's father came over in 1886 to check on his son. Lord Harris recalls how Woods Senior would waylay him on Brighton sea front with reports about his marvellous boy. In all Sam represented Brighton College at cricket, soccer and fives. He remained on the fringe of the college's intellectual activities but contributed to the Art Society, and his picture of a cat chasing some mice earned commendation. Again the college magazine reveals that at an end of term concert, Sam appeared as Gower in an extract from *Henry V*. He had one line: 'Enough, Captain, you have astonished him.' If it remained with him as a quotation, it could at least have been used on the cricket field, perhaps to cap one of W. G.'s excesses.

When he left school, Sam received strict orders from his father back in Sydney. He could try for university but initially he was to spend a year in business. Sam began as an office boy in a bank but left when it was discovered that he could not balance the stamp book. His first

Varsity application was to Oriel, Oxford, who rejected him on the grounds of his spelling and grammar. They might have been more lenient: the Dark Blues never won a Varsity cricket match while Sam was in residence at Cambridge and never topped 200 in an innings. In his four Varsity matches, Sam took 36 Oxford wickets for 318 runs.

He arrived at Jesus in the autumn of 1887. At freshers' fair, he bet a friend that he would be a double blue in his first year. (He had not even decided whether the winter blue would be rugby or soccer.) Sam collected: he became a fixture at wing-forward in the rugby XV and walked into the cricket XI. Academically, he spent his time on a knife-edge though his charm allowed him to soft-shoe his way through vivas. Cardus once said that Sam had his learning from nature and not from books. Randolph Hodgson recalls how despondency spread across the town when it became known that Sam was likely to fail his Part IIs: 'The possibility of such tragedy struck the university to its foundations.' Hodgson remembers Sam in the examination hall: 'He wore a short and tattered gown – an ancient, battered college cap … He appeared to write but little. He seemed to spend the short time he remained within the Corn Exchange in biting his pen. Then, frowning gloomily, he would stride forth… It was said that, in one paper, he had written nothing at all except his name and college.'

Alan Ross picks up the story at the resulting viva: 'The examiners were lenient, and only asked Sam two questions. The first was his name. The second was "What was the name of the first king of Israel?" Sam, who had been doing some desperate if belated study, triumphantly replied "Saul", and was allowed to depart. Dazzled by success, he spoilt the effect by turning round at the door – he did not want all that work to be wasted – and added "Also called Paul".'

The Varsity cricket match of 1888 was ruined by rain. In their only innings, Oxford were reduced to 124 with Sam taking 6 for 48. As a first-year undergraduate, he not only played for the Gentlemen against the Players but also represented Australia in all three Tests against England. At Lord's, with four wickets in hand, the Players needed seven runs to win. Amid mounting hysteria, Sam and Aubrey Smith bowled out the professionals for the addition of one run. Sam's bowling in the Tests was accurate but uninspired. He took 5 wickets at an average cost of 24.2.

In the 1889 Varsity game, he was a shade more expensive than in the previous year. He took 6 for 42 from 20 overs and Cambridge won by an innings. There were nine ducks from Oxford, two of them contributed by Malcolm Jardine, father of Douglas. A. G. Steel raved about Sam in *Wisden*: '… far and away the finest fast bowler

Cambridge has had for many years'. Despite heavy rain, Cambridge coasted to a seven-wicket victory in 1890, and Sammy shared the bowling honours with E. C. Streatfeild.

By now Sam was rooming with the Cambridge wicket-keeper Gregor MacGregor. MacGregor would also become a double inter-national, going on to play Test cricket and represent Scotland many times at rugby. On the morning of the fixture against C. I. Thornton's XI (essentially the Gentlemen of England), Sam treated himself to a breakfast of lobsters and beer. With the lobsters hardly settled, he took all ten wickets for 69 runs.

Having skittled out the best amateur talent in the country, Sam returned to college for dinner. The news had spread and 'Red' Morgan, the Master of Jesus, walked into Hall. Morgan congratulated Sam, adding: 'I wish, Mr Woods you were as proficient with your pen as you are with the ball. I do not believe you know the meaning of the motto of this college which you may notice is inscribed over the door.' The motto in question was SEMPER EADEM (always the same). Still thinking of the lobsters, Sam looked up at the inscription and said in his quiet drawl: 'Yes I do, Mr Morgan, that's the menu.'

Morgan had never forgiven Sam for disrupting one of his wife's garden parties. Sam could turn the most solemn occasion into a Ralph Reader Gang Show, and striding into the party, he noted that Mrs Morgan had hired a cornet player. The cornet player compounded her mistake by playing *Killarney*. The rest can be guessed; Sam's performance was unmelodic and unwelcome. His last Varsity game in 1891 was his most spectacular and he took 7 for 60, forcing Oxford to follow-on. Set a paltry 90 runs to win, the Cambridge batsmen floundered in bad light. They needed two runs when Berkeley bowled Streatfeild and then MacGregor with the scores tied. Sam ran out of the pavilion without bothering to pad up and flicked the first delivery for a one-bounce four.

At rugby, Sam was picked thirteen times for England. According to W. G., he was 'not a good scrimmager' though the *Morning Post* describes him as 'not above doing his share of shoving when it was wanted'. In the loose and in breaking from the scrum, his pace was electric. He broke eleven seconds for 100 yards and describes himself as 'difficult to handle in the open'. One of his few faults was a tendency to make rash attempts at drop goals. He appears to have been capable of rising to whatever the occasion demanded. For Blackheath against Bradford at Park Avenue, Sam found himself the object of some vigorous attention on the part of two opponents. 'What's this you're at?' demanded Sam. 'It's alright,' one of them replied. 'We were told to look after you.' 'Oh! That's your game,' said Sam. Both of the markers were carried off some ten minutes later when Sam slipped one of their combined tackles and two Yorkshire skulls met violently.

Like Dickie Bird (as a player rather than an umpire), Sammy would give his kit away after a bad run. Recalling Sam's team spirit, Frank Mitchell describes how in 1895 England were given a pasting by Scotland. As captain, Sammy was so disappointed he gave away his boots. He was back against Ireland in a new pair two weeks later. The *Somerset County Herald* for December 1897 reports how, having retired from rugby for over a year, Sam promised to help Somerset against Devon. He pulled out a couple of days before complaining that he could not get fit. Reserves were summoned but Sam turned up with his bag just before kick-off and looked into the changing-room. He was plied with reminiscences and within minutes he was unlacing his shoes and asking if he could borrow a pair of pants. Naturally he played a blinder.

Sam is often described as the father of modern wing-forward play. On his retirement he continued his involvement with rugby and did much to improve the scrummaging of the Somerset colts. Back in 1890, he had been a founding member of the Barbarians and he retained a keen interest in the club. Hugh Alison describes how Sam once took the Somerset juniors to Oxford. Alison and Sam took the boys out one evening. Alison retired early but the colts and their mentor returned to college after lock-out. Sam appeared at breakfast with a bandaged hand. Alison recalls the conversation: 'What's happened, Sam?' 'Oh, nothing much,' answered Sammy. 'I was helping my lads over the wall when a beastly little townee came up and wanted to know what I was doing, so I said, "Can't you see? I'm helping these chaps over the wall." "Yus," the townee said, "and if you don't give me something I shall split on you." 'So,' said Sammy, rubbing his injured hand, 'I gave him something.'

At cricket Sam played for Somerset for 21 years from 1886. He was phenomenally quick but was often erratic. Here is C. B. Fry's summation of the finished bowler: 'In his prime Mr Woods was one of the greatest of fast bowlers, and was perhaps the most scientific and artistic of that class who has yet appeared ...' For Randolph Hodgson, his action was 'the embodiment of strength and virile grace'. Sam possessed a well-disguised slower ball and a devastating yorker which he could bowl at will. He was always lively even when rheumatism set in and batsmen often found themselves playing him off the splice.

As arthritis encroached, Sam dropped his pace. He developed his batting, and while the shoulders became hunched, a shambling gait could not disguise massive dignity. Sam mixed bouts of lacerating attack with studied defence. His timing was excellent but he played with stiff wrists and scored predominantly through straight drives. As a fielder he was brilliant at cover-point and fearless during occasional spells at silly-point. His captaincy style was bustling and aggressive. For Ranji, he was 'the best captain imaginable'. Sam treated amateur and pro alike; occasional admonishments were fair and handled with a minimum of fuss. However, as a selector he was occasionally criticized for being unwilling to recruit talent from outside the county.

In the winter of 1891, he toured the United States with a group of amateurs including Herbert Hewett, Charles Wreford-Brown and George Ricketts. All three were appalling sailors and spent much of the outward voyage in their bunks. Sam was concerned, and he dragged the trio upstairs for a dinner of champagne and vegetable soup. His plans went awry when, spotting the soup, an American who was also suffering from seasickness, remarked, 'Say, steward, did you bring this up or did I?' Sam's invalids returned below deck promptly. On the field, Sam performed well with the ball. Many of the games were against teams of up to 22 players. Occasionally deputizing for Lord Hawke (who is alleged to have taken to his bed after eating too many oysters), Sammy was a hit on the dance floor, though in Philadelphia, his over-enthusiasm in a quickstep inflicted a black eye on a partner.

1893 proved an appalling year for Somerset. The county was hard pushed to put up an XI and Sam assisted by gathering together his army of godsons. He took over the captaincy in the following season and remained in charge until 1906. In 1895 Sam and F. S. Jackson bowled unchanged for the Gentlemen from start of play till early evening without a tea interval. As captain, W. G. was criticized for flogging his opening bowlers. (Grace had in fact suggested that he was going to replace Sam, at which Sam had the temerity to tell the Doctor that his bowling was not needed.)

At Hove in June 1895, Sam played his finest innings: 215 not out in two and a half hours. For once he scored all-round the wicket and he was particularly severe on Walter Humphreys. By now he had qualified to play for England and the innings brought him a place on Lord Hawke's tour to South Africa. Soon after their arrival in South Africa, the tourists drove to Grahamstown where they stayed in a farmhouse. In the morning they awoke to find several dozen pigs in their bedrooms. It was the kind of incident that must have got up the patrician nose of Lord Hawke but Sammy found it a scream. C. B. Fry and Sam had shared a cabin on the way out. Charmed by his many eccentricities, Fry adored Sam.

Hawke's party landed in Cape Town just as the country became inflamed by the Jameson Raid. The team was sent north in the hope that cricket might ease political tension. Sam and company arrived in Johannesburg to find that the Wanderers ground had become a hospital. After a few days the tourists were diverted to Pretoria, only a few miles from where the raid had been aborted. Fry and Sammy rode out to inspect the scene. Fry describes Sammy's mount: 'They gave Sammy Woods a known buck-jumper to ride ... Sammy was hurt, but not from falling off. He said, "I suppose you think that this blighter can buck. Let me tell you he's only a pig-rooter."' The players were taken to see Paul Krüger who affected not to speak English and had to be addressed through an interpreter. Krüger was bemused and unimpressed by the presence of cricketers at such a time, and he remained monosyllabic. Only Lord Hawke and Sammy had the nerve to attempt conversation, Sam reflecting afterwards that 'the old blighter was not very hearty'.

After the trip to Pietermaritzburg, Lord Hawke's party offended the hosts by arriving late at a concert. Sammy was in a frisky mood and smoothed things over with his singing. A single verse from Sam's favourite Gus Elen number suffices:

'It really is a very pretty garden,
And 'Ampstead from the 'ousetops can be seen.
With a pair of opera glasses
You can see to 'Ackney Marshes
If it wasn't for the 'ouses in between.'

Later in Pietermaritzburg, Sammy and Fry formed part of a polo team which beat the local Hussars. His team was on foot and equipped with sawn-off mallets resembling hockey sticks. On the way out of King William's Town, C. B. and Sammy visited an ostrich farm. Fry sustained significant injuries when Sammy persuaded him to pluck a tail feather from a cock ostrich. The ostrich was unamused and it pursued Fry for 100 yards at the end of which the future pretender to the throne of Albania had to fling himself through a wire fence. (Fry became furious a few minutes later when he saw Sam offering the ostrich a bun.)

The tourists were undefeated in serious matches, winning all three Tests at a canter. Sam was successful with bat and ball. He made a half-century at Port Elizabeth and his batting average was over 30, while with the ball he took 5 wickets at an average of 25. He always believed that his batting was under-used and he would enquire of Lord Hawke at the beginning of every innings: 'Who's coming in first with me, Martin?'

Sam acted as Assistant Secretary at Somerset for much of the 1890s. The position was a sinecure, allowing the county to keep him at Taunton by treating him as a professional. He was numerate in the most basic sense, and he is often described as a superb whist player. However, he had no knowledge of accounting and little business acumen. This and his appalling level of literacy prevented him from doing any serious work.

Somerset's performance in 1899 was dire, and by now rheumatism had reduced Sam to a trundler. This did not stop him touring the States in the following winter. The outward trip was made in a foul-smelling boat, the *Etruria*. The atmosphere was not improved by the scent of Sammy's cheroot cigars which he smoked all day, beginning at the breakfast table. He was successful as a bowler, snaffling the wickets of several high-class batsmen, but his batting proved abysmal. His aggregate for the tour was 48 runs and in his speech at the farewell banquet, Sam computed his runs against the miles he had travelled, concluding that his scoring was the equivalent of .0012 run per mile.

During a light-hearted game at Bridgwater in 1902, having been buoyed up by some 1876 port, he took all ten wickets for 25 with underarm lobs. Earlier in the year he had visited his family in Australia, ensuring that the trip coincided with MacLaren's Ashes tour. Syd Barnes broke down before the fourth Test and Sam's name appeared on the England team-sheet. He was well past his best and had deep reservations about playing. These were resolved when a few days before the game he caught a chill at the Turkish baths.

In 1907 Sam turned out for Albert Trott's benefit in which Trott took two hat-tricks, so abbreviating the game and, as he put it, 'bowling himself into the workhouse'. With much solemnity, Sammy presented Trott with a straw hatband which he had decorated with a picture of seven rabbits scurrying into their warrens. Trott wore it for the rest of the season. A life-long critic of the stone-waller, it is reported how in a club match, Sam watched a monumentally defensive batsman poking about for over an hour. Sam was asked to dispose of him. Marking out his run he enquired: 'Where will you have it, over the heart, or over the head?' Gilbert Jessop records that the batsman 'lost his wicket the same over, being unfortunate in the matter of a desperately short run'.

Sam's sporting achievements outside cricket and rugby were legion. At soccer he was playing in goal for Sussex within a few weeks of joining Brighton College. He would go on to play for Somerset, Bridgwater Albion and the Corinthians. As a Somerset soccer player, he played at every position from goalkeeper to centre-forward. There is little doubt that he would have been a soccer international had rugby not appealed more. He began playing golf at Burnham and Berrow in 1893, and he took lessons from J. H. Taylor. Working with talented raw material, Taylor, who would win the British Open the following year, soon brought Sammy's handicap down to two.

Sam's charm and general athleticism made him the most popular sportsman in Somerset. He was good looking despite a Desperate Dan chin, and the lady members of Bridgwater Hockey Club insisted that he should captain the newly formed mixed team. Sam brought soccer tactics and fitness to the game. He trained the side himself and for two years, with Sam as centre-forward, it was unbeaten. In later years, his sporting interests widened and he represented Somerset at skittles and billiards. He became a bowls enthusiast in his fifties and played regularly with W. G. Grace at Bridgwater where he helped to establish the town's bowling club.

At the outbreak of the First World War, Sam concealed his age and was in colours by October 1914. He started as a lieutenant with the Somerset Light Infantry in St Austell's where he was appalled by a profusion of teetotallers and Methodists. Sam found himself involved in one of the more ludicrous of the Allied campaigns a few months later, as British battleships sustained horrific losses from submarine attack in the Dardanelles. There had been a notable casualty early on in the campaign when a sub-lieutenant died at Lemnos of sunstroke and blood poisoning. He had been the most successful bowler at Rugby School in 1906, taking 19 wickets at an average of 14.05. Beloved by contemporaries ranging from Henry James to Ezra Pound, he had already written a sonnet which advised them how to remember him. His name was Rupert Brooke.

In a blazing summer, Sam's ship was needed urgently elsewhere. The Hindu stokers had keeled over in the heat and volunteer shifts of seven men were sent down. Sam went into the inferno of a boiler room with six cadets all in their early twenties. After half-an-hour the cadets were carried away senseless. Sam trimmed the coal like an expert for six hours until he had to be dragged away. He was 47 years old. Later he found himself in Khartoum where – incredibly, given his lack of education – he acted as censor. Sam was finally sent home suffering from malaria. He recovered and moved to the Royal Devon Regiment where he finished as a captain in the Labour Corps. He had also spent time in Egypt where a rheumatic hip was worsened by a fall from a runaway camel. Sam revealed to Raymond Robertson-Glasgow: 'I was in charge of a bunch of those sods when they stampeded and made for a cactus forest; so off I rolled, and fell a bit wrong.'

As a consumer of whisky Sam is rivalled among Test cricketers only by Warwick Armstrong. He is said to have drunk a bottle a day and he would rub it into his calves as a cure for cramp. He made sure, however, that younger players drank nothing stronger than beer: 'Whisky and one o'clock in the morning won't suit you, my dear.' In the good times Sam put up at the George Inn, but for long periods his lodgings were little better than hostels. He was hopeless with money and the alcohol made dents in a modest income though he always had a present for the children he met on his daily round of Taunton.

> **If you wanted to know Taunton, you walked round it with Sammy Woods on a summer morning before the match. Sam was Somerset's godfather. He was a lover of life and of nearly all things living. On those walks, he would take you into the back-parlours of little shops and enquire after the youngest son's measles, and whether it had been decided to put Tom into the cornhandling trade. 'Much better let him be a farmer, Missis,' Sam would say,'and marry a fat wife who can look after his money. For he won't, no more than I could my dear.'**

> R. C. Robertson-Glasgow, *46 Not Out*, 1948

Sam retained his strength into late middle-age. In 1923, Somerset won the county rugby championship. The semi-final at Taunton was jeopardized when the Tone burst its banks and the ground flooded. The solution was obvious and we have seen how well he could handle a shovel. At the age of 56, he and a crony emptied every bunker at a nearby golf course. They carried three tons of sand to the ground and the match went ahead. Sam resigned from his position as Secretary of Somerset CC in this year, amid much bad feeling. Despite success on the field, the club's finances were unusually rocky and there was a need for rationalization. Having failed to balance a stamp book, Sam was hardly able to manage the finances of a first-class county.

There are apocryphal accounts of how Sam once saved two lives on a shark-infested beach in Australia. These can be dismissed: on his visits home he rarely strayed from Sydney where such attacks are rare. What is undisputed and narrated in family records is that his physical condition deteriorated in his late fifties after he plunged into the Channel on a winter's day to save a young boy from drowning. He was a strong swimmer, and at Brighton College he had won prizes for diving.

Rarely standing on ceremony, Sam addressed everybody (even W. G.), as 'my dear'. Like the Doctor, Sam was an inveterate practical joker and one of his more high-spirited shenanigans involved attaching a baby's bell to the belt of an opponent. He was often over-boisterous, and on the eve of a Varsity match, while engaged in horseplay with Gregor MacGregor, he knocked the latter clean through a plate-glass window.

As Henry Longhurst once said of Bobby Jones, Sam was 'an uncomplicated man who simply stood up and gave it one'. As a batsman his technique was never subjected to conscious refinement nor did his tactics as a captain stem from calculation. His batting and bowling gave the spectator immediate and simple pleasure, and his hand to eye co-ordination was prodigious.

Sam was never entirely happy unless he was in the open air, and Cardus recalls that when it rained he 'was a lorn, restless soul who chafed like a leashed dog'.

In his youth he hunted on horseback. Later, like W. G., he followed foot beagles and the Doctor often joined him. On such expeditions, Sammy would wait till he and a companion were miles from anywhere and enquire if his friend wanted a cold beer. Having received an understandably pointed answer, Sam would reach into a bush or a stream and produce a couple of bottles; he secreted them all over the county. An occasional if erratic marksman, Sam claimed to have shot at different times grouse, keepers and retrievers.

Obituaries in the local press recall how Sam proved a mainspring of social life in Bridgwater where he served as chairman of the Guy Fawkes carnival. He would get up on stage at concerts and murder Albert Chevalier songs in his rich baritone, often forgetting the words and improvising outrageously. C. B. Fry recalls that having mounted the rostrum, Sammy was unselfconscious and the only debate was whether he would ever step down from the platform.

Not long ago, I met an elderly lady on a railway journey near Taunton. Within five minutes our talk reached Sam. 'Ah,' she said, 'I last met him at a dance when I was eighteen. I had been told I was not to dance with Sam. But I did.'

R. C. Robertson-Glasgow, *46 Not Out*, 1948

With his usual twenty-twenty vision, Benny Green has highlighted this quotation as 'one of the most exquisite dying falls in cricket literature'. Sam died on 30 April 1931. Only his indomitable will had sustained him before he took to his bed. A matter of a few days before, he had been dragging his arthritic limbs into skittle alleys and opining on the crowded county cricket programme. When his condition was made public he received enough fruit to open a stall. The final illness (cancer) was excruciating for onlookers who remembered Sam's immense physicality in his prime. The obituaries are disappointing and few hit the right note. Aware of this, many of Sam's contemporaries attempted their own summation. 'Joseph' writes in *The Times*: 'He may not have been clever or erudite, but he combined the courage of the heroes of old Homer with physical strength and kindliness, and to these was joined the simplicity of a child.'

St John's Church was packed for Sam's funeral and hundreds stood outside in the rain. Close to breaking down, the Somerset wicket-keeper Prebendary Archdale Wickham read the lesson, referring to him repeatedly as 'Smudgy'. In his *Manchester Guardian* obituary, Cardus says he cannot insult Sammy's ghost by quoting statistics. The Test figures are certainly modest and do little to conjure up a naïveté and ardour that are often the hallmarks of a really great and simple man. You can still find the odd person in Taunton who will go rheumy-eyed over Sam Woods. However wild the analogy might seem, the best parallel the writer can find is with Babe Ruth. Here is Paul Gallico on Ruth: 'He played ball on the same enormous scale on which he lived his life, intensely, fervently, and with tremendous sincerity and passion.' Sam's ashes lie in St Mary's Cemetery, Taunton. He remains folkloric.

2
Eric Liddell

b. 16 January 1902, d. 21 February 1945

'But they that wait upon the Lord shall renew their strength; they shall mount up with wings as eagles; they shall run, and not be weary; and they shall walk, and not faint.'

Isaiah 40, v. 31

Eric was born at Tientsin in northern China to a pair of Scottish Congregationalist missionaries. His father, James Liddell, had been a noted gymnast who had given up a career as a draper after being touched with evangelistic fervour in the 1890s. Eric proved delicate as a child, and would regularly burst into tears at the 'Ninety and Nine', a Moody and Sankey hymn which describes the loss of a sheep on a barren mountainside. In 1907, his family returned to Scotland and settled near Loch Lomond. As a six-year-old, Eric was sent to Eltham College. In the next few years he grew in strength and confidence, and at the age of ten he endeared himself to many with his interpretation of the Dormouse in a production of *Alice in Wonderland*.

By 1916 he was showing much skill on the sports field. In 1919 he captained the cricket team and impressed with his fast bowling. Summaries of his rugby performances catalogue steady progress: 'a light wing three-quarter ... gets in some useful kicks' (1916); 'a fast right wing three-quarter ... tackling, kicking and falling on the ball are good ...' (1917); 'His kicking is excellent, and his speed and swerve have decided the issue of several matches ...' (1918). Eric's finest achievements at Eltham, however, were on the track, and in 1918 he clocked 10.8 seconds for the 100 yards, lowering this mark to 10.2 in the following year. Remarkably, as a schoolboy athlete he was overshadowed by Leslie Gracie, the future Scottish rugby captain, who was more versatile and showed greater talent for cricket.

In later years Eric displayed a facility for languages, but in 1919 it was only after intensive cramming in French that he matriculated to take a B.Sc. in Pure Science at Edinburgh University. By the summer of 1920 he had almost given up athletics when he was persuaded to attend training at Powderhall where the university athletes ran with the stadium's greyhounds snapping at their heels. Yet academic work remained his priority, and he was rarely out of the top three in his year. In 1921 he won the 100 and 200 yards at the Scottish Championships and ran an excellent leg to bring his university home in the 4 by 440 yards relay.

Eric played much university rugby in 1920 and 1921. After a successful trial he made his international début against France in January of 1922. The match was played in Paris and the score was one unconverted try apiece. The Scots played an unimaginative game based around their elephantine pack, and there were laughable attempts at place-kicking. Eric played on the left wing, and in the second half he came close to scoring, being smothered while only yards from the line. A few weeks later he lined up against Wales in another moderate game which was locked at nine points all until the closing seconds when the Welsh snatched victory with a drop goal.

In late February, Scotland beat Ireland by two tries to one in gale-force conditions at Edinburgh, and it was Eric who latched on to a Garyowen to give Scotland victory. The wind had blown a Presbyterian minister off the top of a tramcar in the morning, and it made passing almost impossible. The *Scotsman* was dubious about Eric's technical knowledge and noted: 'That he is a great player in the making there is no doubt, but there were times when he showed a rawness in his work and a lack of resource when cornered.'

At Edinburgh in January 1923, he scored a spectacular try against France. The Scottish forwards were dominant throughout but Eric did not impress *The Times* correspondent: 'Liddell ran well, especially when he obtained the last try of the match, but it is difficult to credit him with being anything more than a great runner.' Leslie Gracie was the Scottish captain for the game against Wales at the Arms Park. Eric launched himself on an incisive run early in the first half, but was caught by a crunching smother tackle. In the second, he side-stepped three Welshmen to score a glorious try. With ten minutes remaining, the Scots trailed 8–6 when Eric provided the final pass to set up Gracie for another try. A successful conversion brought Scotland victory by 11 points to 8.

Eric played his last two internationals at the end of the 1923 season. He featured little in Scotland's victory over Ireland by two goals and a try to a single try, and in the Calcutta Cup at Edinburgh, he showed his devastating speed on several occasions but made no impression on a solid defence which formed the platform for an 8–6 English victory.

In March 1923 he had an experience which he described in terms of Saul on the road to Damascus. At the invitation of his subsequent biographer, D. P. Thompson, he addressed a religious meeting at Airdrie. A few days later, Eric would confess to Thompson that 'a new light had come into his life'. (Thompson's biography is the most authoritative treatment of Eric's life to date, and this chapter owes much to it.) As a preacher, Eric's style was hesitant and his voice remained monotone. However, audiences were captivated by his charisma. He seldom became animated, but over six months he built up a repertoire of self-deprecating anecdotes which always hit the right note.

In the summer of 1923, Eric combined his evangelism with track appearances, the highlight being the British AAA meeting at Stamford Bridge where he won both sprint events. In the 200 yards he recorded 21.6 seconds, and in the 100 he clocked 9.7. The 100 yards had been billed as a showdown between Eric and Harold Abrahams, but Abrahams withdrew with a throat infection.

Thus, one of the major scenes in *Chariots of Fire* is pure fiction; the pair never met over 100 yards or 100 metres, their only encounter being in the 200 metres at the Paris Olympics. Similarly, the film's constant assertions that Abrahams encountered anti-Semitism at Gonville and Caius, Cambridge, are inaccurate and shabby.

In the following week, Eric was at Stoke for a contest between Scotland, England and Ireland. He swept the board, winning the 100, 220 and 440 yards, and it is in the 440 that we enter the core of the Liddell legend, a legend that is grounded in hard fact. However far-fetched it may seem, the scene in *Chariots of Fire* where Eric is knocked to the ground but goes on to win, is accurate to the last detail. The *Staffordshire Sentinel* describes how Eric was '... "bored" out of his position and lost several yards – ten yards, or more, many declared – just after the start'. Eric sat on the turf debating whether to get up. He then sprinted after the other athletes, won the race by a matter of inches and collapsed in a dead faint.

In April 1924, he visited the States for the Penn. Relays. Eric finished second in the 220 and 4th in the 100, and the *Philadelphia Inquirer* commented: 'Britain's invaders fared ill at the hands of their Yankee cousins. Eric Liddell, the meteor of the University of Edinburgh, succumbed to Louis Clark in the 220 yards, the latter not only overtaking the Scot, but beating him to the tape by four feet.' This was serious preparation, but his training in the run-up to the Olympics remained Heath Robinson and always took third place behind academic and preaching commitments.

At the British AAA championship in June, he won the 440 yards in 49.6 seconds. In the 220 he was second with 21.7 behind H. P. Kinsman. Unopposed by Eric, Harold Abrahams won the 100 in 9.9. The fact that the heats of the Olympic 100 metres would be held on a Sunday had been common knowledge since January and Eric had been focusing on the longer distances all season. Sadly, this deflates another piece of cinematic legend. Eric was vilified in the press for spurning the chance to win the blue riband event of the Games and there were suggestions that he was being unpatriotic. It would have been easy for him to indulge in a little casuistry and justify his participation in terms of the national effort. He remained true to his principles but avoided any posturing that could be interpreted as being sanctimonious.

On the Sunday of the 100 metres heats, Eric preached in the Scottish church in Paris. He was at the track the next day to applaud Harold Abrahams's victory in the final. Two days later, Eric lined up for the final of the 200 metres on a track dampened by heavy rain. Charley Paddock took an early lead and at the half-way mark he was several yards ahead of a bunch including Eric, Jackson Scholz and Bayes Norton. F. A. M Webster has recalled: 'As the runners approached the finish it looked as though Paddock still had the issue well in hand, but like Lot's wife he looked back, and like Lot's wife he paid the price.'

As Paddock wound up for his trademark jump finish, Scholz flew past him to take gold, and Eric shrugged off Norton to win bronze. David Wallechinsky has noted that Paddock was an intimate friend of Douglas Fairbanks Snr who was in Paris for the Games. He had dined with Fairbanks, Mary Pickford and Maurice Chevalier the night before, and Mary Pickford had taken him on one side for a rousing pep talk. Jackson Scholz would become a pulp novelist, his best known work being *Johnny King, Quarterback* which is indescribably awful.

On 10 July, Eric was uninspired in the eliminations for the 400 metres, but he qualified safely. In the next round he again ran within himself to clock 49.1 seconds. In a retrospective article in the *Leader* magazine, F. A. M Webster describes how on the eve of the 400 metres final, Jack Moakley the doyen of American athletics made a surprising prediction: 'That lad Liddell's a hell of an awful runner, but he's got something. I think he's got what it takes.'

As Eric left for the stadium on the following day, the British team masseur passed him a note containing a garbled version of 1 Samuel 2 v. 30: '... for them that honour me I will honour, and they that despise me shall be lightly esteemed'. In *Chariots of Fire*, the message is delivered by Jackson Scholz. Still sprightly at the age of 83, Scholz gave David Puttnam much advice as the film was shot. When asked if he was willing for his screen persona to deliver the note, Scholz replied: 'Will it make me look good?' An agnostic if not an atheist, he was embarrassed some months later when his mailbox overflowed with letters from film-goers asking for spiritual advice.

The final of the 400 metres took place in the evening and provided respite for spectators who had become bored by the six-mile walk. Eric was still regarded as a rank outsider, and the fancied British competitor was Guy Butler. Eric had been drawn in the outside lane, and the film portrays him saying to one of his rivals: 'I don't suppose I'll see you before the finish.' The writer is hard pressed to think of anything more alien to Eric's nature.

Eric set an electric pace and the *Edinburgh News* report includes: 'Just for a second I feared that he would kill himself by the terrific speed he had set up ...' He hit the 200 metre mark in 22.2 seconds, four yards ahead of a pack that included Josef Imbach, Horatio Fitch and Butler. Imbach was disorientated by the blistering pace; he tripped on a lane rope a few seconds later and the American Coard Taylor also stumbled. Eric entered the straight four yards ahead of Fitch and Butler. He faded at the line but held on to win by three yards in 47.6 seconds.

Eric spent the rest of this year and much of 1925 at the Scottish Congregational College in Edinburgh where he preached with increasing fluency. D. P. Thompson recalls: 'No place was too small, no meeting-house too insignificant, and no audience too unpromising.' In June 1925, Eric boarded the Trans-Siberian railway for Tientsin in Northern China. It was hardly an ideal time to arrive; there were widespread strikes and a weak central government was being undermined by regional warlords. On 23 June, British police opened fire on a rioting mob in Shanghai, creating anti-British feelings that were as strong as at any time since the Boxer Rising. By now Eric's father had become a prominent evangelist for the London Missionary Society and his sister had been teaching for several years.

An army of social historians has pointed to Eric's work in China as a notable example of 'Muscular Christianity', conveniently ignoring the fact that he was employed primarily as a teacher of Pure Science. The whole concept of the Muscular Christian has been done to death, and Eric should always be seen as an individual rather than as part of a movement. His evangelism was tempered by everyday concerns, and he once concluded an interview in the *Belfast Newsletter* with:

'The educationalist must follow on with the evangelist.' He took a keen interest in China's history but he was also committed to its future, and he immersed himself in secular projects including schemes for agricultural reform.

He was of course the most eligible bachelor in expatriate circles and was in constant demand as a mixed doubles partner at tennis parties. His social poise was improving and he is known to have set many hearts fluttering. Later, Eric became an inspirational tennis coach, and several of his pupils went on to represent China in the Davis Cup. He was unable to convert the Chinese to rugby, finally admitting that their physique made the game impractical, but he taught soccer and baseball with much enthusiasm. He lobbied successfully for funds to improve the sports facilities at the college, and a lavish complex was built using the layout of Stamford Bridge.

Running on his own track in the spring of 1928, Eric was credited with 21.8 seconds for the 200 metres, and 47.8 for the 400. If accurate, these times are astounding and would have put him in a dead heat for the gold medal at both distances in the Amsterdam Olympics of that year. He was still only 26, and as a fitness fanatic, he may have remained capable of world-class performances. Sadly, it is difficult to avoid the conclusion that the times emanated from an over-enthusiastic pupil and the school alarm clock.

In autumn of the same year, he competed at the Dairen Athletics Meeting, and the *Peking Times* for 28 October describes how he recorded a creditable 51 seconds for the 400 metres. He would perform a more remarkable feat later in the afternoon. He had turned up at Dairen to run in the 200 which he won comfortably, and initially he had no intention of running in the 400 which was scheduled for 2.45 p.m. Eric's boat back to Tientsin sailed at 3.00 and the track was a ten-minute drive from the dock. We are back in the core of the Liddell legend. After much pleading from the organizers, he agreed to take part in the race on the condition that there should be a taxi with its engine running at the tape. Eric flew home several yards ahead of the field, and without checking his stride he rushed towards his cab.

He was obliged to freeze to attention when a band struck up the national anthem. The cab made good time to the port, but as Eric leapt across piles of crates on the dockside he arrived to find that his boat had pulled out and was 30 yards away from the wharf. The boat was blown back towards the quay, and pausing only to throw his bag on board, Eric took a massive leap and clambered on deck. (The distance was later estimated as at least 15 feet, suggesting that he might have had a successful career in the long jump pit.)

In the summer of 1929 he began to court Florence Mackenzie, the 17-year-old daughter of a Canadian missionary. They became engaged in July of 1930 but Florence left immediately for a nursing course in Toronto. In 1930, Eric won the 400 metres at the North China Championship, beating the German Otto Peltzer. Peltzer encouraged Eric to train for the 1932 Los Angeles Olympics but he gave the suggestion a scant hearing. In August of the same year, he went back to Scotland where he studied for ordination. He returned to China via Canada in the summer of 1932, and in Toronto he gave informal tuition to the British track team which was on its way to Los Angeles.

Eric spent much of 1933 teaching and preparing a home for Florence who returned in March of 1934. The pair married in the same month and spent three deliriously happy years together. In the autumn of 1937, he was asked to go into the field as an evangelist. He bowed to this pressure and went up-country to the village of Siaochang. The new job meant frequent separations from Florence and his two daughters, Patricia and Heather. Eric began to work extensively with the Chinese peasantry and he did much to improve literacy. However, by the end of 1937, the Japanese were in control of Northern China, a turning point having been the Marco Polo Bridge incident in July which marked the onset of full hostilities.

Eric was quick to show his appetite for a struggle when the Japanese began to appropriate fuel supplies. On one occasion, he travelled 400 miles by rail, obtained a consignment of coal and commandeered a barge which he piloted on his own back to the village. In the summer of 1939, Eric returned to Scotland once more. He remained there for a year, during which time he volunteered for the Air Force only to be rejected on the grounds of his age (he was now 37). When it was suggested that a desk job might be found for him, he returned to China in high dudgeon, insisting that he could find more useful work elsewhere.

By the summer of 1941, the likely course of events in Asia was suffi-ciently clear to Eric that he sent his wife home. His evaluation of the situation proved correct in December when the Japanese attacked Pearl Harbor and war was declared in the Far East. Eric did not see Florence again and he never saw his third child. For many months Allied civilians were allowed freedom of movement in Tientsin but they were kept under close surveillance. In October 1942, we find Eric writing to Florence and cataloguing his reading which included *The Grapes of Wrath* and (ironically) *All Quiet on the Western Front*.

In the spring of 1943, the expatriate population of Tientsin was rounded up by the Japanese and transported south to the infamous

Weihsien internment camp. The term 'concentration' would be too
strong as a description of the camp, and there were few cases of
extreme cruelty. However, with internees allowed a living space of
three feet by six, there was rampant disease. Inadequate sanitation
and diet combined to cause many deaths through typhoid and dysen-
tery. Conditions in a similar camp are recreated in J. G. Ballard's
largely autobiographical novel *Empire of the Sun* and in a sensitive and
faithful film adaptation by Steven Spielberg.

The Weihsien camp had a colourful population of 1,800 people of
over twenty nationalities, and it included 500 children and teenagers
who occupied much of Eric's time. Many of the adults were divines,
either Roman Catholic clerics or Protestant missionaries. The following paragraphs will concentrate on the positive aspects of camp life
and the subculture which emerged. It should be remembered,
however, that the pervading atmosphere was one of deprivation.
There are several comprehensive descriptions. The most readable is
Langdon Gilkey's *Shantung Compound* which is refreshingly free from
the cant that pervades other accounts.

Eric had a fast metabolism and it was lack of food which wore down
his prodigious strength. (The average daily intake was 1,200 calories
of poor quality carbohydrate.) Naturally, he followed a demanding
and selfless timetable, and within a few months the spring in his step
had disappeared for good. After only a few days the latrines became
blocked. The Japanese authorities showed no concern and the pipes
were only cleared when a party of Protestant missionaries tied rags to
their faces and strode into an indescribable hell-hole. It was a remarkable feat and needs to be set against some less endearing behaviour
manifested by the missionary population over coming months.

The camp diet improved dramatically towards the end of 1943,
largely due to the efforts of several hundred Belgian monks who
demonstrated stoicism and courage throughout their internment.
They included a large group of Trappists and smaller groups of
Dominicans and Passionists. The Passionists had been conducting
prayers near the perimeter wall when one of their number was struck
on the head by a cabbage thrown over by a Chinese farmer. They
began to conceal large quantities of vegetables under their habits, and
at all times they took these to the communal kitchens. Similarly, the
Trappists struck up a relationship with a local poultry farmer and
brought back up to a thousand eggs a day. (The influx of eggs did
much to restore the Trappists' credibility; they had been released from
their vows of silence and predictably, had sought to make up for years
of abstinence by engaging all and sundry in meaningless drivel.)

The improved diet fostered morale and the inmates found huge reserves of energy. Evening classes cropped up and a dramatic society put on two Noël Coward plays (*Hay Fever* and *Private Lives*). The internees had been restricted as to what they could bring into the camp but many had brought their musical instruments. Various concerts were given, including a performance of Mozart's piano concerto in D minor with a full modern orchestra.

Eric remained on the fringe of these activities but he was tireless in working with the youth club. He also gave science lessons and set 'Oxford' and 'Cambridge' examinations which were accepted retrospectively by the examination boards. Many internees sought to expend their new-found energy by playing sport and Eric was suddenly in his element. He organized a softball league and the matches were watched by the entire camp. Again, the monks were prominent and a team of Dominicans proved unbeatable as they scurried round the diamond in their habits.

Eric also arranged hockey matches for the youngsters but would have nothing to do with sport on Sundays. His charges had little to do at the weekend, and one Sunday they organized a game of hockey with no referee. The match developed into a brawl and Eric observed this. He strode on to the pitch and supervised the rest of the game. We have arrived at the centre of Eric Liddell and found a rare ore. In 1924, his respect for the Sabbath had prompted him to forsake a unique opportunity for fame. Nineteen years later, unobserved on a piece of scrub land in Northern China, he would relax the same scruples with the selfless aim of alleviating the boredom of a group of schoolchildren.

The Japanese guards proved largely humane, but in May 1944 a new camp chief stamped out the illicit food. The diet was reduced to a bowl of stew for lunch and a cup of soup for supper. The camp lost its vitality and conditions became dire in the winter of 1944–5. As morale reached a new low, a consignment of American Red Cross parcels was received, enough for every internee to have one parcel. However, in a frightening display of greed, many of the Americans insisted that since the parcels had come from the States, they should only be distributed to the American population. (This would have allowed each American seven 50 lb parcels.)

After much debate, the authorities decided to distribute the parcels equally. It was the cue for many Protestant missionaries to demonstrate a peculiarly spineless form of hypocrisy. The camp operated a ration card system, and the non-smoking missionaries had always refused to lend out their cards so that a heavy smoker could obtain a few more cigarettes. It transpired that each Red Cross parcel contained a carton of Lucky Strike, and the same missionaries who had refused to let others use their coupons now began to use their cigarettes to barter for luxuries such as condensed milk. It need hardly be added that Eric quietly destroyed his carton. Over a course of three days, he depleted his small store of strength by carrying parcels to the elderly and infirm.

Of all the internees who have published recollections of Weihsien, only Gilkey is sufficiently candid to mention that early in 1944, many of the camp's bored teenage population were found conducting sexual orgies in a basement, the participants being as young as 13. When these activities were revealed, Eric redoubled his efforts at keeping the youngsters occupied, and he organized craft shows and one-act plays. Gilkey's catalogue of the camp's many achievements is tempered by a frank discussion of the human frailty on view, and he changes the names of all the inmates he discusses, though in Eric's case he makes no more than a token effort. Here is his summation of Eric:

It is rare indeed when a person has the good fortune to meet a saint, but he came as close to it as anyone I have known. Often in an evening I would pass the games room and peer in to see what the missionaries had cooking for the teen-agers. As often as not Eric Ridley would be bent over a chessboard or a model boat, or directing a square dance – absorbed, warm, and interested, pouring all of himself into this effort to capture the imaginations of those penned-up youths.

Langdon Gilkey, *Shantung Compound*, 1966

In February 1945, Eric began to suffer from violent headaches. On the evening of 21 February, he died at the age of 43 as a result of haemorrhaging caused by a massive brain tumour. Friends packed Weihsien's church for the funeral while the rest of the camp stood outside in deep snow. The lesson was read by Andrew Cullen, an Eltham schoolmaster who had known Eric since he was ten years old. The main address was given by Edward McLaren who had played rugby for Scotland alongside Eric, and the hymns included 'I know that my Redeemer liveth' and Eric's favourite, 'Be still, my soul'.

Reflecting on the service, David McGavin commented: 'Eric Liddell was the most Christ-like man I ever knew, and there are many who, like me, thank God upon their every remembrance of him.'

Evaluations of Eric as a rugby player often repeat the cliché that 'flying wings' seldom pull their weight in defence. A. A. Thomson has undercut this stereotype with: 'He was a tireless and dogged defender, and when he smother-tackled you, you stayed smothered.' Eric's rugby was by no means limited to an occasional lightning sally down the flank. In his second season he began to demonstrate great tactical awareness, and his handling was always superb. In defence, he could read an opponent's intentions like the pages of a book, and selling him a dummy was like trying to sell poison to a Borgia.

At five feet nine, Eric was below ideal height for the 400 metres, and he would often over-stride. At the Penn. Relays in 1924, his style had reduced the sophisticated Americans to laughter. Eric's posture on the running track was as distinctive as that of Emil Zátopek. His sprawling stride caused his arms to flail and he often lifted his feet so high that he appeared to be performing a goose-step.

The most striking characteristic was a habit of throwing his head back. Sculptress Emma Pover produced a representation of Eric in 1996. She comments: 'It is deliberately Christ-like ... In the last part of a race, Eric almost took flight for God.' The habit of 'running blind' is a trait which Ian Charleson recreates beautifully in *Chariots of Fire*, and without a hint of caricature. (Charleson died of Aids in January 1990. Primarily a stage actor, he is remembered for his acute and sensitive portrayal of Eric, and for brilliant performances as Hamlet which have been favourably compared with those of Gielgud and Olivier.)

Eric's mother-in-law once recalled that he was 'completely filled with the Spirit of Christ ...' One of his favourite sentiments was the need for every Christian to be prepared for 'absolute surrender to the will of God'. His faith was unreflective; he saw spiritual issues with a black and white clarity, but his integrity somehow avoided dogmatism. He was certainly no intellectual, and was interested in people rather than concepts. The diary of a Weihsien internee picks up this theme with: 'He wasn't a great leader, or an inspired thinker, but he knew what he ought to do and he did it.'

Despite bearing a weight of idealism for much of his life, Eric never descended into sterile sainthood; his humour was surprisingly earthy and he cannot be accused of prudery. He parted company with many admirers in his support of the temperance movement, but the severity of his stance on this issue is often overstated. As a preacher, his style was direct, even homespun, and his sermons were never cluttered with obscure allusion.

Eric's grave remained unmarked for four decades. In 1991, Charles Walker discovered it after months of searching. In June of the same year, many Weihsien prisoners returned for a further memorial service, and the site of the grave is now a fitting garden of remembrance. The camp has been converted into a bustling middle school in which the vitality of the pupils contrasts with the arid and bleak surroundings of a region which is best known as the birthplace of Confucius.

Confucius said that when you see a worthy man, imitate him. I think Confucius would have called Liddell a worthy man.

Norman Cliff, *The Independent*, 10 June 1991

One of D. P. Thompson's more perceptive summations includes: '... the clarity of his witness was never dimmed, the strength of his faith was never impaired, the completeness of his self-giving never in doubt.' Eric's talent and monumental integrity are prominent in our conscience through the film. Whatever its shortcomings as documentary, as cinematic art, *Chariots of Fire* is a hauntingly beautiful epitaph to a remarkable man.

3

Denis Compton

b. 25 May 1918, d. 23 April 1997

*'There is a great man who makes every man feel small. But the real
great man is the one who makes every man feel great.'*

G. K. Chesterton, *Charles Dickens*, 1906

On the night that Denis Compton died, a general election was seven
days away. Already aware that the Conservatives were about to take
their biggest drubbing since the Duke of Wellington led them to
defeat after the Great Reform Act, John Major took time out from the
campaign to write a eulogy for the *Daily Telegraph*. 'To watch Denis
Compton bat on a good day was to know what joy was ... I will miss
him greatly as will everyone who knew him. Thank you Denis. You
left memories for all time.'

The Prime Minister's paladin was born in Hendon in a week when
the Allies dropped six tons of bombs on the Bruges dockyard and
brought victory in the Great War significantly closer. Denis's father,
Harry, was a decorator and a competent club cricketer. His wife,
Hilda, was soon making household economies to ensure that Denis
had the best in sports equipment. With the exception of his extraordinary sporting abilities, Denis's childhood was unremarkable. At
Bell Lane Elementary School he was conscientious and widely liked
despite a precocious talent which took him into the cricket team at the
age of 10 alongside 14-year-olds. Weekends were spent playing lamp-
post cricket or taking in Cagney movies at the Hendon Lido.

The young Compton first came to public attention at Lord's in 1932
when he captained a London Elementary Schools side against a team
representing the best public school talent from the same age group.
Denis opened with Arthur McIntyre who would go on to play for
Surrey and England. His inability to judge a run was already apparent. He ran out McIntyre for 44 but stroked his way to a jaunty 112
which caught the eye of Pelham Warner who insisted that he be taken
on by Middlesex.

The versatility was obvious and a few months later Denis played at left-half for England schoolboys against Wales. An Arsenal scout sent a glowing report back to the great Herbert Chapman and Denis was taken on as a weekend apprentice. He left school in 1933 and became a member of the Middlesex ground staff. As a net bowler, his regular clients included the former England captain and Hollywood screen idol Sir Aubrey Smith. By then well into his sixties, Sir Aubrey enjoyed Denis's vivacity and would always ask for him.

Denis's Middlesex début was on the Whitsun bank holiday of 1936 when he made 14 against a Sussex attack including Maurice Tate. He had been picked as a bowler and batted at number eleven. The maiden first-class century was not long in coming; in his sixth match he stroked 100 not out against Northamptonshire. His aggregate for the season was 1,004 at an average of 34.62. There was talk about taking him to Australia for the Ashes tour and Pelham Warner pronounced that he had not seen raw talent like this since the appearance of Wally Hammond. Enthusiasm was tempered by what would be some of Denis's maverick traits, and his captain Walter Robins gave him regular reprimands for absent-mindedness, reluctance to wear a cap and extended conversations with female spectators.

In the previous year he had signed professional forms with Arsenal where he was coached alongside players of the calibre of Cliff Bastin and Ted Drake. Denis's first league match came in September 1936 when he played on the left wing against Glasgow Rangers and impressed the Scots so much that the heady sum of £2,000 was mentioned as a transfer fee. George Allison had taken over at Highbury following the death of Herbert Chapman. Allison already knew that he had found a rare bloom and the offer met with a summary rejection. Denis's league début came against Derby County at Highbury a few weeks later in front of 60,000 and he scored the first goal in a 2–2 draw.

At 19 years and three months, Compo was the youngest Test débutant to date when he made 65 at the Oval against the 1937 New Zealand tourists. His form remained consistent and at times exhilarating in the following year and in June of 1938 he made his first century against Australia at Trent Bridge. Denis came to the wicket after having fallen asleep during a stand between Hutton and Hardstaff. He was dropped by Bradman off O'Reilly before he had scored. However, the runs soon flowed and the *Times* report on his 102 includes: 'Compton looked an artist. The instincts of the great cricketers moved in his strokes ...' In the next Test at Lord's, Denis scored an unbeaten 76 which he always rated as the best innings of his life. Sadly, he was distraught when he dropped Fleetwood-Smith, so costing Ken Farnes a hat-trick. It would be Farnes's last Ashes series; he died on active service three years later and Denis treasured his every memory of him.

Denis's footballing commitments prevented him from making the MCC tour to South Africa in the winter of 1938–9, and on reflection he must have wished he had joined Wally Hammond's party. He failed to hold down a regular place with Arsenal and early in the season he damaged his right knee in a collision with Sid Hobbins, the Charlton goalkeeper. He made a prompt recovery from the resulting cartilage operation but the knee problems had taken root.

In the first Test against the West Indies at Lord's in 1939, Denis was majestic in an innings of 120 during which he dominated a fine pace attack including Learie Constantine and Leslie Hylton. (Sixteen years later, Hylton would be hanged for the murder of his wife.) Later in the year Denis, brother Leslie, Cliff Bastin and other Arsenal players were offered a contract of £100 a week at the Palladium after they auditioned with a head-tennis act.

Denis was called up in the following December and posted to East Grinstead where he served with an anti-aircraft regiment. He was soon transferred to Aldershot and studied to become a physical training instructor. In 1941 he married Doris Rich, the dancer, after a brief courtship. Towards the end of the war he was posted to Mhow in central India where he served as a PT and weapons training instructor, his pupils including the future General Zia of Pakistan.

Between 1939 and 1944, Denis represented England against the home countries in 14 wartime soccer internationals. They were often played before crowds of 80,000 and raised over £6 million for the Red Cross. Programme notes include gems such as: 'In the event of an air raid, cover from shrapnel should be obtained under the stands'. In October 1941, he was part of an English side which beat Scotland 2–0 at Wembley. The home line-up was quite stunning; Denis's team-mates included Joe Mercer, Tommy Lawton, Jimmy Hagan and Stanley Matthews. The opposition was hardly shabby and the names of Bill Shankly and Matt Busby are prominent. Denis had a quiet game but he combined well with Lawton and made some telling crosses. In the following January, England beat Scotland 3–0. Denis set up the second goal when he latched on to a pass from Stan Cullis, beat two men and provided a perfect ball to Lawton.

In September 1943, England defeated Wales 8–3 at Wembley. A match report from the *Manchester Guardian* concludes with: 'Wales had played themselves to a standstill and England in a whirlwind finish put on four goals in five minutes. This was due almost solely to the brilliance of Compton.' The visitors were sadly depleted and in the second half the Welsh outside right, Powell, left the field after breaking his collar-bone. In a delightful gesture, the England reserve Stan Mortensen pulled on a red jersey and did much to keep Wales in the game. *The Times* noted: 'With the ball being continually swung out to the left, Compton had ample opportunity to display footwork and feint, which he was inclined to overdo.'

In his first cricket matches after the armistice, Denis gave much of the nation a tonic and lightened post-war austerity. Sir Neville Cardus recalled: 'The strain of long years of anxiety passed from all hearts at the sight of him. There were no rations in an innings by Compton.' After a domestic series against India in 1946, England toured Australia and New Zealand in the winter of 1946–7 under Wally Hammond. Denis was in sound but hardly inspired form and had little time for Hammond, noting in his autobiography: 'He tended to be individualistic and uncommunicative; worse still, he didn't seem to be part of the side.' Compo produced two centuries during the series, scoring 147 and 103 not out during the Adelaide Test.

Denis's batting in the sun-drenched summer of 1947 beggars description. In first-class cricket he scored 3,816 runs at an average of 90.85. In the Test series against South Africa he made 753 runs at an average of 94.12. Many of his records this year are likely to remain unbeaten and will stand as a permanent memorial. In the first Test at Trent Bridge he scored 163, only to follow this with a stunning 208 at Lord's during which he put on 370 for England's third wicket with Bill Edrich. (This is one record that has gone; it remained the highest stand for any wicket against South Africa until a month before Denis's death when Steve Waugh and Greg Blewett plundered 385 for Australia's fifth wicket at Johannesburg.) A third successive Test hundred (115) came at Old Trafford and in the final match of the series Denis scored 113. The South African bowling attack was modest and a more significant innings was his 139 against Lancashire at Lord's. However it was during this match that particles of bone began to detach themselves from Denis's right knee-cap.

In September he scored his 17th hundred of the season against the South Africans at Hastings, eclipsing Jack Hobbs's 16 centuries back in 1925. The season marked the peak of his popularity and he was nominated Sportsman of the Year, having polled 25 per cent of the vote. The judges enthused about his versatility, and noting his low single-figure handicap, they concluded: 'If he had bothered to take golf seriously he might easily have challenged the omnipotence of Henry Cotton.'

Some of Denis's most glorious hours came in 1948 and the Movietone footage remains ingrained on the collective memory of a now depleted generation. It can make old men see visions. In the first Test against Australia at Trent Bridge, he scored 184 in England's second innings. At Old Trafford, Denis edged a bouncer from Ray Lindwall on to his temple when he had scored four. After several stitches and not a few measures of brandy he tottered back to the wicket sporting an Elastoplast. Lindwall responded with another searing bouncer which Denis negotiated safely. Over three days with extended interruptions for rain, he played the most gritty innings of his career, scoring an undefeated 145.

This Ashes series saw the start of a close friendship with Keith Miller. The pair shared a passion for horse racing and created an elaborate system of hand signals so that they could exchange race results while in the field. When Miller got back to Melbourne a journalist asked him to name the three most beautiful sights in England. The reply was immediate: 'The Derbyshire hills, Princess Margaret, and Denis Compton sweeping the ball from middle stump.'

In the following winter Denis toured South Africa where he scored 114 in the second Test at Johannesburg. His most notable innings was 300 in 181 minutes against North-East Transvaal. Denis clubbed his last 100 runs with what *Wisden* described as 'a bewildering assortment of unclassified strokes'. It remains the fastest triple hundred in first-class cricket. Another high point came in the third Test at Cape Town when he switched from his usual chinamen to the orthodox slow left-arm of his boyhood and took 5 for 70. Denis's marriage to Doris had failed soon after the war and on this tour he met Valerie Platt who would become his second wife in 1951.

By the summer of 1949 the knee was causing him pain and reducing his mobility. His centuries at Headingley and Lord's were high points in a set of dull encounters with New Zealand. By the following winter Denis was despondent about the knee and his general fitness. He was reluctant to return to Arsenal but played a league game against Bolton and was selected for a fifth round FA Cup tie against Burnley. Arsenal won 2–0 and Denis not only set up the first goal but scored the second after a delightful run from his own half.

After beating Leeds United at Highbury, Arsenal faced Chelsea in the semi-final at White Hart Lane. They found themselves 2–1 down with 13 minutes left when a few shimmies from Denis down the left flank produced a corner. Denis curled the ball on to the head of his brother Leslie, and Arsenal escaped with a replay which they won 1–0. In the final, they defeated Liverpool by virtue of two goals from

Reg Lewis. In front of a Wembley crowd of 100,000, Denis had an appalling first half and was consistently closed out by the Liverpool right back Ray Lambert. Compo's own recollections include: 'I think I would have been pulled off if substitutes had been allowed. I was a stone or so overweight at round thirteen and a half and I was quickly out of puff.' He was persuaded by his idol Alex James to sustain himself with a huge slug of whisky and in the second period he tested the Liverpool goalkeeper with a series of crosses and combined well with Joe Mercer to set up Arsenal's second goal.

The hero worship I felt then for Compton cannot be described in fewer than three volumes with footnotes and a full index but those who have been through that sublime phase will know what I mean. You never get over it. Denis Compton once addressed two words to me and if you have a long evening to spare I'll give you the full story.

Melvyn Bragg, *Daily Telegraph*, April 1998

While revelling in the vivacity of his captain, Freddie Brown, Denis could not buy a run on the Ashes tour of 1950–1. His plight touched the Australian bowlers and Bill Johnston once offered him a long hop to get him off the mark only to see him spoon a catch. Bradman even took him to a hotel room, produced a bat and gave him a coaching session. Despite a Test average of 7.5, Denis remained cheerful throughout and he was one of the few batsmen who could read the extraordinary bent-finger spin of Jack Iverson. Only a few journalists and players realized that the discomfort from his knee was now excruciating and a huge intake of pain-killers was dulling his reflexes.

Matters improved in the first Test against South Africa at Trent Bridge in 1951 when Denis showed much grit while making 121. By now he had married Valerie Platt and settled in Buckinghamshire. In the winter of 1953–4, Denis toured the West Indies, a highlight being his 133 in the fourth Test at Port of Spain. Later in 1954 he thrashed a modest Pakistani bowling attack while making 278, his highest Test score. John Woodcock's *Times* report is effusive: 'The Pakistan bowlers were slain at Trent Bridge yesterday as no Test match bowlers have been slain since the era of Bradman, and their executioner was Compton ... The bowlers lay at his feet, baffled as to where to pitch the ball; the fielders had been turned to stone, and the strokes flowed from his bat like a river in spate.'

Denis suffered not only with the knee but with fractured fingers on the 1954–5 Ashes tour and it became obvious that the halcyon days had gone. His highest score came in the final Test at Sydney where he recovered much fluency to make 84. Back in England during the following summer, Peter May's England side faced up to a South African touring party which featured the varied bowling of Adcock, Heine, Tayfield and Goddard. We are now in the Compton apocrypha but it is well documented that Denis turned up at Old Trafford on the eve of the Manchester Test in a tiny monoplane and without his kit-bag. He received an immediate dressing down from May but with an ageing bat unearthed from the bottom of Fred Titmus's trunk he carted the South African attack for 158 and 71.

By the following winter the knee had become arthritic and the patella was removed at University College. It is now a bizarre holding at the MCC museum where it is housed in a biscuit tin and treated with the reverence normally accorded to a saint's finger. Few have the stomach to inspect it and Denis once observed: 'It's a revolting thing. Looks as if rats have been nipping at it.'

Denis's mobility was limited during the 1956 season. However, playing on one leg, he returned for the final Test at the Oval. He was back on his game and scored 94 and 34 not out while making Peter May look like a journeyman. Denis played his last Test cricket in South Africa during the following winter. Scores of 0 and 5 in the final match at Port Elizabeth were a sad way to go out but he had made half centuries in both innings of the game at Cape Town.

Denis once confessed that he only felt really nervous in charity games where he was always the star turn. Visiting his son at Clifton College in 1957, he was persuaded to play for the Parents against the School. He found himself batting against a gangling off-spinner whose height allowed him to deliver the ball from the background of a red brick building. Denis prodded about for a few overs before being comprehensively bowled. To this day the schoolboy rarely travels without a battered match report from the *Bristol Evening Post*. His name is John Cleese. (Decades later, Basil Fawlty would berate Manuel with: 'Well whose fault is it then? Denis bloody Compton's?') Later in 1957, Denis played his last match as a professional for Middlesex, scoring 143 and 48 in fine style against Worcestershire.

He played a few games as an amateur in the following summer but was increasingly distracted by the failure of his second marriage. Some months later, Valerie returned to her native South Africa with their two sons. The award of a CBE this year was treated on the day with appropriate gravitas but the trappings had little meaning. (A week later Denis was seen using the ribbon as a collar for his Old English Sheepdog, Benjy.) He had been somewhat bemused at the award ceremony when Her Majesty greeted him with: 'Mr Compton, how is your poor head?' Denis had travelled down to London on the previous evening and had taken the opportunity of visiting a few watering holes with his cronies. His embarrassment disappeared when he realized that his duel with Lindwall in 1948 had indeed touched everybody in the country.

The enduring memories of Denis's batting will be his sweep and his supposed unorthodoxy. While hardly a text-book player, his technique was in fact grounded in first principles. He certainly had a dominant right hand which accounted for his strength on the on-side. However, Lord Cowdrey's *Wisden* obituary includes: 'His technique was sound and his defence correct; he had the straightest bat in the team, and watched the ball closely on to it.' If he had a weakness it was his reluctance to play straight drives. However, his lofted on-drive was spectacular and he also revelled in a vicious cover-drive which he could place a foot either side of cover-point. His sweep was of course superb but he played it with percentages in mind; Denis hit the ball much finer than is the norm and a downward movement of the bat ensured that he rarely got a top edge.

Denis's status as a truly great batsman was often underlined by C. B. Fry who put him on an equal footing with Victor Trumper. His physical courage was inexhaustible and he was usually able to dig deep and bring out his best form on the big occasion. However, his batting was characterized by a fragile quality which prompted spectators to play every shot with him. Cardus picks up the theme with: 'His cricket has always contained that hint of brevity which is the loveliest thing in the summer's lease.'

Cardus's mention of brevity is a reminder that any Compton innings could come to an unnecessary and unexpected end. With the possible exception of Gerry Weigall, Compo was the worst judge of a run in the history of cricket. There are many hoary chestnuts describing this and they can be passed over here if only to please Denis's shade. A rare gem, however, is J. J. Warr's obituary recollection: 'He was the only batsman I ever encountered who called you for a single and wished you good luck at the same time.'

Denis's bowling has been consistently under-rated. He began as an orthodox slow left-armer with a loping action and a prep-school run up. In 1947 he switched to left-handed wrist spin which he bowled in a similar manner to Michael Bevan in our own time. His turn was acute and his googly difficult to spot. Denis's best bowling perform- ance was for Middlesex against Surrey at Lord's in 1949 when he took five wickets in a day from 30 overs. While this chapter is degenerating into a list of superlatives, it should be noted that his fielding was exceptional. His attention was apt to wander but in first-class matches he pouched 416 catches. He was at his best in the slips but could field anywhere. However, he would occasionally miss a sitter due to his constant chatter with Bill Edrich which could cover anything from a pretty girl on the boundary rope to the chances of a gelding in the 2.30 at Goodwood.

As an outside-left, Denis played 14 wartime soccer internationals and 185 games for Arsenal. Arlott talks of his 'lazy looseness of move- ment' while his Arsenal and England colleague Stan Cullis recollected: 'He was very fast and unorthodox, and capable of shattering opposition sides.' Sadly, Denis was almost totally one-footed. He was somewhat selfish and occasionally proved reluctant to release the ball, wanting to beat one man too many. His acceleration could be decep- tive but opposition full-backs knew that he would rarely cut inside them. Compo was difficult to knock off the ball and had the goal- scorer's instinct as to where a crucial pass was likely to come from.

Despite the media interest which surrounded his performances, Denis is remembered by contemporaries as a superb team man and an excellent tourist. However, sharing a room with him was an unenvi- able experience. Proximity in the alphabet meant that Colin Cowdrey often drew the short straw. Lord Cowdrey has recalled the chaos in hotels, the raids on other players' kit and a regular mad scramble to find his passport: 'He never had any clothes, so he just used to pinch mine. I'd end up losing my shirt, my socks – whole wardrobes of the stuff including my underwear.' Denis was often late for functions even when he was the guest of honour. Similarly, he was always in danger of missing flights and proved a nightmare for tour organizers.

He was dishevelled in general and while the pots of complimentary Brylcreem might have controlled his floppy mane of hair, he never bothered to use them. At five feet 11 inches with broad shoulders, narrow waist and the features of a film star, he spent much of his life fighting off the attentions of women of all ages. However, several of his more grizzled colleagues have recalled that he never once flaunted his sex appeal to them.

Although he often remarked that he found Cardus incomprehen- sible, Denis read many cricket books and had a keen appreciation of the game's origins. His column in the *Sunday Express* was tart and once included: 'I would suggest that Tony Greig's knowledge of the history of the game is less than any former England captain.' Of his contemporaries, Denis had huge respect and affection for Bill Edrich and Keith Miller but his one and only god was Patsy Hendren. In his old age he frequently bemoaned the aridity of modern cricket. He could be splenetic though he recognized Phil Tufnell as one of his own and rejoiced in the advent of Shane Warne.

Denis caught the fancy of millions because he communicated his pleasure to spectators. He would sign his autograph on a toffee paper if a grubby schoolboy required it and was always patient with the tabloid journalists who beat a path to his hotel room. Three decades after his retirement, even the youngest and most brash of Australian tourists would seek him out for a drink at Lord's.

This is not hagiography and the single blot on Denis's character needs to be discussed. His attitude to South Africa was crass, naïve and thoughtless. He toured the country early in his career and was greeted with a wealth of affection which immediately clouded his judgement. Marriage to Valerie Platt (who came from a well-known cricketing family and the very upper echelons of Natal society) served only to blinker him further and he eventually fell out with their two South African-based sons over apartheid. In his excellent biography of Denis, Tim Heald speculates that Compo's loyalty to his friends in South Africa distorted his perspective of the bigger picture.

On the day that Denis made his 300 against North-East Transvaal in the winter of 1948–9, John Arlott had taken a day off from cricket and inspected a Johannesburg township where he saw a black man being knocked to the ground in an act of gratuitous brutality. Years later, the signing of the Gleneagles Agreement brought Denis and Arlott into open conflict. More significant is the tension between Denis and clerics of the integrity of the Rt. Rev. David Sheppard and Bishop Trevor Huddleston. Similarly, Denis's inflammatory attacks on Peter Hain in the 1970s were witless and unworthy of him. They also show that he was ignorant of the fact that Hain not only adores cricket but has played the game to a decent standard for the Arcadia Shepherds. Denis simply wanted to see South Africa playing Test cricket and refused to absorb the larger issues at stake. His stance was misguided and thoughtless. It shows little if any evidence of racism but, sadly, much ignorance.

Denis remained active throughout the 1960s and in the winter of 1964–5 he accompanied the England side to South Africa as a correspondent for the *Sunday Express*. By now he had ballooned to 15 stone but he was persuaded to turn out for a press eleven against a full-strength Western Province side captained by Peter van der Merwe. Unimpressed by Compo's appearance, van der Merwe brought his wicket-keeper on to bowl lollipop medium pace. After Denis had tapped the ball around for a few overs the South Africans realized that they had made a mistake. The damage was done: Denis had his eye in and gave the Test bowlers Harry Bromfield and Jimmy Pothecary a rare trimming, reaching his century at a run a minute.

Having spent the 1960s as a bachelor, Denis married for the third time in 1972. (While Denis and Bill Edrich's stand of 424 against Somerset may be toppled as a Middlesex record, their combined total of eight wives will take some beating.) Denis and Christine Franklin Tobias had two daughters, Charlotte and Victoria. The family spent the next two decades in Burnham, Buckinghamshire. Denis worked as a television summarizer and was never slow to express himself forcibly. He had a column in the *Sunday Express* throughout the 1970s and much of the '80s. However, he rarely wrote more than an entry on a betting slip and would chat perceptively to a succession of ghosts who worked his thoughts up into literate copy.

Denis's health declined gradually; the onset of diabetes placed restrictions on his diet and various hip operations reduced his mobility. His weight increased dramatically, though in evening dress he could still look as sleek as a seal. It is probable that he occasionally drank a little too much in order to dull the pain of arthritis. For those who could remember Denis in his pomp, it was excruciating to see him struggling to walk twenty yards and having difficulty in getting out of his car. However, the charisma stayed with him and Michael Parkinson has recalled: 'He always seemed to turn up in a cloud of dust even when he was walking with a stick.'

In June 1991, Denis hopped about Lord's and opened the Compton stand. He never lost his irreverence for authority but a few weeks later he was overjoyed when he was offered the presidency of Middlesex CCC. He held the post for six years and only handed over the reins a few weeks before his death. Middlesex flourished in this period and their success was certainly due in part to Denis's presence. However, his scathing evaluations of contemporary Test players were hardly constructive. He had little time for Ted Dexter as a selector and still less for Graham Gooch. At a time when Gooch was in dire need of support from the media, Denis's column in the *Sunday Express* included: 'Great batsman, but as a captain, a disaster.' By the summer of 1995 he was becoming particularly acidic. He was often unduly critical of Mike Atherton's abilities as a leader and once accused Ray Illingworth of 'being frightened of his own shadow'.

The grandeur remained intact for a whole generation although a few months earlier there had been a bizarre incident at the Oscar ceremonies. When accepting his best song award for 'Can You Feel the Love?' from *The Lion King*, Sir Tim Rice thanked his boyhood heroes. Inevitably, the list included Denis. There were blank looks all round the Academy of Motion Pictures followed by the question: 'Which movies was he in?'

It was Paul Gallico who told us that statistics never made anyone bleed or weep. For the record: in a first class career spanning 28 years, Denis scored an aggregate of 38,942 runs from 839 innings at an average of 51.85. At Test level he scored 5,807 runs from 131 innings at an average of 50.06.

Denis died at the age of 78 on 23 April 1997 after complications arising from diabetes and a third hip operation. During his final days there was a comet shining brightly over England and few obituary writers missed the significance. Everybody swallowed hard and many wept for their own youth. An impassioned litany in the national and sporting press included David Frith's: 'None could dodge the pain of losing someone who had become a vivid part of one's own life.'

The memorial service was at Westminster Abbey. With the exception of the funeral of Diana, Princess of Wales, it was as charged as anything seen in the Abbey this century and tickets changed hands for four figure sums as 2,000 people crammed into every corner. Past and present from Middlesex turned out in force and Mike Gatting spent much of the service with his arms around a visibly disturbed Mark Ramprakash. (Ramprakash was born twelve years after Denis played his last Test innings.)

As the mourners streamed out into the sunlight there were countless interviews with the great and the good. A *Daily Telegraph* correspondent had the wit to approach a balding, rather scruffy little man who had applied for a ticket through the public ballot. He didn't want to be named but described himself as 'an ordinary ageing cricket supporter'. He commented: 'I came as a small way of saying thank you for the way he lit up those gloomy post-war years with his cricket and his character.' We are back with Chesterton and 'the real great man'.

Earlier in the service, J. J. Warr had introduced a note of levity to his eulogy which Denis would have loved. 'I remember when Ted Heath introduced the three-day week. I asked Compo how he was going to cope and he said: "I'm not going to work an extra day for anybody."'

4
Mildred 'Babe' Didrikson-Zaharias

b. 26 June 1911, d. 27 September 1956

'Babe could tell the rest of the players in a tournament that she was going to beat their socks off and make them like it, because she was not only telling the truth, she was drawing the most fans.'

Harvey Penick, *For All Who Love the Game*, 1995

On 26 June 1911, Hannah Didrikson, a former ice-skating champion, presented her husband Ole with a sixth child, a girl named Mildred. Their daughter would prove a hectoring bore, an insensitive braggart, and the greatest all-round sportswoman in history.

Mildred spent her girlhood in Texas. Her father, a ship's carpenter from Norway, claimed to have rounded Cape Horn 17 times. He settled at Port Arthur on the Gulf of Mexico at the turn of the century, and turned to cabinet-making and the narration of increasingly elaborate nautical stories. He was obsessed with the physical conditioning of his children and created a primitive Nautilus system composed of pulleys and flatirons on which Mildred put in countless hours. At the age of ten, she saved enough money to buy a harmonica and covered her investment through radio recitals. With one bath a week and as much cod liver oil as she could keep down, she was hardly being groomed for stardom.

In her autobiography, the Babe notes: 'Before I was even into my teens, I knew exactly what I wanted to be when I grew up. I wanted to be the greatest athlete ever.' The autobiography is detailed, personable and objective. Together with *Whatta-Gal: The Babe Didrikson Story* by Oscar Johnson and Nancy Williamson, it deflates the myth but preserves the individual. As a teenager the Babe was following the 1928 Amsterdam Olympics and – without even knowing they would be in the States – resolving to be on the American team for the next Games. Within weeks she became a competent hurdler. Her training

consisted of vaulting the hedges in the backyards between her house
and the corner grocery. They were all of a uniform height save one
belonging to a Mr King which was too high. With what would
become a characteristic directness, she went straight round to Mr
King and asked if he would trim the offending hedge. Mr King trotted
outside and performed the necessary topiary.

Port Arthur was dominated by an oil refinery, and Mildred's childhood environment was grim and competitive. It gave her a jungle
mentality which she never outgrew. In a playground scrap, she threw
a punch at a future pro-footballer and laid him out cold. The nickname of 'Babe' came through her prowess at sandlot baseball where
she once hit five home runs in an evening. Managing to find time for
homework after sport, Mildred progressed from Magnolia Grade
School to South Junior High where she achieved B+ grades.

In the 1930s many large organizations poured money into corporate
athletic teams which they saw as a PR weapon. One such firm was the
Employers Casualty Company of Dallas. With a typing speed of 86
words a minute, she was soon on the payroll. Within a month she was
captaining the company's basketball team. Initially, she had been
lukewarm about the offer, and on the night that she was signed up,
Mildred spent her time leaning out of the locker room window and
spitting on to the heads of passers-by. Whatever allowances you make
for her upbringing, it appears strange behaviour for a 19-year-old.

In the summer of 1930 the Babe experimented with the high jump,
employing the old scissors kick technique. In practice one afternoon,
her coach set the bar at the world record height and offered her a
chocolate soda if she could clear it. Mildred sailed over in style. This
proved to be her limit with the scissors kick and she adopted the
Western roll. Track and field were augmented by what was becoming
a mind-numbing range of skills, including diving, swimming stunts
and aquaplaning.

Later in the summer of 1930, she competed in the women's national
AAU championship, winning the javelin and the baseball throw.
Having leapt 18' 8½", she also held the world long jump record for a
few minutes before being beaten by Stella Walsh. At Jersey City in the
same event in July 1931, the Babe took first place in the long jump,
won the 80 metres hurdles in a world record of 12 seconds dead, and
set another world record for throwing the baseball with 296 feet.
(Many Major League outfielders of the time would have been unable
to match this distance.)

It is at this point in the narrative that fiction gives up the race
while truth carries on down the straight. The national athletics

championships of 1932 were held at Dyche Stadium in Chicago. They came in the run-up to the Los Angeles Olympics and doubled as Olympic trials. Mildred was unable to sleep on the eve of the competition and she arrived late. Competing in eight events, she rushed around the arena for three hours. She beat two of her own world records, recording 139' 3" in the javelin and clocking 11.9 seconds in the 80 metres hurdles.

In the high jump, Mildred and Jean Shiley tied with a world record of 5' 3¾". From her eight events, she gained five outright firsts and a joint first. A surprise win came in the shot put where she managed 39' 6¼". In a single afternoon, Mildred had set three world records. As her company's only entrant, she won the team competition by eight points. When cataloguing the victories in her autobiography, she is for once modest enough to gloss over the fact that second place went to a team of 22 athletes from Illinois. Despite these prodigious performances, Mildred was falling foul of many through brashness that would remain with her for over a decade.

She was already proving to be too much of a good thing. On the journey from Chicago to the Los Angeles Olympics, her crass behaviour infuriated the more sophisticated athletes. While the other girls chatted and played rummy, the Babe jogged in the aisle. On the odd occasion that she sat down, the harmonica came out. (Her repertoire was limited to *Home Sweet Home* and *Jack Ass Blues*, and after a thousand miles they began to pall.) In particular, the Babe's inanities were creating an enemy in Evelyne Hall who would take silver in the 80 metres hurdles. Hall recalls Mildred's antics when the train stopped at Albuquerque: 'Babe found a Western Union bike and rode it around the station platform hollering, "Ever heard of Babe Didrikson? You will! You *will!*"' At dinner, she informed bemused executives that she was capable of winning anything except the Kentucky Derby. When the train arrived in Los Angeles, she was lucky not to be helped on a little further into the Pacific.

In the run-up to her events, Mildred proved a nauseating bore. William Oscar Johnson recalls a conversation between Mildred and the urbane swimmer Helene Madison who would win gold in the 100 metres freestyle. Mildred asked Helene what her best time was. When Madison responded, she turned on her heel pausing only to snort: 'Shucks, lady. I can beat that by three seconds just practisin'.' Of the three events in which Mildred competed, it was only the javelin which passed off without controversy. At her first attempt she achieved a flat release and recorded 143' 4". She had wrenched her shoulder while warming up, and made no attempt to improve on this throw which won her gold by eight inches. In the heats of the 80 metres hurdles, Mildred lowered her own world record to 11.8 seconds. With a false start to her name, she followed the other runners rather than the gun in the final. Having steadily overhauled the field, she appeared to hit the tape simultaneously with Evelyne Hall. After much debate, Hall and Mildred were given the same world record time of 11.7 seconds. Mildred was awarded gold and the winning margin was judged to be two inches.

More controversy followed in the high jump. Here Mildred had a grievance. She was now detested by officials as well as team-mates. In the closing stages she found herself in a showdown with fellow-American Jean Shiley. Both girls cleared 5' 5¼", Shiley with the conventional scissors kick and Mildred with the relatively new Western roll. Her technique had not changed throughout the competition, but after the last jump the officials condemned her action as a 'dive'. It was a captious distinction though video evidence suggests that her head was slightly below the rest of her body. The decision to demote Mildred to silver was spineless; she should have been disqualified or allowed to continue the jump-off.

In the aftermath of the Games, the Babe befriended Paul Gallico. Before going on to write *The Snow Goose*, Gallico was one of America's foremost sports correspondents. During the Games he had done much to stereotype her as a sexless 'muscle-moll'. He recanted and took pleasure in charting her transition from tomboyish ugly duckling to a polished femininity. Soon after the Olympics, the Babe could be spotted in extravagant hats and nylons and she began spending a fortune on manicure. Gallico recalls meeting her in Pittsburgh and marvelling at the change. The Babe read his thoughts: 'Yeah, and Ah got silk on underneath and Ah like it.'

The Babe needed to relax in the aftermath of the Olympics, and her thoughts turned to golf. She agreed to play a fourball with Gallico and Grantland Rice who were anxious to assess her potential. With a demonstrable fib, she later claimed that it was her first round. On the back nine, she challenged Gallico to a race up a hill, after which Gallico had to lie down before four-putting. Grantland Rice would later describe the Babe as 'the most flawless section of muscle harmony, of complete mental and physical co-ordination the world of sport has ever known'. On her return to Dallas she received a ticker-tape parade in front of 10,000 people. Opportunities for product endorsements and other offers flooded in, the most bizarre being an enquiry from Amelia Earhart as to whether the Babe would accompany her on a future flight.

In the following year Mildred lost her amateur status. She was totally innocent, and was amazed when she saw herself on billboards endorsing Chrysler automobiles. An appeal to the martinets who composed the Amateur Athletic Union was initially rejected. By the time the apologies were tendered, Mildred had decided that she would indeed turn professional. Later in 1933 she appeared at the Motor Show, sitting on the bonnet of a Dodge coupé while playing the harmonica. In the following winter, she embarked on a barnstorming variety act at theatres in New York where, sporting a panama and high heels, she would sing a burlesque of *I'm As Fit As A Fiddle and Ready for Love*. She would then don a tracksuit, jump a few hurdles and hit plastic golf balls into the stalls, rounding off the show with harmonica solos. (The repertoire was becoming more urbane and now included Cole Porter's *Begin the Beguine*.)

Mildred's hand-to-eye co-ordination made her a proficient billiards player and she played exhibitions in the early 1930s. The depression was at its height and the scandal over her alleged professionalism had tarnished what was already a dimming star. On one occasion she was so hard up that she considered performing a stunt in which she would race against a horse. As the result of a bet, she once pitched the first inning in an exhibition match between two major league baseball teams, the St Louis Cardinals and the Philadelphia Athletics.

More extravagant were her appearances for the itinerant House of David baseball team whose members sported extravagant beards since they were not permitted to shave. The House of David was an inane American cult whose 500 members set up a chaste, teetotal colony at Benton Harbour, Michigan in 1903, describing their mission as being to unite the Lost Tribes of Israel in preparation for Judgement Day. They soon attracted hordes of sightseers whereupon their leader, an engaging rogue by the name of Benjamin Purnell, built a ball-park and charged for admission. From these games Purnell selected a first-rate touring team. Amid much ridicule, the Babe followed the team and pitched at the beginning of every game.

In the mid-1930s Mildred saw tennis as her best chance of riches. She was dismayed to find that as a legacy of the javelin injury, she was unable to serve overarm. She redoubled her golf training and played her first tournament in November of 1934. In preparation for the following season, she hit over a thousand balls a day and was obliged to tape her hands. She was not only incredibly long off the tee, but displayed magical touch around the green. Targeting the Texas State Championship as her first real tournament effort, she beat Peggy Chandler by two holes. Chandler was the epitome of the

amateur golfer and there is much of her in Fitzgerald's characteriza-
tion of Jordan Baker in *The Great Gatsby*.

The encounter between Chandler and Mildred was pure theatre as
the latter's raucous comments sent shockwaves along the genteel fairways of the River Oaks Country Club in Houston. Chandler herself
had confided to a journalist: 'We really don't need any truck drivers'
daughters in our tournament.' Only a matter of weeks later the
USGA, without any explanation and to widespread derision from the
sporting press, decreed that Mildred was a professional and effectively ruled her out of women's golf. Undeterred, she embarked on a
series of best ball exhibition matches with Gene Sarazen. She received
the considerable sum of $150 for these matches and insisted on being
paid in one-dollar bills.

In December 1938, she married George Zaharias, a gargantuan and
charismatic professional wrestler whose antics earned him the nickname 'The Crying Greek From Cripple Creek'. Zaharias promoted
wrestling in Denver and had a string of muscle men touring the
States. He would caddie for the Babe, occasionally testing wind direction by blowing smoke streams from a Havana the size of a vaulting
pole. George was a glutton and Philistine, and his hotel room resembled the delicatessen counter at Macy's. Johnson and Williamson
report that he bought cheese by the wheel and beer by the crate. His
less endearing habits included submerging slices of bread in olive oil
before swallowing them whole. Unsurprisingly, he later ballooned to
28 stone. The Babe was hardly a connoisseur herself and always made
a point of shovelling caster sugar into her champagne.

The couple met at a golf tournament when a waggish promoter put
the wrestler and the Olympic star in a threesome with a Presbyterian
minister. Zaharias began dating her immediately and the couple
honeymooned in Australia. During the sea passage, the newly-weds
realized that people in third class were having a better time than those
in first. They asked to be downgraded; the holiday picked up immediately and Mildred sat in on harmonica with the ship's band. George
rarely lost sight of the possibility for making a quick dollar, and he
arranged golf exhibitions around Australia for his wife and wrestling
bouts for himself.

George and the Babe kept on golfing together after their marriage.
Time magazine describes how she once hit a terrific tee shot. George
was determined not to be upstaged; he wound himself into a run-up
which took in some of his wrestling moves and spanked the ball five
yards further than his wife. The Babe turned to him: 'I always said I
could fall in love with a man strong enough to out-drive me.' Despite

his appearances in pro-celebrity tournaments, George seems to have been unable to understand match-play scoring. Over dinner in New York one evening, while his wife was playing in the Texas Open and suffering an abysmal run of form, a Reuters wire was delivered to him. George perused it and announced: 'Babe lost but it was real close, 10 and 8.'

By the end of 1939, Mildred was keen to regain her amateur golfing status. With George a wealthy man, she spent three years competing in professional tournaments but refused all prize money. By this time the shoulder injury had healed and Mildred turned to tennis again. She played up to 17 sets a day at Beverly Hills, many of them with Louise Brough who became a firm friend. Mildred soon reached championship standard but was amazed when her application to play in the 1941 Pacific championship was turned down. In an asinine interpretation of professionalism, the authorities decided that as a former professional athlete, she counted as a tennis pro even if she had never played a set of tournament tennis before. Hugely disappointed, Mildred never touched a racket again. She turned briefly to ten-pin bowling at which she soon excelled, and found a lifelong friend in Harold Lloyd, the silent-movie comedian, who was obsessed with the game.

Mildred was desperate to succeed at amateur golf, and she began a monumental practice régime. In pro-ams, Mildred appeared with Bing Crosby and Bob Hope. Social partners included Joe Louis who was capable of scoring in the mid-seventies. Tournament golf came alive in 1946, and over 36 holes the Babe trounced a Mrs Sherman 11 and 9 to win the US Women's Amateur at Southern Hills, Oklahoma. It was the first of a remarkable string of victories that would run through to 1947.

In June of this year she set her sights on the British Open Amateur Championship. Having stood up in a train all the way from London to Edinburgh, she arrived at Gullane several days early. Her length off the practice tee excited attention from the press, and entering into the spirit of a phenomenally friendly welcome, Mildred accepted invitations to meagre afternoon teas from the humblest of villagers.

The Babe was immaculate with her woods for most of the tournament and she hardly missed a fairway. Her short game was also on song and the *Scotsman* highlighted her 'almost sinister concentration when she sized up the surface of the green'. When she began the final she had lost only four holes in six rounds. The Babe loved a rowdy audience and she notes how she decided to 'loosen up those galleries', encouraging spectators to make more noise. Winning her second match 4 and 2, the Babe performed trick shots on the final holes and sent the crowd wild. Mildred's predictions as to her performance on a hole were often gauche but she seldom failed to deliver. The crass one-liners of the 1930s were evolving into genuine wit. When asked by an unctuous opponent if she objected to a ball being picked up from casual water, Mildred replied, 'Honey, I don't mind if you have it dry-cleaned.'

She adjusted rapidly to links conditions and regularly equalled or bettered men's par. By the final day, the spectators numbered over 5,000 as Mildred took on Jacqueline Gordon. For once her driving was wayward and the match was tied at lunch. In the afternoon Mildred went out in 36 and beat Gordon 5 and 4. Massive crowds applauded for 15 minutes after which she hurdled a stone wall and sang a highland song. In the following week she made a brief tour of other Scottish courses, playing St Andrews with a thousand people walking behind her. In an exhibition match at Gleneagles, the Babe reverted to her vaudeville days and performed standing somersaults. She went home on the *Queen Elizabeth* and in New York she was reunited with George. On Fifth Avenue, the Babe donned a kilt and performed the Highland Fling, while in Denver she appeared in a carnival procession with a train of floats representing the various stages of her career.

By now the financial incentives to turn professional again were overwhelming. Mildred signed with Wilson Sporting Goods. She made movie shorts and an instructional book appeared in her name. Having contributed an introduction and posed for the photographs, Mildred farmed out the text to a hack and it is doubtful if she even looked at the proofs. If challenged, she might have echoed her friend Paul Gallico who once told her that the only way a book will take strokes off your golf score is if you use it to tee-up your ball in the rough. A series of general sporting exhibitions followed. These included an appearance at the Yankee Stadium where to the accompaniment of *Take Me Out to the Ball Game*, she hit fungo fly balls into the crowd before playing third base during in-field practice and pitching to Joe DiMaggio.

Mildred's achievements at golf in the next few years were prodigious. She was the top money-earner from 1948 to 1951, winning the US Women's Open in 1948, 1950 and 1954. More importantly, in 1949 George Zaharias saw an opportunity for a women's professional golf tour, and with backing from Wilson, a fledgling tour was in operation by the end of the year. It grew to become the present LPGA. In the late 1940s, George wound down his own business interests and the couple quarrelled over bookings. The marriage became rocky and there was talk of a divorce. During her alienation from George, the Babe grew close to Betty Dod, a tour rookie. A fine guitar player, Betty would accompany the Babe's harmonica in jam sessions as they travelled across the country.

Betty Dodd proved to be Mildred's only friend on the road. It is hardly surprising. The tour's finances were rocky, and its experienced manager Fred Corcoran agreed to take a salary of a dollar. However, the Babe still insisted on appearance money. She could be savagely competitive and parsimonious at the same time. Introducing herself to fellow golfers, the Babe (already well on the way to career prize-money of a million dollars), would teach them how to play rummy and play a few lightning hands. She would then announce that the novice owed her a by no means nominal sum and insist on payment.

Mildred continued playing golf in the early 1950s. Her credentials as a double international rest on the basis of a tour to England as captain of the US Lady Professionals. Playing a series of foursomes and singles against the British Amateurs at Sunningdale, she part-nered Betsy Rawls to crush Philomena Garvey and Jean Donald 11 and 9. Lewine Mair has described the Babe's ensuing singles match against Garvey. The contest was originally scheduled for one round and the Babe lost by two holes. The organizers decided to extend the game to 36 holes. With the match all-square at the 35th, her approach to the 18th landed stone dead though not before it had taken deflec-tions from a tree and the clubhouse wall. Mildred holed out to take the match.

By early 1953, Mildred's game was in inexplicable decline. In April the woman who had raised thousands of dollars playing in benefits for the American Cancer Society learnt that she had cancer herself. As she lay in a hospital bed in Beaumont, Ben Hogan was winning the Masters. Mildred received a telex signed by 40 sports writers in the press tent at Augusta. With the cancer apparently localized, there was hope that a colostomy would lead to permanent recovery. By the middle of June she was hitting mid-irons round the Tampa Golf Club and a few weeks later she was featuring prominently in competitions.

In her first tournament after the operation, she shot 82 and 85. On the third day she was five over par after as many holes. Seeing her three-putt from four feet, her playing partners told her to pick up if she felt ill. The response was a retort, 'I don't pick up the ball!' and a two under par back nine. Back in the limelight, Mildred was received by Eisenhower and nominated as Associated Press Sportswoman of the Year for the sixth time. At a tournament in Oklahoma, she was presented with a palomino horse which she insisted on riding on to the green. She became a tireless fund-raiser for the American Cancer Society and spent much time in hospices.

In 1955, we find Mildred writing her autobiography and building a house in Tampa with the architects working from her own highly competent drawings. Seemingly buoyant, she worked alongside the electricians and plumbers. In July 1955, doctors discovered a new strain of cancer in her pelvis. While finishing her memoirs in the following September, she was still talking about a total recovery and more golf, concluding: 'My autobiography isn't finished yet.' It was. After wasting away for a year, the Babe died in September 1956 at the age of 45. The headlines were predictable: 'Babe steals home'. Betty Dodd had been at her bedside for months. The pair were still stomping their way through blues numbers, and only weeks before her death, Mildred recorded a gramophone record of harmonica solos and plugged it shamelessly on the Ed Sullivan Show.

During the final months, Sam Snead and Ben Hogan organized prayer vigils for her. Harvey Penick had been among her greatest fans. Having been invited to coach her one day, he had simply watched in awe. Penick remembers a meeting with George Zaharias: 'When I saw George shortly after her funeral, we both broke down and wept in each others' arms.' (Things turn around: in April 1995, most of the tears that Ben Crenshaw shed as he donned the green jacket at Augusta were for Penick, whose coffin he had been carrying four days earlier.) In the 1970s, George's diet caught up with him. He suffered massive heart attacks and spent his last years in a wheelchair. Destined to die in her mid-forties, the Babe had revealed in the foreword to *Championship Golf*, 'I expect to play golf until I am ninety; even longer if anybody figures out how to swing a club from a rocking chair.'

5

Albert Neilson Hornby

b. 10 February 1847, d. 17 December 1925

'It is little I repair to the matches of the Southron folk,
Though my own red roses there may blow;
It is little I repair to the matches of the Southron folk,
Though the red roses crest the caps, I know.
For the field is full of shades as I near the shadowy coast,
And a ghostly batsman plays to the bowling of a ghost,
And I look through my tears on a soundless – clapping host,
As the run-stealers flicker to and fro,
To and fro:–
O my Hornby and my Barlow long ago!'

Francis Thompson, 'At Lord's', 1907

The quotation is a cliché but it remains a touchstone for the affection in which this benevolent despot was held during a county cricket career which spanned 32 years. The title of the poem is a misnomer. Thompson was not at Lord's in 1907 when he wrote it, and his tears were the by-product of an addiction to opium which killed him in the same year. He had been invited to the Middlesex vs Lancashire fixture but illness had prevented him from attending. The piece was written to thank friends who had issued the invitation. As a 19-year-old medical student, he had been a spectator at Old Trafford in 1878 when Lancashire had played Gloucestershire and the 'run-stealers' had put on a first-wicket stand of 108.

Ten years later, having flirted with the medical profession and the priesthood, Thompson was sleeping under newspapers on Victoria Embankment. He was rescued by the journalist, Wilfred Meynell, who tracked him down through a laudanum supplier and published his poems in *Merry England*. Meynell spent years attempting to combat Thompson's habit and regularly persuaded him to take cures at Storrington Priory. Thompson's work is characterized by sentimental and mystical pronouncements. It is frequently rhapsodic but can be arrestingly beautiful. Many of the poems concern the tension between sacred and profane love and it is ironic that he should be best remembered for a piece on such a comparatively pedestrian subject as a pair of Lancashire batsmen.

Thompson's hero, Albert Hornby, was brought up at Poole Hall in Cheshire where his family were successful cotton merchants. In 1851, his father, William, became mayor of Blackburn and six years later he was elected as a Conservative MP. Hornby senior was a popular club cricketer and huntsman, and his sporting feats earned him the nickname of 'Th' Gam' Cock'. He is commemorated in a bronze statue at Sudell Cross in Blackburn.

Albert was sent to Harrow in 1862 and he immediately excelled as an athlete. He was double jointed with a high degree of ambidexterity, and he quickly gained a reputation as a superb fives player. He was admired by boys of all ages for his agility and alertness, and it was these attributes which earned him the nickname of 'Monkey'. Many Harrovians remembered him for a fight with a boy called Crampton on the school's infamous Milling Ground. Years later, Lord Dunedin recalled his staying power under pain: 'Crampton was the taller boy and fought well. But "Young Monkey" won simply by his power to endure punishment.' At cricket, Albert attracted attention by the aggression and unorthodoxy of his batting, but his performances against Eton were undistinguished. He played in 1864 and 1865, scoring 19 and 27 respectively.

The Monkey spent a fortnight at Oxford University in 1865, having gone up with the intention of spending his whole time on the sports field. It was explained to him that he would be required to do a modicum of work and he promptly returned to Blackburn. Here he proved shiftless and an embarrassment to his father, the *Nantwich Guardian* noting: 'Those responsible for him tried to turn him into a business man; being unable to expel nature, they failed.' Production at the family cotton-mill fell off immediately since the Monkey would lure staff away to play cricket.

In his late teens, Albert played a curious brand of football which was a mixture of rugby, soccer and the Eton and Harrow field games. The side was organized by his father and variously known as Brookhouse or 'Hornby's Team'. It should be remembered that these were the earliest days of soccer and rugby, and neither game had been codified. The pitch was located behind the Hornby residence, and by 1872, Albert was acting as captain. The *Sports Telegraph* recalls a match against a team from Bolton in which the play proved 'vigorous', and the injuries were so horrific that Brookhouse refused a return fixture.

Albert was also playing soccer at this time. In January 1878 he represented Blackburn Rovers against a touring Partick side which was defeated 2–1. A match report in the *Blackburn Standard* includes: 'Hornby distinguished himself by his activity and excellent dribbling.' Albert played regularly for Blackburn in the late 1870s, and obituarists recall how his rugby instincts once got the better of him and he did a Webb Ellis to the amusement of players and crowd.

On one occasion, a noted barracker at the Rovers became particularly raucous. Albert instructed the referee to stop the game, strode on to the terraces and ran the man out of the ground by the scruff of the neck. There were few sports at which he did not try his hand and he would take on all-comers in boxing booths at local fairs, frequently giving away five stone in weight. He also competed in sprint, hurdle and quarter mile events, and followed a hectic schedule. As a 21-year-old, Albert was at the kill in an otter hunt at five in the morning, followed a fox until nine o'clock, and was on the cricket field at eleven.

The Monkey made his county cricket début in 1867 for Lancashire against Yorkshire at Blackburn, where he failed with scores of 2 and 3. He did not play for Lancashire in the following year but turned out for Cheshire. In 1869, he played a full county season for Lancashire and headed the batting averages with 31.1. In the autumn of 1872, he toured North America with a strong team of amateurs. The party was organized by Robert Fitzgerald of the MCC who chronicled the trip in *Wickets In The West*. On the outward voyage, W. G. suffered badly from seasickness and his humour was not improved by the presence of a hundred waifs from the Brompton Orphanage. Albert proved hyper-active and excelled at deck games. He even created some of his own, and would keep the orphans amused with prodigious broadjumps. Humour on board the SS *Sarmatian* had a schoolboy quality and Fitzgerald records that he was obliged to interfere when he heard a seasick colleague being greeted with: 'Boiled mutton and capers, or stewed tripe this morning, George?'

The Monkey's performance was poor throughout. A rare success was in an exhibition match at Toronto where he kept wicket and made five stumpings. The *Toronto Globe* notes that a banquet of the night before had gone on until three in the morning, and that 'Hornby's wicket-keeping could not be surpassed'. Albert had a sufficiently clear head to stump W. G. from the second ball of the day.

His performances in other matches were disappointing. He was by no means focused on cricket and was anxious to take advantage of social opportunities. His brother had visited Canada in the previous

year and had compiled a photograph album of débutantes. Albert
had perused this and left the team regularly in order to meet local
belles. At Hamilton, it was decided that the game should be
completed in one day, however poor the light might become. As dusk
settled, the Monkey disappeared into the pavilion. He emerged some
minutes later, lay down in the slip cordon and lit a candle.
Fitzgerald's account includes an evocative period touch. At a banquet
after the Hamilton game, he met a brother of Dr Livingstone, and
notes: 'He believes in Stanley which was cheering.' (Fitzgerald need
not have worried; Stanley had found Livingstone in the previous
October, and was struggling back to Zanzibar.)

Albert's form worsened when the team moved on to the States. He
made a 'pair' at Boston and shelled several catches including a sitter
in front of the grandstand at Philadelphia. After receiving a repri-
mand from his captain, he organized a net session which is described
by the *New York Herald*: 'A. N. Hornby, when at practice, kept in
almost incessant employment a large force of small boys to procure
the balls which he hit clean over the fence.' The party headed back for
England in late September. Catering on the voyage home was
Spartan, and Fitzgerald notes that the tourists' staple diet was
sardines. W. G. must have consumed these like plankton.

In July 1873, Albert produced one of his finest innings, making a
fluent 104 for Gentlemen vs Players. He also ran 20 yards at full speed
on the square leg boundary to take a remarkable catch which
dismissed Ephraim Lockwood. The 1875 season saw a series of fine
opening stands with Richard Barlow. Against Yorkshire at Old
Trafford, the pair had their finest moment. In the final innings of a
tense Roses encounter, Lancashire were set a target of 146 against the
clock, whereupon Albert and Barlow knocked off the runs without
offering a chance.

The Monkey's rugby career has received little attention since his
death. He played mainly as a full-back but was competent at three-
quarter. His teams included Preston Grass Hoppers, Manchester,
Lancashire and England. He did not turn to rugby until he was
nearing 30, but he became a regular full-back for the 'Hoppers in the
mid-1870s. 'Fearless', 'wholehearted', 'irresistible' are the adjectives
used by opponents and team-mates. One of the most remarkable
things about the Monkey is that he was barely five feet eight inches,
and yet his rushes were so powerful that he often had two or three
jerseys ripped during the course of a game.

He found the social aspects of rugby well suited to his zest for
physical activity and he became a regular on the Grass Hoppers'

annual tour. In 1878, the Hoppers visited Ambleside. As his team was leaving the clubhouse after the game, Albert spotted the local Volunteers in the act of turning out for a church parade. He encouraged his colleagues to 'fall in' behind the Volunteers, variously armed with brooms and poles. On reaching the church, the troupe turned round and charged en masse back to their hotel, causing uproar in the streets.

Albert had played his first international against Ireland at Kennington Oval in February of the previous year. It was the first international between teams of 15 players, the original number having been 20. Albert played at three-quarter. He scored an unconverted try in the first half, *The Times* commenting: 'Hornby was conspicuous for his excellent drop kicks and for a dextrous run, which he finished by obtaining a try.' England dominated the game and won by two drop goals and a try to nil. Albert would play in another eight internationals. In the following March at Edinburgh, Scotland won comfortably by a goal to nothing, though Francis Marshall comments: 'The good running and tackling of A. N. Hornby and L. Stokes at three-quarter back kept their opponents at bay until the last ten minutes.'

Albert's first international during the 1881 season was in February at Blackburn against an Irish team depleted by internal bickering. He made the final pass for England's first try and scored the second. Despite some inept conversion attempts, England won by two goals and two tries to nothing. In March he played at Edinburgh in front of a crowd of 10,000 which saw the Calcutta Cup match drawn at a goal and a try apiece. Incredibly, the English team was weakened by the absence of H. H. Taylor who missed the train from London.

In March 1882, he skippered his country against Scotland at Whalley Range. Albert and A. E. Stoddart are the only men to have captained England at cricket and rugby; it is a distinction which they will surely retain. England were beaten at home by Scotland for the first time, going down by two tries to nothing. It was not a happy game for the England captain and would be his last international. Francis Marshall recalls: 'Hornby was unequal to the task of keeping the Scotsmen out. His tackling was good, but in fielding and punting he was far removed from his best form.'

The Monkey was 35 and a knee injury was robbing him of his pace. (There is however, a credible legend that in the following year he declined an invitation to play against Scotland on the grounds that it would interfere with his shooting which was going particularly well.) In his history of the RFU, O. L. Owen summarizes him as 'a fast and daring attacker who combined a diehard spirit with an elusive corkscrew run'. His principal sporting loyalty was to cricket but he never lost touch with rugby. He became President of the Lancashire RFU in 1884 and also refereed major games including the 1890 North vs South fixture in which he allowed a controversial try by the North.

> **It would have been impossible for him not to have brought his peculiarly pugnacious personality into play on the rugger field. He probably had a hand-off like an on-drive for six and he must have been as hard to stop as a north-country stone wall in motion.**
>
>   A. A. Thomson, *Rugger My Pleasure*, 1955

The highlight of the 1878 county cricket season was the fixture between Lancashire and Gloucestershire at Old Trafford. It is this game which Francis Thompson remembers in 'At Lord's'. The Grace brothers attracted great interest and 28,000 people attended over three days. Albert dominated Lancashire's second innings and *Wisden* is almost familiar with its readers: 'Just fancy, one man making 100 out of 156!' On the third day, the ground was ridiculously over-crowded and the seating and catering facilities proved inadequate. The spectators staged a riot and Albert strode into the mêlée where he made a citizen's arrest.

In 1878–9, the Monkey toured Australia under Lord Harris as part of a team that played a fully sanctioned Test but was far from being representative. It had only two professionals in Emmett and Ulyett, and no specialist wicket-keeper. The Monkey shared a room with W. G. It is common knowledge that the Doctor was no fan of soap and water, and Albert's habit of taking a cold shower in the morning sent shivers down W. G.'s spine: 'Oooh, Monkey, you do make me shudder!'

The single Test was played in Melbourne in January. Spofforth produced match figures of 13 for 110 and took the first hat-trick in Test history. Albert fell to him in both innings for 2 and 4, and Lord Harris's team slumped to a ten-wicket defeat. In Australia's first innings, Albert produced an extraordinary bowling spell of seven consecutive maidens. In the run-up to the Test, he had boxed a few exhibition rounds with Jem Mace, and an interesting description of the fight emerges from the otherwise inane platitudes of Lord

Harris's memoirs: 'Though not tall he was a pocket Hercules, muscular, hard, and as active as a cat; but, though doing his best, I do not think he touched Mace's face once.' Mace was a British fighter and one of the last of the bare-knuckle merchants. After a tour of the States in the early 1870s, during which he won the unofficial world middleweight championship, he had settled in Melbourne where he became a publican.

On 7 February, the tourists began a game against New South Wales. Tempers flared on the second day when a rumour flew round the ground that Emmett and Ulyett had described the spectators as 'sons of convicts'. The *Australasian* notes that 'rowdyism became rampant'. In front of a restless Saturday crowd, the NSW captain, Billy Murdoch, was adjudged to be run out by a fine margin. There was immediate uproar. The *Australasian* continues by reporting that the crowd included a 'well-known and ill-favoured bookmaker' who by now had almost certainly lost heavily on the match. The bookmaker and his cronies instigated a pitch invasion which was taken up from all sides of the ground. Two thousand people flowed on to the outfield, and when a mob surrounded the wicket, Lord Harris was struck with a whip.

Popular versions of ensuing events are exaggerated and it is often reported that the Monkey offered to fight the whole crowd. He did, however, floor Harris's assailant and drag the man into the pavilion. (The legend is that he used the ruffian as a battering ram to force his way through the spectators.) A local paper described how the Monkey's shirt was torn from his back as the rioters tried to rescue the captive. Albert ploughed through the spectators and handed the 'larrikin' to the authorities. There were two more riots later in the day and the game was abandoned.

At the beginning of the 1881 domestic season, Albert scored three centuries in as many weeks. For Gentlemen vs Players at the Oval, he started brilliantly and with his score on 20 he made a towering hit from the bowling of Ted Peate which the six feet three inch William Gunn plucked out of the heavens while leaning over the boundary rail. The Monkey was unimpressed: 'Only a damned giraffe could have got near the thing' was his trenchant observation. Lancashire, with Hornby in charge, won 13 of their county matches in this season and drew the other three. They won the championship comfortably, their captain making 1,531 runs at an average of 41.14 which prompted *Lillywhite* to describe him as Grace's 'one superior'.

In the following season, Australia toured England under Murdoch. Albert's achievements in the previous season earned him the England captaincy, and in the single Test at the Oval, his side dismissed Australia for 63. The English team was stacked with batting and Albert held himself back to number ten. Having made two runs, he was bowled by a massive off-cutter from Spofforth. His side was dismissed for 101 and Australia responded with 122 during which Albert made some inspired bowling changes.

Much of the mystique of the ensuing innings is worn out now but the events retain some magic. England required 85 to win and as the Australians prepared to take the field, Spofforth uttered the famous words: 'This thing can be done.' Albert decided to open with Grace and the pair were getting ready in mid-afternoon when a spectator by the name of George Eber Spendlove fell to the ground and began vomiting blood. Events in the next ten minutes have been the subject of much hyperbole, but W. G. certainly removed his pads and attended in a professional capacity.

Not for the first time, W. G. lost his patient and ten minutes later he was padding up again. The Monkey was soon back in the pavilion for 9, bowled once more by Spofforth. W. G. and Ulyett steadied the ship and England needed only 34 runs with 8 wickets in hand. It was at this point that Spofforth became unplayable and the England dressing room turned into a circus. Alfred Lyttelton and Alfred Lucas played out 12 maiden overs during which Charles Studd walked around gibbering and wrapped in a blanket. Studd was among the finest batsmen in the country and had already made two centuries against the tourists. Unaccountably, his captain held him back to number ten and he did not face a ball.

England lost two wickets with the total on 70, and another two when the score was 75. The Surrey secretary, C. W. Alcock, recalled: 'Men who were noted for their coolness at critical moments were trembling like a leaf.' As last man, Ted Peate could only totter to the wicket after a liberal dose of champagne. Later, Peate himself noted: 'Steel's teeth were all in a chatter; and Billy Barnes's teeth would have been had he not left them at home.' Studd and Peate needed to make eight runs for victory when the latter was bowled by Boyle. Australia had won by seven runs and the famous mock obituary appeared in the *Sporting Times*.

Later that year, Lancashire won the championship for the second time in succession. The Monkey had injured his shoulder in a riding accident early in the season and finished with a modest average of 28.1. In June 1884, Albert played for the North against the Australians and made a sparkling 94. In the absence of Lord Harris and Alfred Lyttelton, he assumed the captaincy for the Old Trafford Test but rain washed out the first day and produced an undistinguished draw.

In the 1884 Varsity match, the Oxford player George Kemp was wanted to go in to bat but was found lying on his back reading Molière. Albert heard about the incident and pronounced: 'If that man had been my son, I would have disowned him on the spot.' Like W. G., Albert had little time for books. The *Nantwich Guardian* notes that while at Harrow, 'he failed to secure a reputation as a scholar', and Home Gordon picks up the theme with: 'How the "Monkey" had stayed in the school was amazing, for he was profoundly illiterate and rather proud of the fact.' After his fortnight at Oxford, it can be safely said that the only book he ever opened was *Wisden* which he carried at all times in his kitbag.

In 1876, Albert had married Ada Ingram, a daughter of Herbert Ingram, the founder of the *Illustrated London News*. She bore him four sons: Albert Jnr, George, Walter and John. None of them manifested the distressingly æsthetic tendencies of George Kemp. Albert Jnr (A. H.) inherited much of his father's aggression but a modicum of the talent. He proved a successful captain of Lancashire between 1908 and 1914, and his fielding was world class. George had a superb record in the Boer War and died in 1905 as a result of his wounds. Walter fell on the Western Front only six days before the Armistice. The youngest son, John, acquired many of his father's eccentricities and spent 20 years as an explorer in Northern Canada, returning regularly to England with specimens of Arctic wildlife which the Old Man proudly displayed in his home. He died of exposure in 1927 during an ambitious expedition.

Albert's favourite son was George, and the pair would play in minor games at Old Trafford. During one of these matches, George fumbled a simple catch and a cry of 'Oh, my! What will Pa say?' came from the crowd. The Monkey stopped the game and was soon causing uproar in the stands as he hunted down the culprit.

It was in July 1886 that Albert played his finest innings when he trounced a Surrey attack including Lohmann and Abel for a glorious 161 runs at Liverpool. In 1891, after taking the county to second place in the championship, he made the first of many retirements from the captaincy, intending to stand down in favour of Archie MacLaren. MacLaren was unable to play regularly in the following season, and the Monkey returned as joint-captain with Sydney Crosfield for another few years. He was in his mid-forties but was enjoying a successful spell in the Third Cheshire Regiment where, according to the *Cheshire Courant*, he proved 'a popular officer and a clever shot'.

He remained argumentative and there is a choice anecdote in the *Courant* obituary: 'An older generation of Cheshire people will recall as the writer does, a match which Mr Hornby ran on The Rodee at Chester with Lieutenant Woodyatt. This match, the outcome of a mess-room argument, was run over a distance of 440 yards level, and Mr Hornby won by a yard. On that day the regiment appeared to a man to be shouting for Mr Hornby, and the crowd also, so great was his fame on other fields, were on his side.'

There had been another example of crowd favouritism way back in 1868. It was in this year that Charles Lawrence brought a group of Australian Aborigines to England. The party played club games throughout the country with creditable results and created a sensation with demonstrations of native dances and boomerang throwing. In the game against East Lancashire, Albert scored 117 and took nine wickets in two innings with his lobs. The Aborigines would also take on their hosts at European athletics. It will come as no surprise that the Monkey was quick to take up the challenge.

Albert stepped up for the 100 yards sprint (first prize £1) in which he faced two of the tourists in Johnny Cuzens and Charley Dumas. He came second by a yard and cheerfully lined up for the high jump which the *Blackburn Gazette* describes with: 'Next came the running high jump, won by Mosquito at 4 ft 11 ½ in. Charley, Dick-a-Dick and A. N. Hornby competed with the winner. Mr A. N. Hornby took the lead and kept it, much to the admiration of the spectators until the last two elevations, which Cuzens alone seemed capable of clearing.' The applause became ecstatic when Albert took the lead in the 150 yards hurdles and retained it to beat Dick-a-Dick by a few inches. Sadly, the water bucket race was cancelled but Albert spent the rest of the evening hurling cricket balls at Dick-a-Dick from close range, the Aborigine fending these off with a small shield.

The Monkey remained a prominent figure for much of the 1890s, and a profile in *Baily's* magazine begins: 'It would hardly be possible to find a more complete embodiment of the general, and happily still growing, taste for physical culture than Mr Albert Neilson Hornby, cricketer, football player, and sportsman in the best sense of the word.' Three months earlier he had been badly injured while hunting with the South Cheshire Hounds, *Cricket* noting '… he was thrown and had three ribs broken. He remounted and saw the run out, but collapsed at the finish.'

In 1894 he was elected President of Lancashire CC and he remained in this office until 1916. He may have proved useless as a business-man in his father's mills, but as a county administrator he was shrewd and forward-thinking. He persuaded the club to purchase the lease on Old Trafford at the turn of the century, and Lancashire flourished on the field and in the ledger book under his guidance. Archie MacLaren was not a success as captain, and the Monkey occasionally filled the breach in 1897 and 1898. In his final game for Lancashire at the age of 52, the Monkey played electrifying tip-and-run to make 53 against a competent Leicestershire attack.

As a batsman, Albert's technique was primitive. The *Daily Telegraph* obituary concludes that he was 'neither sound, finished or stylish'. However, he had a wide range of strokes and almost certainly invented the reverse sweep. While struggling to make his mark in county cricket, a youthful Archie MacLaren came to his captain for advice. Albert's counsel was simple: 'Keep your left shoulder up and say your prayers.' He had a bustling presence at the wicket and scored predominantly off the front foot and through the 'V'. He certainly recognized a half-volley when he saw one and was often dismissed through a wild slash early on.

There is little doubt that he was one of the most consistently fast scorers in the history of the game. Of all the bowlers he faced, Albert struggled the most against Fred Spofforth, though he was hardly alone in this. He always batted bare-headed and when questioned on this, he recalled how he had once been given out when his cap fell on to the wicket: 'There are enough ways of getting out, without adding to them.' He disliked being surrounded by close fielders and had regular run-ins with E. M. Grace who used to crouch near to the bat on the leg-side. A. A. Thomson recalls an exchange: '"If you stay there E. M., I'll kill you." "Kill away" was E. M.'s reply.'

Apart from an extraordinary spell in the 1879 Melbourne Test, Albert did little as a bowler. His ambidexterity allowed him to bowl his lobs with either hand, and for Harrow Wanderers he is reported to have bowled with both hands in the same over. When bowling right-handed, his stock ball was a leg-break, and he appears to have been difficult to get away. As a fielder, Albert was enthusiastic and given to raucous appeals. His experience as a boxer made him remarkably quick. He would normally hover in the covers where he often fooled batsmen with his ability to throw with either hand.

As a captain the Monkey was out of the same drawer as W. G.; one of the 'can't have it, shan't have it, won't have it!' school. His authority on the field was unquestioned and he captained England with W. G. as his subordinate. As a tactician he was as sharp as they come and the *Sports Telegraph* obituary includes: 'At cricket, a man had to be very wide awake to get the better of A. N. Hornby.' He had a rare gift of instilling enthusiasm into his team but his encouragement was always measured and specific. He could be a monumental disciplinarian and Don Davies recalls that 'Lord Hawke was a turtle-dove in comparison'.

Nevertheless, much of Albert's brusqueness was a front. He thought deeply about the manner in which he handled his players and on occasion, he proved diplomatic in trying circumstances. He was not, however, very tolerant of personal preferences. Straight out of Harrow, a confident young Archie MacLaren once announced that he was competent in any position except point. (Archie fielded at point for the rest of the match.) Claims to have been the first captain or wicket-keeper to do away with the long-stop are legion, but George Pinder often stated that he and Albert were the pioneers in a North vs South game.

Despite being semi-literate, the Monkey had a significant career in local politics. His family was steeped in Conservatism and he became the first county councillor for Nantwich in 1893, remaining on the council until 1906. During this period he fought a constant battle with what he saw as the effete Liberalism of the borough. Albert was also Chairman of the Crewe Conservative Association for several years, though many were disappointed with the quality of his speeches. However, his colleagues were duly impressed when he performed miracles in pacifying an enraged delegation of cobblers. After an AGM, he is reported to have apologized for the brevity of his speech and promised 20 minutes on tariff reform at a later date. Of course the speech never materialized. In the mid-1880s, he was repeatedly asked to stand for Parliament. The pressure mounted in the run-up to the election of July 1886 until he finally deflated many hopes with the emphatic declaration, 'Not in my line!' Lord Salisbury's composite majority of 118 members in the 1886 Parliament did not include the Monkey.

For A. A. Thomson, Albert was 'a man of wrath'. He could certainly be truculent, and the *Manchester Evening News* summarizes him as 'a great gentleman who could be a great autocrat'. Thomson's verdict comes from an evocative if fanciful chapter in his *Odd Men In*. He continues: 'If he did not like what a sports writer had said of him, he did not pen him a pained note. He did not write to *The Times*, pleading for higher standards of objectivity in sporting journalism. He simply darted up the steps of the press-box at Old Trafford, seized "the feller" by the collar – anybody who offended Hornby was always "the feller" – and ran him down stairs, out of the ground, and probably out of Manchester altogether.'

Whatever his attitude to journalists, the Monkey was remembered with affection by a generation of farmers who rode alongside him with the Cheshire Hounds, and he is known to have given liberally to their needy tenants. He always displayed the common touch but a few reminiscences suggest an element of bigotry. Home Gordon recalls how he once opined: 'I have only known one gentleman who was a Radical and he was a crossing-sweeper.' It was probably little more than a *bon mot* and he is remembered for the respect he showed for the Lancashire 'professors'. Thus, in marked contrast to Lord Harris, the Monkey, when emerging from the gate reserved for amateurs, would always walk over to the professionals' entrance point and accompany them to the wicket.

There is a rare anecdote which gets us very close to the core of Albert Hornby. The *Manchester Evening News* for May 1892 describes how Albert mingled with the crowd during an interval for rain at a match between Lancashire and Sussex at Old Trafford. 'Mr Hornby noticed a group of about 30 deaf and dumb boys, shivering and looking disconsolate at the lack of entertainment. Determined that they should not be deprived of all the pleasures of life, he conducted the whole party into one of the refreshment tents, and gave the waiters orders to let them feast till they could feast no more.'

Albert spent many years at a spacious mansion in Nantwich where he had a cricket pitch laid that was close to county standard. He remained a fearless rider to hounds until late in life. Neville Cardus recalled that he 'went after a ball rather as he went at a ditch in the hunting field'. The analogy is evocative but it can hardly be the result of observation. There is as much possibility of Cardus having follow his idol on a hunt as there is of the Monkey having accompanied Sir Neville to a Hallé concert. In the early 1920s, Albert was involved in a serious riding accident. As he returned home from a hunt along the Chester High Road, his horse fell and rolled on him. The incident set up internal complications from which he never recovered.

Arthritis was also gaining a hold but he remained a familiar figure at rugby internationals and he is reported to have been unimpressed by the advent of the trainer's sponge bag. 'We had to attend to our own in my day.' He continued to visit Old Trafford wearing an extravagant soft felt hat emblazoned with the Lancashire colours, and he would give caustic evaluations of the play. As the Grand Old Man of Lancashire cricket, his appearances on the ground were always greeted by ecstatic applause. By now he was helpless, but he insisted on viewing proceedings from behind the bowler's arm. He could not gain access to his favourite vantage spot in his wheel-chair, and fellow double international Harry Makepeace would place him under his arm like a child and carry him to the seats next to the old press-box.

The Monkey died on 17 December 1925, and the *Nantwich Guardian* reports that 'he expired after drinking a cup of tea'. The funeral was held in Nantwich. There were as many farmers present as there were sportsmen; organists queued up to play one hymn each and there was much squabbling among the clergy as to who should read the lesson. In the area of the church reserved for Lancashire CC, three generations of cricketers wept openly. As Harry Makepeace and Cecil Parkin dropped red roses into the coffin, 200 people stood outside the church in driving sleet. It was a fitting tribute to an authentic immortal.

6

Reginald 'Snowy' Baker

b. 8 February 1884, d. 2 December 1953

*'We don't go for strangers in Hollywood unless they wear a sign
saying that their axe has been ground elsewhere, and that in any case
it's not going to fall on our necks – in other words, unless they're a
celebrity. And they'd better look out even then.'*

F. Scott Fitzgerald, *The Last Tycoon*, 1941

By the time the 36-year-old Snowy Baker moved from Australia to
Hollywood in 1920, he had already ground his multi-faceted axe with
distinction. He had represented Australia at four sports. It was a pedigree that might have satisfied even Fitzgerald's Celia Brady. Sadly,
Baker was a venal and florid egotist, a scheming and manipulative
businessman, at best a rogue and at worst a crook. He remains the
greatest all-round athlete in the history of Australian sport.

He was born in Darlinghurst, Sydney, to George Baker, a civil
servant hailing from Limerick, and Elizabeth Baker, née Robertson.
George Baker lived to 92 and was a fearless rider into his eighties. In
his youth he was a first-rate swimmer and athlete. George encouraged his boys to be versatile sportsmen, his favourite maxim being:
'Activity is the law of life. Idleness means decay.' In an interview with
the Sydney *Daily Telegraph*, only a year before his own death, Snowy
recalled his father's glorious exit: 'He came home one morning from
his walk and said to our mother, "Darling, I fear it is all over." He put
his arms around her, shook hands with us all, stretched himself on his
bed and was dead within ten minutes.'

Baker was the third son in a family of five boys and a girl. He soon
acquired the nickname 'Snowy' on account of his blond hair and pale
skin which verged on the albino. His household featured twelve dogs,
two monkeys and a koala bear. The Bakers were affluent and he had
his own pony as soon as he could walk. As an adolescent, Snowy was
dutiful though hardly an altar-boy. He would orchestrate his brothers
in varied pranks, often targeting his sister, Jean. Rebellion against his

parents and their class came in his mid-teens, by which time he was acting as a bookie's runner at the Randwick Racecourse and priding himself on being the quickest sprinter between the pitches. He became a favourite and was soon carrying out dubious errands for high-rolling gamblers. The canker was in the rose.

His sporting talent surfaced early on at Crown Street School. At the age of 13 he won the 100 and 200 yard *open* swimming championships of New South Wales, being one of the first swimmers to use the crawl. As a track athlete, he excelled at distances ranging from 100 yards to a mile. He was the leading schoolboy athlete in the city and won the Sydney all-schools championship in 1898. As a rugby half-back he was consistently brilliant. Snowy and his brothers were taken for daily swimming lessons at the Woolloomooloo Baths. Here they were introduced to Peter Jackson, the ex-Australian world heavyweight champion. The boys acquired a keen interest in boxing and their father employed a string of fighters to instruct them. In 1899, at the age of 15, Snowy graduated from junior rugby with the Warrigals to the senior Eastern Suburbs side where he held his own at half-back. By now he was fully grown; he weighed a shade under eleven stone throughout his life, and his height was five feet nine inches.

Snowy was never an academic, and his journalism in later life was the work of an army of sub-editors. He did however have a talent for technical drawing, and in his late teens he was employed as a draughtsman. He would come to work late and exhausted from sports events, and few employers would accede to his constant requests for leave. He could sleep on a meat-hook and was often discovered taking a nap in broom cupboards or sprawled over his drawing board. After an extended period with the Colonial Sugar Company, he worked on several dockside projects. He certainly passed technical drawing examinations but never attended Sydney University. Still less did he win multiple blues, as is often stated.

In 1902, Snowy joined the New South Wales Lancers. He progressed to the rank of sergeant and proved superb at military games and novelty events. In the All-Australia gymkhana he came second on three occasions. He was also earning fame as a water polo-player and high diver. Over two years he won 40 swimming events, and was only beaten by the great Dick Cavill for the Australian 100 yards title. With his brother, Harald, he formed part of a team which set a world record for the 4 x 500 yards freestyle relay.

In the summer of 1904, 'Darkie' Bedell-Sivright led a tour of Australia by the British Lions. On 18 June, the tourists played New South Wales. At the age of 20, Snowy lined up as a half-back. The home team was frequently caught offside and it went down 27–0. However, the match was notable for much creative play in the loose. Snowy combined well with the Futter brothers and had an attempt at a drop goal charged down. Tempers became frayed in the second half. Fired up by Denis Lutge, a ferocious Sydney wharf labourer, Snowy and several of his team-mates were involved in a slanging match with the English forward Denys Dobson who was sent off for foul language. Dobson warrants a moment's digression. Twelve years later he died in Nyasaland, from wounds inflicted by a charging rhinoceros. The glorious legend is that his old rugby master at Cheltenham College commented: 'I always said that he had a weak hand-off.'

A fortnight later, Baker made his international rugby début in the first Test between Australia and the tourists. His side lost 17–0, but the game was by no means a rout. The Australians had 14 men on the park within a few minutes. However, they had the better of the first half and were inferior only in handling. Snowy's captain, Frank Nicholson, decided to run with the wind in the first half but his side made little impression on a superb British defence. The Sydney *Daily Telegraph* had stationed a reporter on the Sydney Hill, and his copy details conversation between the spectators: '"My colonial word – they're shaking up John Bull". "Snowy'll get his head kicked off" said one, as that sturdy player dropped on the ball in front of three British forwards.'

Baker's sporting timetable at this period is staggering. Seven days after his international rugby début, he lifted the New South Wales middleweight title when he defeated Andrew Carter at the National Sporting Club. The Sydney *Daily Telegraph* reported: 'Carter was sent down three times in the first round by right-hand punches, and ere that particular couple of minutes had expired, Carter's seconds threw in the towel ...' A fortnight later, Australia played the British Isles at the Brisbane Exhibition Grounds in the second Test. Snowy had travelled up to Brisbane by train with Denis Lutge, and the pair's high spirits had caused havoc with the railway stewards. The tourists won an indifferent game 17–3, amid poor handling from both sides. Great Britain proved superior in scrummaging and in the loose, but Snowy was superb throughout and the *Brisbane Courier* notes: 'Snowy Baker did some great defensive work at half ... his rush stopping was excellent.' Snowy was selected for the third Test but withdrew through injury. His rugby career was effectively over.

In August 1905, he won the Australian amateur middleweight title. The Brisbane *Daily Mail* reports how, in the final, he gave Albert

Scanlan seven pounds and a beating: 'Baker allowed Scanlan no peace during the early part of the last round and although Scanlan was game enough, he was overpowered.' The *Courier* describes the closing seconds: 'Hitting was fast and heavy, and though Scanlan was outclassed from the start, he fought a splendid battle and took severe punishment without a flinch.'

In 1905, Snowy joined the Mercantile Rowing Club and competed in junior fours and eights. His water polo team had held the New South Wales championship since 1903 and would retain it until 1906. In this year, he retained the Australian amateur middleweight title. In December of 1906, he left Australia for England to take part in the 1907 British amateur boxing championship. He was now the epitome of Australian manhood and his good looks had created an army of female admirers. A thousand people assembled at Sydney's Circular to see him off, and some of the more ardent groupies hired a launch in order to pursue him to the Heads. Years later, in an interview with the Sydney *Daily Telegraph*, he described how when the boat stopped off at Port Said, he was encouraged to share a bottle of scotch with his cabin-mates. A strict teetotaller, he stuck to local tap water. When the boat docked in London, Snowy was the first ashore, being stretchered off with a severe bout of typhoid which was almost certainly caused by contaminated water.

He was unable to take part in the boxing championship and was obliged to spend several months convalescing. He endeared himself to the British swimming authorities, and in the summer of 1907 he spent several months touring Europe. In addition to his appearances in the pool, he gave demonstrations of wrestling, boxing and gymnastics. He broke the Danish 50 metre freestyle record, won an international 500 metre event in Sweden and also took the Finnish diving title.

Sadly, Baker suffered an almost laughable succession of illnesses as soon as he returned to London. He had decided to stay in Europe and compete in the 1908 British amateur boxing championship, but he contracted enteric fever in some squalid lodgings. Within weeks of recovering, he came down with pneumonia and returned briefly to Australia for some much needed sunshine. He was back in London in July for the opening of the 1908 Olympics.

Two days after the opening ceremony, Snowy came sixth in a heat of the 'fancy' spring board diving for which his illnesses had made him unprepared. He was also handicapped by a lack of formal competition in Australia. A week later, he formed part of an Australasian team which eased to victory in a preliminary heat of the 4 x 200 metres freestyle relay in 11 minutes 36 seconds, a full 17 seconds ahead of Denmark. Snowy's split-time was 2 minutes 59.8 seconds. Later in the day, the Australasians struggled to come fourth in the final. They were probably the strongest team in the competition but were all suffering or recovering from illness. The Australasians had been in last place as Snowy began the third leg and it had been his brilliance which hauled them into the reckoning.

The Olympiad dragged on for four months and Snowy was largely inactive in August and September. He performed in a few boxing and swimming exhibitions but became increasingly bored. The tedium was relieved on 19 October when Australasia won gold in a debased rugby competition. Many countries had withdrawn and the only other còmpetitor was the host nation which fielded the Cornwall side. It is surprising that Snowy did not form part of the Australasian team. He contented himself with cheering on his compatriots and scream- ing abuse at his close friend, Robert Craig. A vaudeville impressionist and a spectacular eccentric, Craig had brought his pet carpet snake, Bertie, over to London.

A week later, the Olympic boxing competitions began in Clerkenwell. Snowy breezed past William Dees in the first round. Throughout the event, Snowy was subjected to a ridiculous schedule which appalled even British observers. He and Walter Child were the only boxers required to fight in the second stage since all the other competitors received byes. He was obliged to enter the ring only a few minutes after his first bout for a fight which went the full three rounds. Snowy won on points but not without a struggle. He gained the decision by virtue of a savage right which lifted Child off his feet and into the press corps. In the next round he beat William Philo inside 60 seconds, flooring his opponent with a left uppercut.

In the final, Snowy found himself fighting fellow multiple inter- national, Johnny Douglas, who would go on to captain England at cricket and win an international cap as an amateur soccer player. Douglas was fresh, having had a bye in the first round and reasonable intervals between his subsequent fights. There are many newspaper accounts but the course of the bout is difficult to follow. The fullest reports are in the *Morning Leader* and the *Sporting Life*, although the two correspondents seem to have been at different fights. What does emerge is that Snowy did much work with his left jab in the first round which he won comfortably. He took a short count in the second which may have been the result of a slip. At the end of the third, the judges could not reach a verdict and an extra round was ordered. Snowy landed a huge roundhouse left in the closing seconds and Douglas rocked visibly.

Nevertheless, Douglas shaved the decision on points but the Australian had won the bout on many cards. As president of the Amateur Boxing Association, it was Johnny Douglas's father who placed the medal round his son's neck. Baker might have smiled ruefully at the schedule and the judging. There is a perennial myth – which Baker subsequently endorsed – that it was Old Man Douglas who refereed the fight. This is demonstrably untrue; the bout was controlled by Eugene Corrie. Since Baker was generous in defeat and never sought to undercut Douglas's victory, his mistake on this matter can only be attributed to a failing memory. There is a more credible legend that the pair boxed bare-fisted at the National Sporting Club a few days later and that Douglas was knocked out cold.

Snowy left for Australia shortly afterwards and docked at Fremantle on 12 December, confiding to local journalists: 'Yes, I lost the boxing championship, and I think the better man won.' Eleven days later he sparred at Rushcutters Bay with Tommy Burns. Burns was in training for his world heavyweight bout with the American negro, Jack Johnson. Snowy was chosen as the referee but had to stand down when Johnson objected to his blond hair. The fight would prove to be one of the most savage encounters in the history of boxing with racial overtones which make Schmeling-Louis in 1936 and its own attendant bigotry look like a piece of gentle milling at the Oxford and Cambridge Club. Amid horrendous chanting and crowd violence, Johnson butchered Burns for 14 rounds until police stopped the fight.

Snowy already had a small interest in Rushcutters Bay Stadium, being in cahoots with the arena's doltish and grasping owner, Hugh McIntosh. Snowy is often said to have promoted the Burns-Johnson fight. He certainly played a minor rôle in publicity but Harry Carpenter has assured the writer that the involvement was minimal. However, he soon formalized his relationship with McIntosh.

In January 1909, he opened a gymnasium and health academy. The 'Baker Postal Course of Physical Culture' became a rage across Australia despite spectacular platitudes such as: 'Try to be bright and see the "silver lining" in every cloud, as bright spirits and happiness are helpful to health and strength'. Two months later, Snowy married Ethel Kearney (née Mackay), the vivacious and trig widow of Augustus Kearney, a notable Victorian physician and a first-rate tennis player. Ethel possessed an hour-glass figure and an engaging manner with Gilbert and Sullivan arias. She was also a fine tennis player and a superb horsewoman.

Towards the end of 1912, Baker became increasingly active at Rushcutters Bay and in December he bought a majority share-holding from Hugh McIntosh. In the following month, the London *Sportsman* reported his purchase: 'Snowy Baker should be the very man to run a show like the Stadium. He is not only an experienced boxer, but the best all-round athlete in the Colonies. He is a tactful, affable young fellow, well educated, and a great favourite "down under" with all classes. Here's good luck to him, for he is one of the best.'

By contrast, here are the more accurate conclusions of Ruth Park and Rafe Champion who include a damning summary of Snowy in their biography of Les Darcy: 'A self-made man, he was ruthlessly hard with other sportsmen who came under his authority. Blessed with plentiful hubris, a confident manner and undoubted courage, he was valued by his master Hugh McIntosh ... and disliked and feared by the sporting world, which called him "The Great I Am".' Rushcutters Bay had originally been the site of a Chinese vegetable garden and only basic hospitality features had been built under McIntosh's ownership. Snowy and brother Harald poured much money into the venture; they rationalized the catering facilities and soon numbered among the moguls of sporting life in Sydney. W. F. Mandle has noted that initially, Snowy refereed major fights wearing green trousers and a bizarre felt hat, later changing to a more restrained tuxedo.

Early in 1913, he staged fights between touring British welter-weights and (laughably) advertised these as being for the world championship. He later made the boxers fight outside their weights and withheld purses on ridiculous pretexts. By now he had become a bizarre compound of Douglas Fairbanks Snr, Charles Atlas and Don King. Towards the end of this year, he called a conference to rational-ize championship boxing rules and bring them into line with American standards.

It soon became obvious that Rushcutters Bay required additional funding. Snowy went into partnership with John Wren. Snowy's senior by 13 years, Wren remains a scoundrel of the first chop and one of the most colourful characters in Australian history. He had been sent to work in a wood-yard at the age of 12 but soon became a small-scale usurer and bookmaker, launching a 'tote' which would later net him £20,000 a year. In a meteoric rise, he became a millionaire through projects as diversified as a cycling stadium, his boxing ventures with Snowy and a frock shop in Sydney.

Early in 1914, Snowy went on a six-month tour of Europe in the hope of persuading more boxers to fight in Australia. His targets included Georges Carpentier with whom he had discussions in Paris. Ted 'Kid' Lewis signed up immediately and sailed for Australia having been promised several lucrative bouts in Sydney. Morton Lewis's biography of his father reveals that Snowy made Lewis fight well above featherweight, was parsimonious with expenses and slippery on contractual details. On one occasion, Lewis lost a ludicrous points decision in a bout where the referee had been his opponent's brother-in-law.

By now, Baker's duplicity was becoming common knowledge. His conduct prompted Dave Smith, a former Australian middleweight champion, to form the first trade union for boxers. Many of the activities at Rushcutters Bay were unsavoury, the most repellent being bouts where young boys would fight each other from within sacks. Naturally it was impossible to judge how much punishment the lads were taking and the contests only terminated when one of them collapsed. Meanwhile, Snowy continued to coin money from a succession of major fights. His lifestyle became increasingly extravagant and he careered round Sydney in a canary-yellow Rolls-Royce with brass snakes coiling along the mudguards.

In the early months of the war, Snowy was involved in a car crash which caused spinal problems and (perhaps conveniently) kept him out of the conflict. He began screening movies at the stadium and became interested in the technical aspects of film-making. He remained a grasping opportunist and Rushcutters Bay saw much open soliciting by prostitutes. In the summer of 1915, this and a flagrant disregard of safety regulations attracted the attention of the *Sydney Morning Herald*. The resulting outcry nearly saw the arena closed.

Snowy paid off a few city councillors and in August he arranged for Les Darcy to fight Jeff Smith, a competent and intelligent American welterweight who had already fought an exhibition against Georges Carpentier. The first two rounds were savage, with the two boxers exchanging low blows and rabbit punches. Harald Baker was in charge of the bout and towards the end of the second, he disqualified Smith for persistent fouls. Snowy immediately announced that he would be holding on to Smith's share of the purse and that it would be donated to the Soldiers' Relief Fund. He always fancied himself as a litigant but in Smith he was trying to pluck a bird of his own feather. Smith sued Snowy for $Aus2,320, and film evidence was supporting his contention that both fighters were at fault when Snowy dug into his slush funds in order to silence him.

As the war continued and the Anzacs sustained massive losses, Rushcutters Bay came under fire from the press; the boxers and the younger spectators being branded as shirkers. Ostensibly to improve morale, Snowy spent much of 1915 in a tour of the country performing acrobatics on his grey horse, Boomerang. The show-stopper was a routine in which he manipulated a 36-foot stockwhip. In autumn of the following year came the murkiest episode in a shabby life.

At the time, the 20-year-old Les Darcy was the finest middleweight in the world and a proven money-spinner. In October of 1916, only four days before the Australian Prime Minister Billy Hughes introduced a conscription referendum, Darcy left Australia for America as a stowaway. That he was avoiding the draft is indisputable but it is now accepted that he had no long-term intentions of staying out of uniform. He had been reared in grinding poverty and was looking for a large pay-day in order to support his widowed mother and ten siblings, including a crippled brother. Baker and John Wren vented their spleen by calling Darcy a shirker and whipping up a frenzy of vilification in the press. Meanwhile, Snowy, who never saw a day's active service, was orchestrating massive recruitment rallies through his 'Sportsmen's Thousand' campaign for which he desperately needed Darcy as a figurehead.

It is worth noting that Darcy had already joined up in Brisbane but his mother had intervened on the grounds that he was a minor. He later made efforts to join both the American and Canadian forces and did in fact enlist with the US Aviation Corps. By 20 May 1917, Darcy lay dead in Memphis at the age of 21. Even when Darcy joined the Aviation Corps, Baker vented his savage and witless spleen by suggesting that he was gambling on the war being over before he had completed his training. Recent research has proved that Darcy died of pneumonia and septicaemia. There is of course a persistent legend that he died of a broken heart.

In July 1917, *Truth* magazine launched an exposé of Baker's part in Darcy's demise which prompted him to take out a libel case. He dropped the suit eight months later when the magazine recanted. The scandal dragged on and he soon realized that Darcy's mother was likely to expose him. In October, he asked for an enquiry to be held at Maitland and brought his high-calibre lawyers to meet (and intimidate) the Darcy family. In an inconclusive verdict, the enquiry more or less cleared Baker. It is likely that much money changed hands under the table. Superb research on Darcy by Katharine Moore and Murray Phillips reveals an article in the *Sporting Globe* published 30 years later. It recalls an exchange between Baker and Dave Smith at Darcy's funeral. Baker is said to have confessed: 'On my arrival at the cemetery, Dave drew me aside and asked me not to go to the graveside as feeling was running so high against me that some of the unruly ones were threatening to dig a grave and bury me alive.'

There was widespread media coverage of Snowy's own attempts to enlist, most notably in August 1917 when the Sydney *Referee* reported that he had been rejected for the third time as a result of the spinal injuries he had received a few years earlier. As already mentioned, there remains a scintilla of doubt over the legitimacy of these injuries. Three months later, and firmly established as a screen idol, Snowy was diving 80 feet to rescue his female co-star. The anomaly did not go unnoticed:

My word, didn't Snowy Baker cop it at this time. 'Why don't you enlist, people were saying, you're so keen on everyone else joining up?' Baker gave as good as he got. He had courage, I have to give him that. His story was that he had tried to enlist. Only a bad back kept him away from the Front. But it didn't keep him out of the movies, we all noticed. His athletic stunts were as hair-raising as ever.

Eric Pearce – quoted in *Home Before Dark: the life story of Les Darcy*, R. Parke and R. Champion, 1995

In the final years of the war, Rushcutters Bay had been little more than a large movie hall. Snowy was quick to realize that his athleticism and good looks held out the promise of a fortune in the burgeoning Australian film industry. In the autumn of 1917, he went into partnership with the theatrical entrepreneur Edward Carroll. After a chequered career as a railway clerk, fruit-seller and hotel proprietor, Carroll had moved into film and theatrical management, acquiring the rights to the first Australian feature, *The Story of the Kelly Gang*.

Snowy's first film was *The Enemy Within*. It went on general release in 1918 and the cast included Gerald Harcourt. Snowy plays secret agent Jack Airlie opposite 16-year-old Lilly Molloy. An appalling actor, he is carried at all times by some slick direction and his incredible stunts which he devised and performed himself. He is supported by an Aboriginal assistant as he launches a crusade against hordes of baddies who are loosely identified with the International Workers of the World Movement, popularly known as the 'Wobblies'. The film reflects contemporary paranoia about subversion and introduces what will be the staple diet of all Baker's movies, his thrilling rescue of the heroine. When Molloy is taken prisoner by the villains and tied to some wave-lashed rocks, Snowy evades heavy gunfire as he plunges to her rescue.

The Jazz Singer was some ten years away and Snowy's films are of course silent. Most of them are charming, ingenuous romps in which he grins from ear to ear while performing stunts which become increasingly distanced from the plot. By 1919, he had formalized his relationship with Carroll. They bought into the Southern Cross Feature Film Company and formed Carroll-Baker Australian Productions. In sharp contrast with his partner, Carroll appears to have been a businessman of unquestionable integrity.

The pair brought in the American director Wilfred Lucas, and in 1919 they cranked out *The Lure of the Bush*. By now Snowy's acting had improved and he approached competence as a station-hand. The film may have inspired sections of Laurel and Hardy's *A Chump at Oxford*. Snowy plays the eldest son of a pioneering Australian family. He is sent to England, and after a public school education he returns to Australia with monocle, plus-fours and a riding crop. Anxious to relearn the ways of bush life, he gets a job as a jackeroo. He alienates the other ranch hands but soon becomes their hero when he defeats the senior station hand in a superbly orchestrated bout. His co-star, the delectable Rita Tress, had been disowned by her family when she left the upper echelons of Sydney society for a film career, but she achieved significant success through her competent acting and superb equestrian ability.

Snowy's next move was predictable; in the autumn of 1920 he moved to Hollywood. Given the similarities in their acting careers, he was introduced to Douglas Fairbanks Snr who was working on *The Mark of Zorro*. Fairbanks's prowess with a stockwhip in this film is the result of intensive tuition from Snowy, and the pair became close friends. Snowy spent many hours with voice coaches but was unable to make the transition to talkies. He was given a few walk-on parts in Fairbanks movies and performed occasional stunts on Boomerang who had travelled over with him. However, he was more notable in Hollywood as a coach in horsemanship and swimming.

A few years and several bad movies later, Snowy bought a ranch and built a lavish mansion which he adorned with gum-trees and passion fruit vines. He had a brief turn in vaudeville, performing athletic feats on the Orpheum Circuit and also promoting wrestling. He was ready to return to Australia when the Riviera Country Club in Santa Monica offered him a lucrative position as its director. He was a huge success in the rôle and began giving polo lessons to the film community. (He once recalled that Will Rogers was his most gifted pupil while Spencer Tracy was the most obstinate.)

Snowy's marriage was essentially happy but there were occasional bust-ups. He still had an eye for a shapely calf and a fine pair of eyes, and would occasionally get a little frisky with Mary Pickford. These overtures were normally halted by a friendly slap from Fairbanks who was quite capable of taking care of himself. Fairbanks was first-rate as a boxer, fencer, wrestler and acrobat, and adored spending time with athletes. The relationship with Fairbanks was enduring. In a letter to the author, Douglas Fairbanks Jnr has recalled how his father would introduce Snowy at dinner parties: 'Ladies and gentlemen, I give you the greatest all-round athlete in the world.'

In March of 1932, Snowy made a brief visit to Australia. His aim was to find work as a journalist for the forthcoming Los Angeles Olympics and he touted himself around newspaper offices in Sydney. The *Referee* signed him up eagerly and preened itself on having secured such an excellent judge. In a front page spread it recalled Snowy's feats at the turn of the century: 'There may have been an ancient Greek his equal, but we doubt it … the greatest all-round athlete, amateur or professional, that Australia ever produced.'

Snowy was at the quayside to meet the Australian Olympic team and he entertained many of the youngsters at his ranch, also taking them to parties where they met the likes of Joan Crawford and Greta Garbo. There was much innocent flirtation, his favourite companion being Philomena 'Bonny' Mealing who would win silver in the 100 metres backstroke.

Snowy installed himself at the front of the press tent in the Colosseum Stadium, employed an impressive team of copyboys and pecked away at a battered Remington. Mary Pickford fluttered around and he kept the wires to Sydney positively buzzing with some lively if jingoistic froth. He had little to report in terms of Australian performances – three golds, a silver and a bronze – during an Olympiad which belonged to another subject here, Mildred 'Babe' Didrikson. Drinking nothing stronger than seltzer, Snowy could party all night with Fairbanks and his cronies at Pickford but arrive at the track early in the morning with a clear head.

In 1943 (at the age of 59), Snowy was still captaining the Californian polo team. In the same year, he performed wonders as an equestrian instructor to Margaret Lockwood who had landed the lead rôle of a highwaywoman in *The Wicked Lady* while scarcely knowing how to sit in the saddle. Some months earlier, his pupils at the Dupry Stables had included a 10-year-old Elizabeth Taylor who had been thrown during the filming of *Lassie Come Home* and required some fine-tuning for her rôle in *National Velvet*. He was obviously superb with children, and a 10-year-old Shirley Temple received instruction in the saddle for *Susannah of the Mounties*.

In 1945, he rode in a steeplechase against a field of 15 and won on the bridle by five lengths. However, his mind was dulling and three years later he retired from his position at the Riviera Country Club. He had always been devoted to his stepdaughter, Joan, and was inconsolable when she died later in this year after fracturing her spine in a show-jumping accident. He retired to an apartment on Irving Boulevard in Los Angeles where he became something of a recluse. However, he remained amenable to journalists. In 1950, he gave a long interview to the Sydney *People* in which he claimed to be performing double somersaults from the high diving tower and giving riding lessons at the Beverly Hills Saddle Club.

Despite being quietly spoken, Snowy was given to vacuous aphorisms which he took for wit. He remained clear-eyed and spry into his sixties, taking great pride in his magnificent upper body. A retrospective profile in a 1932 issue of the Sydney *Referee* includes this verdict on his rugby: '... tremendously courageous. He was a rare tackler, a relentless rush-stopper and as hard a player for his weight as has been seen in the game.'

In his final years, Snowy became desperate to return to Australia but Ethel, who was crippled by arthritis, was unable to make the journey. He made a short visit to Sydney in June of 1952 and had a seizure during the flight. His contemporaries were convinced that he had come home to die. However, he recovered in a sanatorium and gave a long interview to the Sydney *Daily Telegraph*. He was insistent that readers should know that he had maintained his physical condition, stressing that he still weighed 162 pounds as on the night of his fight with Johnny Douglas.

Sadly, he was suffering from progressive atrophy of the spine and arteriosclerosis. Two years later he died in Los Angeles of cerebrovascular disease. He remained an atheist to the last and there was no funeral, only a simple cremation. What religious convictions he had were shattered by the death of his stepdaughter. He retained this stance even when he knew himself to be terminally ill, a reassuring challenge to H. L. Mencken's assertion that there are no atheists in foxholes.

The obituaries constitute a vomitous whitewash of a shabby life. Baker had obviously employed a superb PR agent while in

Hollywood, and many of his more squalid actions have only been unearthed as a result of persistent interest in Les Darcy. This chapter is hardly revisionist history but it seeks to undercut the comfortable, avuncular image which he successfully nourished from 1920. As a man, he was fraudulent, grasping and manipulative. He is without doubt the most versatile athlete his country has produced. As a sporting icon, he belongs in the upper tier of the Australian Pantheon. Put him with Les Darcy, Victor Trumper, Keith Miller, Richie Benaud and Phar Lap.

7
Charles Burgess Fry

b. 25 April, 1872, d. 7 September, 1956

'Alice laughed. "There's no use trying," she said: "one can't believe impossible things." "I daresay you haven't had much practice," said the Queen. "When I was your age, I always did it for half-an-hour a day. Why, sometimes I've believed as many as six impossible things before breakfast."'

Lewis Carroll, *Through the Looking-Glass and What Alice Found There*, 1872

The facts can be easily documented but not without disbelief. Anybody studying Fry hovers in the limbo between fact and fancy. Here are some of the impossible but eminently true things: six consecutive centuries followed by an 82 two days after playing in the FA Cup Final; coming within a whisker of preceding Baden-Powell as the founder of the Boy Scout movement; candidature for the throne of Albania; a share of the world long jump record; cricket and soccer for England and 40 years as the nominal head of a naval training ship where a barbaric wife held sway over a régime that caused untold misery.

The subject is a polymath endowed with mind-numbing talents. With the possible exception of politics, he would have succeeded in any walk of life he chose and indeed he chose quite a few. Few people have set their sights on such a variety of targets and achieved them with such ease and dignity, and yet the myriad achievements fall short of the awesome promise displayed as a youth.

Charles Fry was born near Croydon into a comfortably but by no means prosperous family. He became a voracious reader of fiction and spent his boyhood acting out scenes from the novels of Fenimore Cooper. Cricket, athletics and fishing came into his life in the same summer and in his autobiography he describes how he made a static 17 not out on the village ground, favouring the leg side. Athletics commenced with victory by a foot in the high jump at a village fête. The realization that he would be a prodigious long jumper occurred on an evening walk when Dan the family dog appeared foaming at the mouth. Reports of hydrophobia prompted him to leap over a hedge and shin up a nearby tree, only for Dan to save himself by lapping up a basin of water proffered by the phlegmatic Fry senior. 'I was astonished at the distance I had cleared from the top of the bank over the intermediate hedge. That is how I found out that I was a long jumper; and it also shows the value of a really ugly dog like Dan.'

C. B.'s early schooling took place at Hornbrook House. Initially it was a chaotic establishment with no pretensions to preparing its pupils for public schools, and no organized games. Drastic change came in 1883 when it was sold to a son of Dr Pears who had raised Repton to prominence. The elder boys were cleared out, the diet improved, and Latin appeared on the curriculum. Cricket lessons were introduced under the direction of H. G. Wells's father who, in a moment of inattention at square leg, was knocked cold by one of the youngster's soon to be famous pull shots. Soccer was also taught and C. B. played for West Kent FC in a men's league at the age of 12. His aptitude for classics won him a scholarship to Repton two years later. An archetypal public school, it was chosen years later as the setting for *Goodbye Mr Chips*, with Fry invited to advise on sports scenes.

In 1889, he set a school long jump record of 21 feet which stood for 28 years until it was shattered by Harold Abrahams. In the following summer, his parents sent him to Paris in the hope that his spoken French would improve. He lodged below the Arc de Triomphe and attended lectures at the Sorbonne. It was a period of much student unrest, and as he emerged from a class one afternoon he was literally swept into a riot. He appears to have enjoyed proceedings and appeared at the front of the ranks. Largely neglected by his tutor, he revelled in café life which centred on Emile Zola and Claude Monet.

In 1890 he tried for scholarship examinations at Oxford, and was awarded Wadham's senior scholarship ahead of F. E. Smith, the future Lord Birkenhead. He had not gravitated Jude-like to the shimmering spires, nor did Oxford constitute, as it did for others, an indulgent finishing school or an intellectual greenhouse. He arrived in October 1891 with his wits and three pounds in his pocket, and many vacations were spent in tutorships. With little parental help, it was a struggle. Like Thackeray, C. B. might well have entitled the Oxford chapter of his autobiography 'How to live well on nothing a year'.

In between sporting commitments, Fry took a spectacular first in Classical Moderations after two years and an even more spectacular fourth in Greats a little later. This rare failure came about through the serious illness of his mother and melancholia induced by financial worries. As an undergraduate, his extraordinary physique was captured on the photographic plate by Edward Farquhar Buzzard – a first-rate soccer player himself – who persuaded him to appear naked in a series of poses which formed the core of a book that remained the definitive guide to artistic anatomy for many years.

C. B. became a ubiquitous figure at Oxford and was active in the Drama Society, appearing as one of Portia's suitors in an 1895 production of *The Merchant of Venice*. In a remarkable display of loyalty to the production, he insisted on performing in the Saturday matinée while under pressure to play soccer for the Corinthians, an appearance that would have done much to guarantee him an international cap. Other highlights as an undergraduate included being interviewed by Max Beerbohm for the *Idler*. Totally at ease, and greeting Beerbohm in a dressing gown, he held forth on subjects ranging from German unification to croquet.

In early 1892, C. B. appeared in his first Varsity soccer match at left back as Oxford lost 5–1. He had already represented England against Canada in December 1891 in a fixture which many soccer historians refuse to accept as a legitimate international. He would play in three subsequent Varsity fixtures, captaining a strong team in 1894 which lost 3–1, primarily due to a thaw at Oxford during some severe weather. His team turned up at Queen's Club with wet weather studs, only to find the ground like an ice rink and the Cambridge team ideally equipped with felt-barred boots.

Repton's concentration on soccer meant that Fry had not played rugby before he went to Oxford. He became active in college rugby, and it was not long before his athleticism saw him into the Oxford XV at wing three-quarter. He subsequently proved good enough to play for Blackheath and the Barbarians and to be considered for the England team. A high point of his short career was three tries for Oxford against the Barbarians in 1894, after which he was cheered on every inch of his walk back to Wadham.

As a cricketer Fry arrived at Oxford 'a known man'. In the freshmen's match, a distinctive century guaranteed him a place in the eleven. His first Varsity game in 1892 was a fluctuating affair in which the Cambridge batsman Gerry Weigall ran out three partners including his captain Stanley Jackson, sending Jackson to the danger end with the immortal: 'Get back Jacker, I'm set!' In the first innings, Fry came in at first drop with the Oxford score on 0. After a hesitant start he scored 44 in partnership with Malcolm Jardine. Poor batting coupled with Weigall's calling obliged Cambridge to follow-on, and although the Light Blues amassed 388, Oxford coasted to victory.

In 1893, miserable batting by Oxford created an unremarkable match which Cambridge won by 266 runs. When Oxford batted a second time, C. B. contributed 31 to a total of 64. In 1894 he replaced Lionel Palairet as captain. In the first innings he made a patient century. Oxford's ninth wicket went down with the captain on 83, and R. P. Lewis tottered to the wicket with a pallid countenance. Lewis surprised everybody by blocking out a few deliveries and allowing C. B. to move to three figures. In the second innings, C. B. was not called upon as Oxford eased to victory by eight wickets. A finger injury in the run-up to the 1895 game rendered him almost incapable of holding a bat. He was played for his bowling and took 6 for 78 in the first innings.

C. B. turned out three times in the Varsity athletics fixture, winning the long jump on each occasion. As a 100 yard sprinter with no starting blocks, he clocked 10.2 seconds and a wind-assisted 10 seconds dead. His most notable athletic performance occurred on 4 March 1893, when for Oxford against the London Athletic Club he recorded 23' 6½" in the long jump. The legend (which C. B. frequently reinforced) is that it was made in between puffs of a cigar. Countless occasional essays suggest that this leap not only broke the world record but was unbeaten for 21 years. In fact he equalled the record which had been set in Detroit by the American J. Ruben a few months earlier. Still less did it stand for two decades, being broken by the Irishman J. J. Mooney a year later.

It was after he left Oxford that Fry began to specialize. He turned out a few times for the Barbarians but showed little interest in continuing with athletics and devoted himself to cricket and soccer. In 1895 he played occasional games for Sussex, and on the recommendation of Ranji, he was selected for Lord Hawke's tour of South Africa in the following winter where he flourished with an aggregate of 750 runs at an average of 34. He played in the first two Tests at Port Elizabeth and Johannesburg, scoring 43, 15 and 64. Opportunities to play regular first-class cricket in the years immediately after this tour were limited. He scratched a modest living during a two-year stint as a classics master at Charterhouse. He recalls that the school would not allow him to take cricket classes and that he narrowly escaped being taught himself by the head boy. He was anything but conscientious and was often absent in London. He did, however, spend hours in a barn where pupils hurled cricket balls at him as he tried to enliven footwork that had already been condemned as static.

As early as 1892, Fry's bowling action had been, as the Victorian hacks put it, 'a matter for grave concern'. In June 1898 at Hove, he was no-balled nine times running. He was called in his first over and proceeded to serve up round-arm deliveries with an obviously stiff elbow, only to hear Jim Phillips condemn another eight balls. In the second innings he appeared with his right arm in a splint and swathed in enough bandages to eclipse Claude Rains in *The Invisible Man*. None of this tempted Billy Murdoch to allow the experiment by bowling him. Ranji wanted to write a treatise on batting with one eye; Fry would have enjoyed knocking off an essay on how to bowl with your arm in traction. The incident marked the end of his bowling career.

Later that summer, at the age of 26, Fry married the disgraced Beatie Sumner who was his senior by ten years. In the late 1870s, and barely out of her teens, Beatie had turned many heads on the Gloucestershire hunting circuit. A superb horsewoman who exuded a potent cocktail of tomboyish sexuality, her conquests included Charles Hoare, a wealthy banker who, in his early thirties and married with five children, was twice Beatie's age. As a young woman, Beatie had been an honorary whip with the Duke of Beaufort's Hounds and the subject of a characteristically mannered portrait by G. F. Watts. Hoare's wife was adamant in her refusal to allow a divorce. A tempestuous affair horrified both families, culminating in a scandal that engrossed Victorian society. Having separated from his wife, Hoare lived openly with his young mistress for several years.

Even when married to Fry, Beatie compounded her disgrace by vacillating openly between the two men in the early years of the century, though by this time the sexual aspect of the relationship with Hoare had evolved into a quasi-religious fervour. At 36, Beatie was still charismatic but she was a fading attraction and significantly overweight. By contrast, if such things had existed, Fry would have been near the top of a *Cosmopolitan* list of the most eligible bachelors for 1898. One of the most promising young men of his generation, he was also broke. There was no family money, cricket as an amateur barely covered his expenses, and professionalism was unthinkable. Sports journalism offered modest remuneration. Hoare was anxious that Beatie's past should be submerged in a respectable marriage and he almost certainly engineered the union. The marriage offered C. B. leisure to play cricket and probably a dowry put up by Hoare.

In 1885, Charles Hoare had founded what was to become the *Mercury*, a training ship on the Hamble River which prepared boys for naval careers. C. B. gives a brief history of the school in his auto-biography. What he chooses to say about Hoare is generous to a fault;

a fellow polymath with a passion for architecture and similarly touch-
ing eccentricities, Hoare designed the *Mercury's* theatre along the
lines of the Wagner Theatre at Bayreuth, and certainly produced large
numbers of qualified naval cadets.

Marriage to Beatie may have released Fry from schoolmastering but
it would impose restraints for many decades. That the core of Charles
Fry's life constituted a waste of extraordinary talents is a familiar but
inevitable judgement. In the first year of his marriage we find him
ostensibly editing, but in fact writing, *The Book of Cricket*. A lavish
coffee table volume, it teems with photographs but the biographies of
the players are trite and unrevealing. The only time he allows himself
some stylistic freedom is when, let down by another contributor, he is
obliged to write a portrait of himself, concluding that he is 'slightly
too theoretical ... no cutter ... a very intermittent off-driver' and
having 'a confidence in his back play which is not always justified'.

Between 1899 and 1910, Beatie bore Fry three children; two
daughters in Charis and Faith, and a son, Stephen. There has been
speculation that Charis may have been by Hoare. Stephen became a
Royal Navy officer and afterwards Director of Broadcasting in
Palestine before running a hotel with his American wife. He played
cricket for Hampshire intermittently in the 1920s with a modicum of
success and his son Charles Jnr also turned out for the county.

By early 1899, Fry was contributing articles to the *Athletic News*, the
Express and the *Captain*. He was introduced to Thompson Seton, the
founder of an American forerunner of the Boy Scout movement. In the
Captain, Seton saw the ideal mechanism for bringing his organization
to Britain, the idea being eventually scotched by Fry's misgivings as to
the underlying disciplinary content of the organization and the
suitability of the British countryside. Seton's ideas had fuelled C. B.'s
boyhood Fenimore Cooper fantasies but he did not see them as practical. He admits that the ultimate success of Baden-Powell's
movement proved him wrong and he lists being in some other guise
the first Scoutmaster as among his 'might-have-beens'.

Despite the demands of journalism, Fry remained active in cricket
at the turn of the century, and in 1899 he scored 1,500 first-class runs
at an average of 42 which brought him a place in the Test team. The
1899 Ashes series produced four draws and an Australian victory,
and he played in all five Tests. He was undaunted by a home début at
Trent Bridge which saw him opening with Grace in what transpired
to be the Old Man's last Test appearance, and he top-scored with 50 in
the first innings. He failed at Lord's, scoring 13 and 4, while at
Headingley he batted once, scoring 38. In the fourth Test at Old

Trafford, he failed again with 9 and 4 but he scored a fine 60 at the Oval.

He enjoyed a successful spell at right-back with Southampton at the turn of the century, and in March 1901 he played for England against Ireland at The Dell. England won a lacklustre game 3–0, C. B. describing it as 'aimless and vague and watery'. His performance was no more than competent and he did not retain his place. Later in 1901, he had his most prolific run as a batsman, scoring six consecutive centuries between 15 August and 14 September.

We now enter the core of the legend. The attempt at the seventh century was delayed until the beginning of the 1902 season when, playing for London County against Surrey at the Oval, he was caught with his score on 82. This innings came only two days after he had been involved in a gruelling FA Cup final replay against Sheffield United. The first leg had been a dour affair that was drawn at one goal apiece. The replay proved more attractive and Ernest Needham, an accomplished cricketer for Derbyshire, proved too much for Southampton. Needham provided the assist for Sheffield's first goal and after Southampton had equalized through 'Jigger' Brown, he also scored the winner, latching on to a weak headed clearance from C. B. to shoot from long range.

Later in the summer, Joe Darling's Australians toured England. C. B. failed miserably in the first three Tests with scores of 0, 0, 1 and 4 and was dropped after the third game. After the second consecutive duck, *Punch* enquired: 'What did C. B. Fry? – Two duck's eggs.'

In 1904 he was invited by George Newnes to set up his own paper, *C. B. Fry's Magazine*. With no technical knowledge, he set to work enthusiastically and sought out J. M. Barrie in the hope that the playwright would produce a piece for the first issue. The painfully reserved Barrie thawed more than usual, picking Fry's brains on cricket technique, but he provided him with nothing better by way of an interview than a suggestion to try E. V. Lucas, the essayist.

There was no shortage of offers from a diverse group of contributors, and a scheme for publishing the reflections of Hilaire Belloc on a walking tour of Morocco was only prevented by Belloc's ill-health. More extravagant features included a study of Theodore Roosevelt's young son who, it appears, once interrupted a White House meeting by entering it on stilts. The magazine continued until 1913 when Fry fell out with his publisher. A sideline involved promotion of the game diabolo in which a curious object consisting of two cones, joined at their points, was spun the length of a piece of string attached to batons.

He enjoyed another full season of county cricket in 1904 and, as a pioneer of the motor-car, would chug sedately to county matches in a 12-horse-power Clement-Talbot. Though no mathematician, he lapped up all kinds of engineering. Similarly, he once gave a quick lecture on the principles of radio communication to an astonished Marconi. Having devoted the winter of 1904 to journalism, he describes 1905 as his happiest season of Test cricket as the nation revelled in the captaincy of Stanley Jackson. The series was a resounding success for Fry who averaged 58 in his four matches, scoring 73 and 36 not out at Lord's and a glorious 144 at the Oval which featured some magnificent driving.

In 1907, in collaboration with Beatie, Fry produced the novel *A Mother's Son*. It has been completely ignored by his biographers, and warrants some discussion. Primarily the work of Beatie, it is something of a pot-boiler, lurching from the trite romanticism of the penny-dreadful to moments of genuine pathos. Beatie was a voracious reader of 19th-century fiction and the book abounds in its floating debris as she assembles a depressingly derivative cast. In the manner of David Copperfield, Mark Lovell loses his father and is brought up by a saint-like mother. She is aided in this by a local grandee who owes much to Fielding's Squire Western.

The backdrop is stratified into those possessing the stiff upper lip and those displaying the subservient forelock. Shortly after a successful career at Oxford, the hero is doomed by heart disease. With just enough time to produce an heir, he dies in his early twenties, leading a suicidal mounted attack on the Boers for a small wager while scores of unwilling infantry are wasted behind him. The passage reads like one of Michael Palin's *Ripping Yarns*, the distinction being that while Palin is looking for laughs, the Frys are playing it as straight as C. B.'s forward defensive.

A few weeks after the publication of *A Mother's Son*, C. B. was at Lord's for the first Test against South Africa. He scored 33 in the opening game and 54 in the second innings of the subsequent match at Headingley. In the final Test at the Oval, he raced to a chanceless 129 which he considered to be his best ever innings. The winter was spent in his first serious stint on the *Mercury* as Beatie absented herself to nurse Charles Hoare who was now fatally ill. In the period of Hoare's stewardship, while strictly disciplined and absurdly Blimpish, the *Mercury* was a happy and successful establishment where the cadets enjoyed a healthy curriculum that combined seamanship with a regular education.

Fry and Beatie took control of the academy on Hoare's death. The

Denis Compton, the twentieth century Everyman. The original Brylcreem Boy, he scored 5,807 Test runs for England, was a wartime football international and an FA Cup winner for Arsenal.
(left, Keystone Collection; below, Hulton Getty)

(below) Alfred Lyttleton, cricketer and footballer for England, was Cabinet minister under Arthur Balfour.

(right) Reginald Spooner played ten cricket Tests for England and was a leading stylist of his generation.

(left) Maurice Turnball, Glamorgan's greatest cricket captain, played cricket for England and rugby and hockey for Wales.
(Roger Mann)

(below) Kenneth Gandar-Dower brought cheetahs back from Kenya to race against greyhounds. He played tennis and squash for England and was also a poet, journalist and aviator.
(Hulton Getty)

(left) 'O my Hornby and my Barlow long ago' - Albert Hornby was celebrated in cricket's best known poem and captained England at rugby and cricket. He refused an England rugby cap because 'it would interfere with my hunting.'

(right) Lottie Dod revolutionised women's tennis. She won five Wimbledon singles titles and was a hockey, golf and archery international.
(Hulton Getty)

(below) Snowy Baker not only represented Australia at rugby, boxing, swimming and diving, he was also a major silent film star and equestrian coach to Elizabeth Taylor and Shirley Temple.
(Australian Film and Sound Archive)

(above) Frank Mitchell - England rugby captain while a Cambridge undergraduate, he later played cricket for England and South Africa.
(David Frith)

(above) A cricketer for England and Australia, Sammy Woods also captained England at rugby.

(below) Andrew Stoddart captained England at cricket and rugby.

(below) Patsy Hendren, a wartime international footballer, scored a total of 3,525 Test runs for England and had an average of 47.
(Sussex County Cricket Club)

Reginald Foster is the only man to have captained England at cricket and rugby.
(David Frith)

school needed to attract wealthy patrons and establish itself as a charity. Fry achieved both objectives, unashamedly pulling in favours from his influential acquaintances. To a man, Fry's obituarists point to his work on the *Mercury* as a piece of altruistic public service. The myth of the post-Hoare régime was exploded in 1985 by the publication of Ronald Morris's *The Captain's Lady*. A fine piece of urbane and balanced iconoclasm, it begins by exploring the relationship between Hoare and Beatie and continues with dispassionate accounts of life on the *Mercury* from its inception in 1885 to closure in 1968.

Morris describes how with Fry retiring and uninterested, Beatie degenerated from an athletic, Betjemanic figure into an ogress, ruling over a Dickensian system and subjecting the boys to extraordinary hardship and corporal punishment. The whole ship lived in fear of her as she personally oversaw the chastisements. Fry claims that he and his wife gave many thousands of their own income to support the academy. Since C. B. was an example of that frightening phenomenon, a rich man without any money, and Beatie's legacy from Hoare was modest, this should be regarded with suspicion. The ship was its own profit centre and the naval authorities paid handsomely for each boy who could enter as a midshipman.

Morris suggests that Fry was largely ignorant of what was going on, and was only known to strike a boy on one occasion and with justification. He was certainly wrapped up in a different world. In 1943, we find him trying to extract from the Brains Trust and from James Agate a true definition of the word 'rhythm', taking the Greek noun 'Ruthmos' with its original meaning of 'flowing' as his starting point, and proceeding to discuss the rôle of pattern in the metre of the Psalms. Meanwhile, in bizarre rituals some 500 yards away, boys were being strapped against a cannon and flogged to within an inch of their lives.

One of the *Mercury*'s few redeeming features was a commitment to music, the music teachers being of a different breed to the naval staff and the standards of tuition exceptionally high. External help was needed given that C. B. was tone deaf. (Years later, when travelling to Australia, he would muscle in on an otherwise dulcet octet and produce much disruption by bellowing his way through *Little Dolly Daydream* while his colleagues struggled to maintain the melody of the *Lily of Laguna*.) Morris records that in 1897, Beatie had returned from a trip to Bayreuth with a passion for Wagner. Neville Cardus reinforces this when he describes being invited to the *Mercury* to see the boys perform extracts from *Parsifal*. There is no record of what Sir Neville thought of the operatics but it can be hoped that he was not

tempted by his *Guardian* colleague Sam Langford's quip at a
Manchester production of the work: 'Amfortas is the wisest man here
tonight, he's brought his bed with him.'

In 1912, Fry brought out his classic instructional book *Batsmanship*
which runs to over 200 pages of purely technical discussion of the
various strokes. It is not an easy read, being remarkably dry and
containing no general reflection. Cardus describes it as 'the sort of
book Aristotle might have written if he had ever heard of cricket'. It
undoubtedly found the bookshelves of the greats, and Douglas
Jardine, while still at prep school, is said to have argued with a master
on a point of technique, citing Fry to reinforce his point. The book is
largely orthodox in its doctrine, and it was greeted favourably by the
establishment. Any student trying to carry out all of the instruction
would be incapable of co-ordinated movement having arrived at the
wicket. The sole historical exception is 'Swot', a bookish classmate of
Michael Parkinson who is said to have swallowed it whole and
achieved a surprising level of competence.

A few weeks after the publication of *Batsmanship*, Fry took over the
England captaincy for the Triangular Tournament of 1912. Many saw
his appointment as coming a decade too late. In his memoirs he notes:
'I was not popular at Lord's, being regarded in the light of a rebel.' He
distrusted tradition as an end in itself, an attitude which the MCC
often interpreted as truculence. Initially, Lord Harris offered him the
captaincy on a match by match basis. It was not a currency he under-
stood, and as befitted the grandee in him, the suggestion was
summarily dismissed. Like Miss Otis, he sent his regrets. The MCC
climbed down, giving him control for the whole series.

In the first match, England coasted to victory against the South
Africans by an innings. The more eagerly anticipated meeting
between England and Australia at Lord's was ruined by rain. The
England captain batted only once but he made a competent 42. With
minimal help from its captain, who scored 10 and 7, the English side
defeated South Africa comfortably at Leeds. As the appalling summer
continued, the fixture between England and Australia at Old Trafford
was washed out, while at the Oval, England defeated South Africa by
10 wickets.

Although he rapidly gained the respect of his players, Fry's lofty
mannerisms did little to endear him to the public, and the press was
seriously questioning his competence as he led England into the
deciding game at the Oval. The Australian captain Syd Gregory was
aware that his team were underdogs, and he was willing to risk all by
starting the match on a quagmire. Fry steadfastly refused to start until

the wicket was half-playable and the game began in late afternoon when he elected to bat. The score was 109 for 2 when he strode to the wicket. His entry was greeted with catcalls and he was dismissed a few minutes later for 5. Despite a fine 62 from Woolley, England were all out for 245.

C. B.'s second appearance at the wicket followed the loss of Rhodes and Spooner from consecutive balls with the England total on 7. Again he was greeted with shrieks of derision, but he appears to have been charged with adrenalin or to use his own charming vernacular 'very much on the job'. England was fortunate that another downpour took some venom out of the wicket. Her captain was always a good wet wicket player, and with assistance from the equally tenacious Johnny Douglas, he laboured to 79 and took the home side to a total of 175 and a lead of 309. Australia disintegrated to 65 all out and predictably, Fry had transformed himself from villain to hero in the eyes of a fickle Oval crowd which entreated him to join the other players on the balcony. He never emerged despite Ranji's entreaty to 'do the noble thing'.

The appalling weather and unpleasantness at the Oval had combined to create an unfortunate end to a disappointing series in which he had demonstrated fine leadership and acute tactical insight. As a skipper he had proved approachable and resourceful. It was his last Test match.

Fry spent the war years supplying the Merchant and Royal Navies with cadets. In 1920, his close friend and Sussex team-mate, Ranji, was invited to attend that much maligned product of 1920s idealism, the League of Nations. The Prince's decision as to who he should take as an aide was not difficult. C. B.'s own view of the League was objective; he saw it as an executive arm of the naïve certitudes that had produced the Treaty of Versailles, but was happy to make his excellent French available to Ranji. While extensively employed as a speech-writer and social organizer, he had time to look around him and he describes being enraptured by various colourful delegates including Paderewski who had forsaken the concert platform for the Polish premiership.

The most memorable moments occurred when an Albanian delegate, a Christian bishop with a stunning physical similarity to W. G. Grace, became one of many to be impressed by Fry's bearing as he flew around Geneva performing his multifarious duties. At the beginning of the First World War, the acting King of Albania had been a German who had the good sense to vanish at the onset of hostilities. By 1920, with their throne vacant, the Albanians were looking for a figurehead monarch and ideally 'an English country gentleman with ten thousand a year'. The bishop thought he had found his man and an interview was held. The bishop was impressed and Fry describes himself as having been 'well in the running for the billet'. Ranji was either unwilling to come up with the money or reluctant to lose an invaluable assistant, and the fairy tale never materialized.

The experiences in Geneva gave C. B. a taste for politics, and in the 1920s he stood for Parliament as a Liberal on three occasions, contesting seats at Brighton, Banbury and Oxford. Many occasional essays descend into spiralling eulogies and simply list these campaigns as another aspect of the man's all-round achievements. While he polled 20,000 votes at Brighton in 1921, the candidatures were in fact conspicuously unsuccessful. On his day, his occasionally brilliant rhetoric could make opposing political candidates sound as though they were opening a garden fête. Too often, however, an unwillingness to close and extensive classical quotation saw him lapse into rambling monologue.

By the late 1920s, we see the first hints of a mind beginning to doubt its own perceptions and a massive nervous breakdown followed in 1930. The symptoms were unusual and have been researched thoroughly by Ronald Morris: 'His behaviour was bizarre – he was said to have run naked along Brighton beach, and at home he hugged his possessions in fear of them being stolen by imaginary thieves. For the first few years of the 1930s he had to be looked after by a nurse, often staying at a house in Maidenhead made available to him by Ranjitsinhji.' In conversation with the present author, E. W. Swanton speculated that Ranji's death in 1933 may have been instrumental in prompting C. B. to snap out of his illness.

By 1934 he had recovered completely and one of his first public appearances was at the marriage of his son Stephen. Earlier in the year, representatives of the German Youth Movement had visited England and approached their opposite numbers in the Scouts. Perhaps through good fortune or some hazy suspicion that this was not the kind of liaison it wanted, the Scout movement had shown neither interest nor civility. The Germans renewed the project by approaching Fry who was well known for his work on the *Mercury*. They asked him if he would visit Berlin and meet the leaders of the Hitler Youth Brigade. He commissioned the help of his old Wadham colleague, John Simon (by now Foreign Secretary), and elicited interviews with leading figures in the Scout movement. On the condition that he would be allowed an interview with Hitler himself, he travelled to Berlin in late April.

It seems that C. B. had his critical faculties blunted from the outset. His first formal audience was with Rudolf Hess who proved ingratiating and at the end of the interview C. B. invited Hess to stay with him in Hampshire. He congratulated himself on a favourable German reaction to an initial memorandum and was oblivious to any attempts at curbing his enthusiasm. He thought nothing of Alfred Spender's refusal to serve on a liaison committee and was glowing in his evaluation of von Ribbentrop who acted as interpreter during the long-awaited interview with Hitler. The meeting was conducted in the Reich Chancellery and it appears that he swallowed whole the Führer's assurances that the uniform of the Youth Movement had no military significance and that German Jews permeated all aspects of communism.

The description of his visit to Berlin coincides with one of the few rambling sections of the autobiography, with the narrative flitting between analysis of Berlin in the 1930s to mild flirtations with Teutonic lovelies in the hospitality boxes at Lord's. Fry closes his observations on Hitler with a banal quotation from Ovid's *Metamorphoses*, the sentiment being that it is right to be taught by the enemy. For once he is demonstrating more classical education than sense. The unrepentant attitude and cheap reassurance, despite ample opportunity for revision, have appalled many contemporary writers.

Perhaps Fry's judgement was unhinged by the manifold calls on his time. Within a few weeks of returning from Berlin, he was busy covering the Ashes tour to England by Bill Woodfull's Australians. His thoughts formed 'colour' pieces in the *Evening Standard* which complemented the factual reporting of a youthful E. W. Swanton. Fry dispensed his regal reflections in a column entitled *C. B. Fry Says*. Despite being laced with Greek, the pieces are among his finest writing, and the sentences fire off like darts. Prompted by the author, Mr Swanton recalled the scene at the opening match of the tour at Worcester as if it was yesterday: 'I can see Charles Fry now. He was talking non-stop to anybody who would listen, while scribbling his thoughts on flimsy sheets of A5 paper. By mid-day, the *Standard* was screaming for mercy. He had already given them 1,500 words!'

The conversation and hospitality in Fry's box at Lord's during this period have become legendary. Guests included James Agate, Arnold and Clifford Bax, Harold Begbie and Edmund Blunden. Like a good chat show host, Fry had the ability to make his guests interested in each other. Copious amounts of champagne and chicken were dispensed by his manservant Jimmy Brooks. A retired music hall comedian of the Max Miller school, and a veteran of Flanders, Brooks performed duties ranging from driving the Bentley to checking classical references and phoning through the copy. Fry continued as a columnist for several years, and from a London base he produced reflective articles on the 1936 Olympics.

Soon after the Olympics, C. B. made his one visit to Australia as an *Evening Standard* correspondent on Gubby Allen's Ashes tour, where, not without some bickering, he shared a booth with Douglas Jardine. Always innovative and occasionally eccentric in his dress, his presence on the voyage out was a Barnum and Bailey affair as, bedecked in garb that varied from short leather trousers to a bath towel resembling a toga, he held forth on subjects ranging from the prospects of the forthcoming series to the origins of iambic verse. Cardus seems to have been one of the few to have had C. B.'s measure. He notes that the only occasion when C. B.'s clothing approached normality was at the costume ball when he appeared as a scoutmaster. Greeting him the following morning, by which time C. B. was sporting a bizarre scaled green tunic, Cardus was able to observe: 'Glad to see you back in fancy dress, Charles.' E. W. Swanton has recalled that C. B.'s normal garb was a voluminous Norfolk jacket, Harlequin tie and extraordinary trousers which buttoned at the ankle.

He was not above occasional displays of ridiculous pomposity during the tour of Australia, the most notable occurring at a public banquet which he left in high dudgeon on observing that his place card read '*Mr* C. B. Fry'. He never saw an hour of action at sea, and his title of Captain (which he would occasionally inflate to Commander), was a nominal one. Returning to England via the States, Fry spent several weeks in Hollywood where he spent many hours flirting with Mary Astor on the set of David Selznick's *The Prisoner of Zenda*.

In 1946, Fry became a widower when Beatie died after a fall. Taking time out from the *Mercury*, he joined the BBC team for the third Test match against India at the Oval. In his obituary of Rex Alston, Frank Keating recalls Alston's experience of working with Fry. 'He had the pleasure of sacking C. B. Fry, cricketing eminence. Fry was foisted on me as the first cricket "inter-round summarizer" in 1946. At the end of the first over, I brought him in saying, "What do you think, Charles?" On air, I ask you, this difficult little pipsqueak raised his voice to me and said to the nation, "Charles? My name is not Charles to you, sir, but Commander Fry. If you get that right in future, I will begin to answer your questions." Odd blighter – no, of course I never used him again.' This is Fry at an asinine extreme, the only redeeming circumstance being that he was distraught by the loss of Beatie. There were also frequent disagreements in the commentary box with John Arlott, though Arlott once recalled how Fry was instrumental in persuading him to continue writing poetry: 'Did he think I might become a poet? He thought for a moment and then said "I think you are already – but you will be a better one".'

On Beatie's death, Fry made token attempts to take over the running of the *Mercury*. His heart was never in it, and he soon left for London and a flat on the Finchley Road. By the early 1950s he had retired from public life but had not given up writing. A series of polemic articles included pleas that the Russians should be persuaded to take up cricket.

Fry was obsessed with the concept of grace. Like Arthur Ashe, many years after him, he discussed it at every conceivable level; physical, intellectual and moral. C. B. once described batting as 'a dance with a stick in your hand'. He recommended dance lessons for all as a cure for self-consciousness, regarding a knowledge of how to move effectively as having a great influence on the whole being. In a letter to James Agate, he describes studying dancing for four years under Josephine Bradley, then the best ballroom dancer in the world and to become a close friend. Similarly, in his biography of John Arlott, David Rayvern Allen recalls how as a dancer, Fry was 'inclined to take such long and imperious strides that his partners found it very hard on stockings'.

A most remarkable man, Charlie. You know, he was in his late seventies when he took out a bird I knew, took her to a night club and gave her a magnificent dinner, and danced with her afterwards, enthusiastically – modern dancing – and she said to me, 'And do you know, he's seventy-eight and he didn't have a piss for five hours'. By now John's shoulders were shaking with laughter. 'Terribly observant of the girl'.

David Rayvern Allen, *Arlott: The Authorised Biography*, 1994

In 1955 Fry appeared on *This is Your Life*. When asked what were his proudest moments, he highlighted the occasions on which *The Times* had published his poetry. With many of the guests commenting on his gifts for leadership, he was asked later in the programme if he considered himself to have been a great cricket captain. The reply came in a flash and has an unusual and disarming modesty. 'Of course I was a great captain. I had great bowlers.'

This rare television interview was among his final public appearances. After a short illness, C. B. died from an infection of the urinary tract on 7 September 1956. The obituaries were lavish but the final summation can be left to Cardus, writing when Fry was in his pomp. 'No living English musician, critic or performer of my acquaintance is half the work of art to look at and to *experience* as C. B. Fry. In himself he is a national gallery and a theatre and a forum.' Perhaps we can indulge in one flight of fancy. As he sat on the set of *The Prisoner of Zenda*, he might just have caught a piece of dialogue, and thinking of the Albanian bishop, smiled ruefully, as Douglas Fairbanks Jnr tells Ronald Colman that 'Heaven doesn't always make the right men kings.'

8
Charlotte Dod

b. 24 September 1871, d. 27 June 1960

'The fascination of what's difficult
Has dried the sap out of my veins, and rent
Spontaneous joy and natural content
Out of my heart.'

W. B. Yeats, 'The Fascination Of What's Difficult', 1910

When Henry V arrived at Calais in the autumn of 1415, he did so in the knowledge that his archers, on whom he was staking everything in the little scrap that lay ahead at Agincourt, were under the tutelage of Sir Anthony Dod. It left Henry free to respond to the Dauphin's insulting gift of a consignment of tennis balls. Clutching our link between the Dod family and tennis balls (archery will become a major theme later), we can move to the old Worple Road ground in London SW19, where on 6 July 1887, a direct descendant of Sir Anthony won her first Wimbledon singles title for the loss of only two games. She would go on to represent England at hockey and golf, and Great Britain at archery.

Charlotte 'Lottie' Dod was born at Bebington, Cheshire, into an engaging family of sports fanatics headed by Joseph Dod, a successful cotton broker. Lawn tennis had been invented three years after her birth. The Dods were immediate converts and their home boasted grass and shale courts. Lottie began playing with her brothers and sister when she was nine, and her prowess earned her the nickname of 'The Little Wonder'. None of the Dod children attended school but they were well educated by a succession of tutors. Tennis was only part of a sporting timetable which included croquet, golf and bowls.

Lottie compiled a scrapbook of her sporting achievements. This is kept at Wimbledon and is a gold mine for researchers; much of the material quoted here is taken from it. She has also been the subject of a biography by Jeffrey Pearson to which this chapter is greatly indebted.

In 1883, Lottie and her sister Anne won the Consolation Doubles at the Manchester tournament and a local paper commented: 'Miss L. Dod, who is only eleven years old, played from the back of the court with skill and judgement.' Her first notable tournament was the 1884 Northern Ladies' Doubles at Liverpool, where she was a runner-up with Anne, losing a marathon best of five sets match. She entered the tournament again in 1885 and on this occasion she and Anne won the doubles. More remarkably, at the age of 13, she reached the final of the singles where she stretched the Wimbledon champion Maud Watson before going down 6–8, 5–7.

Lottie made her first real impact on the tennis world in 1886 when she gained revenge over Maud Watson to win the West of England Championship at Bath. Her backhand survived an onslaught and she displayed superb movement and a mature all-court game. At the Buxton tournament in the same year, the lady competitors played the gentlemen at cricket, the gentlemen batting left-handed and with broomsticks. In front of 2,000 spectators, the ladies were set a target against the clock which they reached with two minutes to spare. Lottie scored 14 runs, having previously taken a hat-trick with some teasing lobs.

At the beginning of the 1887 season, she travelled to Dublin for the Irish Championship at Fitzwilliam Square. In a keenly contested final, she defeated Maud Watson 6–4, 6–3. The Fitzwilliam Square Club was among the first to build an indoor court with electric lighting, an achievement which owed much to the pioneering work of a Mr O. E. Woodhouse who is gloriously described in the Badminton Library as being 'equally distinguished as a lawn-tennis player and electrician'. By now Lottie had Maud Watson's measure, and later in June, she destroyed her 6–2, 6–1 in the Northern Championship at Manchester.

In July of the same year, Lottie played in her first Wimbledon. She had to play only two matches and eased her way to the challenge round where she met Blanche Bingley. (At the time, the holder simply waited for a challenger to emerge from the rest of the field.) Miss Bingley was a determined retriever with extraordinary court speed. She would go on to win the title another five times but she was unable to live with Lottie's ground strokes. The first four games went with serve, whereupon Lottie launched into the most glorious burst of sustained hitting that tournament tennis had seen, winning the next ten games to take the title 6–2, 6–0.

Lottie had impressed all with her technical ability and sheer athleti-cism. Her victory is somewhat debased by the absence of Maud Watson, and the fact that there were only six competitors. However, she had beaten Watson three times earlier in the season and there is little doubt that she had established herself as the foremost tennis player in the country. She had been 15 years and 285 days old when she won the title, and she remains the youngest Wimbledon singles winner. The nearest challenger to date is Jennifer Capriati whose age was 15 years and 96 days when she breezed past Martina Navratilova in 1991 to reach the semi-finals. (Lottie's distinction was kept intact by Gabriella Sabatini who dispatched Capriati two days later.)

Lottie was less dominant in 1888, and she was hard pushed by Blanche Bingley at the West of England tournament and the Northern Championship. The two women met once more in the challenge round at Wimbledon and on this occasion Lottie achieved a comfortable 6–3, 6–3 victory. In 1889, Lottie declined to defend her Wimbledon title. Years later she would explain why in an interview with the *Lady's Pictorial*: 'I was yachting in Scotland with friends, and we were having such a good time that I could not make up my mind to leave.'

In 1891, Lottie displayed exceptional form in coming through to the Wimbledon final where she defeated Blanche Bingley for the loss of three games. She was scheduled to play Lena Rice in the challenge round but when Rice withdrew, Lottie was awarded the title by default. The *Field* report concludes: '... when Miss Dod set herself going it was at once apparent where the championship was destined. A few years ago Miss Dod retired in order to give some other lady a chance. I am afraid she will require to do so again, or else she will frighten her less gifted sisters away.' At Wimbledon in 1892, Lottie brushed aside Blanche Bingley once more, this time for the loss of only two games.

At the Dublin tournament in the same year, she suffered a rare defeat at the hands of Louise Martin. Martin played an excellent serve and volley game throughout, and a break for rain allowed her valuable respite. Lottie gained revenge for this defeat a few weeks later in the Northern Championship at Liverpool where she defeated Martin for the loss of one game in under 30 minutes. This should have produced a challenge match against the holder Miss Stanuell who, having witnessed Lottie's awesome form, decided to take her hat and her leave. At the same meeting Lottie won the All England mixed doubles with her brother Tony. (The mixed would not be contested at Wimbledon until 1913, since when two brother and sister combinations have won the title, John and Tracy Austin in 1980 and Cyril Suk and Helena Sukova in 1996.)

By now Lottie's interests were widening. A cutting from the *Irish Cyclist* for September 1892 describes her summer holiday: 'Miss Lottie

Dod, the champion tennis player, is at present sojourning at Portrush, indulging in the pastime of golf. She has learnt to ride a safety, and is very keen on taking to cycling. Miss Dod is the very picture of healthy, muscular womanhood, brown as a berry, and with the regular athlete's eye. Whatever she takes up in the way of pastime she means to excel at.' Despite this new enthusiasm, she stuck with tennis for another year, and in the challenge round at Wimbledon in 1893 she faced one of her sternest tests to date when Blanche Bingley won the first set 8–6. Lottie recovered to win the next two sets 6–1, 6–4.

Lottie gave up tournament tennis at the end of this season, primarily out of boredom after such a long stretch of dominance. She devoted herself to golf, playing at Moreton Ladies. Golf was one of the few sports at which Lottie did not possess prodigious natural talent. She laboured to develop a swing that involved a healthy body turn but was always mechanical and she was often obliged to resort to crude methods for counteracting a pronounced slice. She made her début in the 1894 British Ladies' Championship at Littlestone, Kent, but lost in an early round. This defeat prompted her to begin a heavy schedule of tournament play, and in May 1895, in the third round of the British Championship at Royal Portrush, she claimed the notable scalp of Sybil Whingham. In the fourth round, she was brushed aside 4 and 3 by the eventual winner, the exquisitely beautiful and graceful Lady Margaret Scott.

Jeffrey Pearson describes how in December 1895, Lottie travelled to St Moritz where she indulged in every winter sport imaginable, including cricket on the frozen lake. The Cresta run was only a minor challenge and she also showed an aptitude for mountaineering. She completed her holiday in the New Year with a cycling tour of Italy during which her party travelled from Genoa to Rome. She returned to St Moritz in the following November and trained assiduously for the Men's Skating Test which she passed early in 1897. In the summer she took off for Norway and, with minimal experience, she made several impressive climbs in the Romsdal Valley.

The 1898 Women's Golf Championship at Great Yarmouth was one of the most keenly contested to date. Lottie's semi-final was against Elizabeth Neville. She was immaculate from tee to green but she could not hole a putt of any consequence and eventually went down by the odd hole, *The Times* commenting: 'Miss Dod exhibited unsteadiness on the greens, although her play was quite equal to that of her opponent in driving and approaching.'

By the late 1890s, Lottie had acquired a passion for hockey. She developed into a bustling utility player with a heavy shot and was a prolific scorer for the Cheshire county team. She made her début for England at Richmond in March 1899, playing at inside-right in a 3–1 victory over Ireland. A match report in the *Gentlewoman* includes: 'Although Miss Dod is somewhat behind the others in the matter of pace, she is surprisingly quick and powerful in her strokes and tricky in dribbling and passing. She is a very strong player.'

In May 1899, Lottie travelled to Newcastle, County Down for the British Golf Championship. Newspapers of the day are dominated by the Dreyfus case which was reaching fever pitch and had escalated into clashes on the streets of Paris. None of this would have been uppermost in Lottie's mind as she came through some tough matches before facing May Hezlet in the semi-final. On the front nine she topped many of her drives, and was inaccurate with her club selection. After the turn, she repeatedly found sand and was beaten 4 and 2.

Both Jeffrey Pearson and the English Women's Hockey Association give sketchy accounts of Lottie's appearance in a hockey match against Ireland in March 1900, claiming that no detailed records of the game survive. Even cursory research at Colindale revealed a substantial report in the *Dublin Sporting News*. The game was played on 1 March at Anglesea Road, Ballsbridge, and Lottie scored twice in a 2–1 victory for the visitors. A Miss Olme scored for Ireland early on, and the home side retained its lead until early in the second half when Lottie scored with some reverse stick-work. A few minutes later she put her side into the lead, and the report includes: 'Miss Lottie Dod was the best of the forwards.'

In 1900, Lottie again reached the semi-final of the Ladies' Golf Championship at Westward Ho! where she was defeated on the final green by Mrs Wilson Hoare. In the following year, her eccentric swing began to take a toll on her lower back; she suffered from sciatica for many months and played no sport. However, she remained active and contributed a chapter to the Badminton Library. Her recommendations include hitting the ball flat at all times and attacking the net after a suitable approach whenever possible.

As a crowd-pleasing exercise before the 1904 Ladies' Golf Championship at Troon, the home countries played a series of internationals, and Lottie captained the English ladies. She struggled in her first match against the Scottish captain Elie Glover, but came through on the last green. On the second day she was drawn against the Irish captain May Hezlet, and having gone out in 39, she was one up at the turn. After a poor run on the back nine, she was beaten 2 and 1.

In the tournament proper, she won her semi-final against Dorothy Campbell by the comfortable margin of 4 and 2. In the final Lottie faced May Hezlet, and by virtue of some superb putting, she was two up by the tenth. A crowd of 5,000 spectators included swarms of unruly schoolchildren and hundreds of dock-workers who had deserted the Clyde and travelled south for the day. Lottie found herself one down at the 17th tee. Hezlet missed from three feet on the 17th green, and the pair went to the 18th tee all square. Lottie's drive was rifle-straight, and coming through one of the biggest tests of her nerve to date, she laid her approach stone dead and single putted to win the championship by one hole.

At Cromer, in May and June of 1905, the field for the British Championship contained half a dozen high quality American players including Georgina Bishop, and Harriet and Margaret Curtis. Prior to the championship, the British Ladies took on the Americans and Lottie captained a strong team which boasted players of the calibre of May Hezlet, Dorothy Campbell and Molly Graham. The home side triumphed 6–1, but it was Lottie who sustained the only defeat. She had not spared herself by playing the American captain, Georgina Bishop. Lottie is widely considered to have been nerveless, but even she may have been overawed by the media attention that the matches attracted. Lottie was three up at the turn but she consistently missed fairways on the closing holes. The score was all square on the 18th green, but the American closed out the game on the 20th.

The Curtis sisters had formed the backbone of the American team, and the name will have registered with golf enthusiasts. Many years later, the competition was formalized as the Curtis Cup. On the following day, England took on Scotland. Lottie may have been drained by her match of the previous afternoon, and she was uninspired as she lost to the Scottish captain Molly Graham. Further defeat followed a few days later against Ireland, when Lottie was beaten by May Hezlet. It was hardly ideal preparation for the British Championship which began two days later. Lottie struggled into the fourth round where she went down 4 and 3 to the eventual winner Bertha Thompson.

By now it will be apparent that Lottie's talents were Elizabethan in their variety. In 1906 she announced that she had given up golf and would be concentrating on archery. In the previous year, she had moved to Newbury where she joined the Welford Park Club. Archery had been a consuming passion for generations of Dods stretching back to Sir Anthony and Agincourt. Having decided she would excel at another sport, it was not long before Lottie was featuring prominently in the Grand National Archery Meeting, and in the spring of 1908 she won the Southern Counties Ladies' Championship at Beddington Park.

In July she became a treble international when she competed at the White City for the Olympic archery title. On the first day Lottie performed superbly to head the event with a ten-point lead over Sybil 'Queenie' Newall. On the second, she faltered slightly and Miss Newall triumphed by a margin of 46 points. Queenie was 53 years old and she remains the oldest woman to win an Olympic gold medal. Lottie continued with archery for a few more years with a good measure of success, but in 1911 her home club at Welford Park was closed down and she gave up the sport.

In 1913 Lottie moved to Bideford with her brother Willy, and they became prominent members of the Royal Devon Golf Club. Shortly after the outbreak of war, Lottie gained nursing qualifications, and she made repeated applications to be stationed in France. These were unsuccessful; she was now 43 and the sciatica was coming in prolonged bouts. She was posted to a hospital in Chelsea where her work resulted in a Red Cross medal. After the war, she played regular club tennis at Roehampton and became a fixture at the Wimbledon Championship. Lottie also renewed the musical interests of her youth, and joined the London Oriana Madrigal Society, later becoming its Honorary Secretary. She had a fine contralto voice and was a competent pianist with a great love of Debussy.

In 1926, Lottie began to combine her madrigal singing with recitals as part of the Bach Cantata Club under the baton of Charles Kennedy Scott. The club had as relaxed a notion of what constituted a cantata as Bach himself and it performed a wide variety of the composer's music, most notably an annual recital of the Christmas Oratorio. As a contralto, Lottie would have had few if any opportunities to sing solos but by now her personal ambitions were burning less brightly, and she was happy to be part of an overall sound.

With encouragement from Thomas Beecham, Kennedy Scott had founded both the Oriana Madrigal Society and the Cantata Club. He was a keen sportsman and was overjoyed when he was introduced to Lottie. His pleasure was redoubled when he realized that she had a first-rate voice and the pair became close friends. Lottie appeared with the club at St Margaret's, Westminster, throughout the 1930s in performances which were characterized by Kennedy Scott's manic desire to reproduce the exact sound of Bach's own day. On several occasions, the club was accompanied by Albert Schweitzer, the missionary and explorer whose own wide-ranging talents established him as a first-class organist and a world authority on Bach's choral music. Kennedy Scott was also a close friend of Vaughan Williams who heard Lottie sing and was said to be impressed with her voice.

When not involved with singing, Lottie did much work at a girls' club in Whitechapel, playing the piano at drill and teaching the youngsters various ball games. She also gave lessons in part singing to a group of Girl Guides in the East End, and her pupils won several competitions. In the late 1930s, she spent many weekends at Westward Ho! and bought a house there with Willy. She renewed her involvement with the Royal North Devon Golf Club and featured regularly in the monthly medal. Lottie remained a keen follower of tennis and did not allow herself to lapse into a roseate view of the standards of her own era. Lance Tingay has underlined this and he recalls how in 1939, she revelled in the unbridled aggression of Alice Marble, pronouncing her the finest woman player of all time. Jeffrey Pearson notes that during the Blitz, it was not until 1942 that Willy persuaded her to leave London. Brother and sister spent the late 1940s at Westward Ho! and Lottie served as Lady President of the Royal North Devon Club at the end of the decade.

She returned to London in 1950 and bought a flat in Trebovir Road, SW5. Willy joined her two years later and Lottie became a familiar figure as she tripped down the Earl's Court Road to buy fruit. As her mobility declined, she turned to bridge. In his autobiography, N. L. 'Pa' Jackson, the founder of the Corinthian Football Club, notes: 'I have it on good authority that she is one of the best bridge players in London.' Willy joined his sister in London in 1952 and the pair lived together until Willy's death two years later. Lottie's own health was failing; she gave up the flat and spent time in various nursing homes on the south coast.

Physically, Lottie was solidly built, even stocky. She was hardly a 'great big mountainous sports girl', but there is something Betjemanic about her physicality. Like Maureen Connolly, her anticipation was uncanny and she never seemed to make a hurried shot. Her ground strokes had the pace and authority of her male contemporaries, and her footwork was superb. Lottie always served underarm; this was hardly due to inability since her overhead smash was awesome. At the net, she did not punch the ball according to contemporary wisdom but took Agassi-style lunges with controlling backspin. She chased down anything at which she could throw herself, and once criticized her opponents' stomach for retrieving: ' Instead of running hard, they go a few steps and exclaim, "Oh, I can't", and stop.' As a doubles partnership, Lottie and her sister were among the first players to attack the net in tandem. She was neither self-conscious nor demonstrative on court, and was playing the 'inner game' a hundred years before it acquired a vast and pretentious literature.

On the tennis court, Lottie's clothes were as revolutionary as her play. In view of her age, the authorities relaxed the strictures of the day and she was allowed to wear a calf-length skirt in place of the normal bustle dress. For an era in which piano legs were draped, it was a significant departure from the norm and as daring as Billie Tapscott's stockingless legs of 1929 or 'Gorgeous Gussy' Moran's lace knickers of 1949. Lottie also rejected the regulation straw boater for a peaked cap. Despite her manic urge to excel at sport, she was quintessentially feminine and there was nothing tomboyish about her. She displayed consummate dress sense and would spend hours decorating her tennis outfits with elaborate pattern work.

Lottie slipped away peacefully and almost unnoticed by the British press on the evening of 27 June 1960. The legend is that she had been listening to radio commentary from Wimbledon during the afternoon. It is easy to deride her victories; she came through only three matches to win her first Wimbledon title in 1887, and in the early days fields for major tournaments could be as small as six. In the years in which she was the reigning champion at Wimbledon, her challenger might have played several hard matches. There is little doubt, however, that she would have reached the highest levels of tennis and her other sports in any era. In her own time she was close to being unbeatable on the tennis court, and in eleven years she was defeated only five times in singles. Virginia Wade, who is an avid student of her predecessors, is mindful of Lottie's stature, describing her as 'the first player to approach the fitness and athleticism of the men'. Lance Tingay has identified Lottie as the outstanding female sportswoman of the 19th century. After a respectful nod to Kitty Godfree, the present writer would nominate her as the greatest all-round woman athlete in the history of British sport.

9
Maurice Turnbull

b. 16 March 1906, d. 5 August 1944 in action.

'Now you will not swell the rout
Of lads that wore their honours out,
Runners whom renown outran
And the fame died before the man.'

A. E. Housman, 'To an Athlete Dying Young', 1896

Under a heading 'Normandy Battle Is Won', the *Western Mail* for 12 August 1944 includes the following: 'A broken German army is fleeing towards the Falaise Gap. It is today being savagely attacked from the air.' The Normandy landings had brought victory nearer but at huge cost. The death toll included a 38-year-old major in the First Battalion of the Welsh Guards, a victim of machine-gun fire during fighting outside Caen. Of all the casualties posted home that month, news of Maurice Turnbull's death was perhaps the most widely mourned. His sporting talents were self-evident; he had played cricket, rugby and hockey at international level. That he was urbane, witty, articulate, and as good as few men have been since the Fall simply piled on the agony.

Maurice had been born into an affluent Penarth family headed by Philip Turnbull. The family was close-knit and had descended on Cardiff during the coal boom whereupon several members made a fortune out of a shipping business. In addition to playing cricket for Glamorgan, Philip also found time to represent Wales 13 times at hockey. Five of Maurice's brothers would play rugby for Cardiff and the family was synonymous with sporting life in the city.

The Turnbulls were devout Catholics and in 1917 Maurice was sent to Downside, a leading Catholic school in Bath. He prospered among the Benedictine tutors and his impact on school life was immediate. He skippered the junior cricket XI in his first year, and in 1918 he also captained the lower-school rugby XV. Within weeks of his arrival he was the choir's leading treble. Maurice broke into the cricket XI in

1921. He opened the batting regularly with his brother Lou, and the pair played alongside each other for the school hockey team. In the 1923–4 season he captained the school rugby XV and the *Raven* summarizes his performance with: 'M. J. Turnbull filled the position of scrum-half, and played consistently, equally good in attack and defence.' He was also active in the boxing ring; a report in July 1923 including: '… very quick on his feet and uses his left well'. He won prizes for history and also became president of the literary society.

Of course Maurice quickly became the school's wonder batsman. In the damp summer of 1924 he played in only two matches. Against Blundells he made a resolute 81 and against Bruton he clubbed a glorious 184. His county début was against Lancashire at Swansea, where at the age of 18, he made a polished 40 runs to top-score against an attack that included McDonald and Parkin. The academic year of 1924–5 was an uninterrupted triumph. He became Head of School and Captain of Games. In March 1925 he not only played rugby for the full Somerset XV against Devon but also scored four goals as the school defeated the Cardiff Hockey Club. The range of his interests remains dizzying and in April he featured as Samuel in *The Pirates of Penzance*: 'M. J. Turnbull's Samuel was a capital sketch. He ably and humorously carried out a well-conceived idea of the character.' In the summer term, Maurice made 1,323 runs in schoolboy cricket.

In October 1925 he went up to Trinity, Cambridge, to read history. In the first winter he concentrated on hockey at which he was an inside-right and not a goalkeeper as is frequently stated. In the third week of term he performed well in trial matches but was not an immediate choice for the university. He would go on to represent Cambridge on many occasions, but a combination of injuries and international duties kept him out of the starting line-up in Varsity hockey matches.

In May 1926 he scored 97 in the Freshmen's cricket match and two months later he won his cricket blue amid scrappy batting from both sides in atrocious weather. Maurice fell to William McBride for scores of 18 and 20. He suffered a leg injury in rugby training at the beginning of the 1926 autumn term. As a result he missed the Varsity rugby game (for which he was by no means a certainty) and did not recover in time for the cricket match. In 1928, he was unable to break into the rugby and hockey teams and had a disappointing Varsity cricket match.

In the Christmas holiday of 1928–9, Maurice proved a prolific scorer for the Cardiff Hockey Club. In February he formed part of a Welsh side which played Scotland at Dunfermline. The visitors won by a single goal which *Hockey World* describes with: 'The Welsh left wing tackled the Scottish defence, and the ball was slipped across to the right, where Turnbull pounced upon it, and by a neat flick he beat Robb.' A fortnight later, Wales were defeated 3–0 by Ireland at Abergavenny where many of their forwards proved inept. Maurice was one of the few players to come away with credit. The team regrouped and later in the month it put up a creditable fight against England at Bristol. The game was played at lightning pace and in the second half the Welsh forwards tired. The visitors went down 4–2 but could easily have been swamped. The game proved to be the end of Maurice's international hockey career.

In 1929 he captained the Cambridge cricket XI against Oxford and his side was on the winning end of a draw. Batting at number six, Maurice played valuable innings of 27 and 32 not out. His dismissal in the first innings stemmed from over-exuberance, and *The Times* reported: 'Turnbull tried to hook a rank long-hop into Mayfair, and, missing it, was bowled off his pads.' He left Cambridge later in the same month. In an eight-week term he had scored 1001 runs. His final degree was a 2:2, this being a reflection of his contribution to many walks of university life rather than a verdict on his intellect.

His form for Glamorgan in the same summer was modest but he was seen as captaincy material and he was taken to Australia and New Zealand in the winter of 1929–30 with the England team. The social programme was hectic; most of the tourists knew how to drink, and Dubonnet and pink gin were consumed in vast quantities. Many of the ensuing details come from *The Book of the Two Maurices* which Turnbull wrote in conjunction with Maurice Allom who had been a Cambridge contemporary. They contribute alternate chapters and style themselves as Big Maurice (Allom) and Little Maurice (Turnbull). The book is graceful, anecdotal and a sustained joy. Allom was an accomplished author but his passages pale in comparison with Little Maurice's limpid prose.

Maurice already had an interest in wine and while in Adelaide he became a fan of local vintages, dragging reluctant team-mates around the vineyards. In an obituary tribute, Johnny Clay would recall that during a fixture against Middlesex, a 19-year-old Maurice 'sent for the majestic wine waiter of a London hotel and administered a rebuke on the quality of the claret ...' A few eccentricities were emerging and Allom recalled that despite scorching heat, Maurice was rarely seen in Australia without a trilby and an umbrella.

As the most eligible bachelor in the party, he was besieged by what we would call groupies and what he dismisses as 'flappers'. Maurice's form was poor at Melbourne where he was dismissed by the finger-spin of Bert Ironmonger and Don Blackie. However, he recovered with a fine century against New South Wales, putting on 265 for the fourth wicket with Frank Woolley.

In mid-December the party moved to New Zealand. Scores of 2 and 0 in provincial games were hardly ideal preparation for his international career which began at Christchurch. He batted only once and was dismissed for 7. Maurice did not play in the three subsequent Tests. As a permanent drinks-waiter, he found débutantes queuing up for a chat, and notes: 'Ardent women wanted us to write risqué rhymes in their autograph books. They reminded me of bees around honey: no time for philandering here.' At Wellington the team was linked by wireless to the UK along the primitive Pacific cable of the day. First up to the microphone was the Nottinghamshire bowler Fred Barratt. Everybody was expecting something profound, or at worst a heart-felt message to loved ones at home. Old Fred's gravelly tones crackled along the ocean bed: 'How did Notts. Forest do in t'coop to-day?' After an appalling run in New Zealand, Maurice came good in the last match at New Plymouth where he made a superb 79 before being run out.

The Book of the Two Maurices ran to several editions. An evaluation appeared 35 years later and the review includes: 'It is not easy for this reviewer to be objective about it, for his copy was, at that time, the most expensive book he had ever possessed, bought with a schoolboy's carefully hoarded sixpences.' The reviewer is John Arlott, and David Rayvern Allen has noted: 'The fearless, hard-hitting Turnbull was one of the Gods of John's youth.' Arlott was still a policeman when his hero died. Decades later, he would still go rheumy-eyed when Maurice's name was mentioned. The pair had a great affinity of interests, most notably their passions for wine and contemporary verse. If Maurice had lived they would surely have found shared pleasure in many poems and not a few bottles.

In 1930, Maurice was awarded the Glamorgan captaincy. During his first season in charge he scored 1,520 runs at an average of 32. *Wisden* selected him as a cricketer of the year, and its profile mentions 'a well-balanced mind, a charming personality and a thorough knowledge of the game ...' Despite his personal success there were stern challenges ahead: he was faced with a motley squad and diminishing gate receipts. In the early days the gulf between Glamorgan and the established counties was immense. Wilf Wooller used to sigh and recall: 'Yorkshire only ever booked a hotel for two nights when they came to Cardiff.' The bulk of the Glamorgan side were little more than sound club players, and *Wisden* once concluded: 'In the first few seasons, Glamorgan were like no other side; some will say it was no side at all.'

In the winter of 1930–1, Percy Chapman toured South Africa with a mediocre team. The first tour diary had been successful and there was much interest in a second. Maurice did not disappoint, and in *The Two Maurices Again*, his wit and intelligence are as honed as ever. By now the authors are supremely poised, and a spoof review on the fly-leaf from a Rear Admiral Browne includes: 'I select this as my book of the year. This is no mean praise as I only read one book a year.' The voyage out was a riot; poker schools abounded and Maurice Leyland fleeced everybody at billiards. Mrs Chapman proved a treasure; she held her own with the men at deck-tennis and even performed on the piano, stomping her way through an endless repertoire of Gershwin songs.

The party arrived at Cape Town in November. The boys could not have been expecting much from their skipper in the Tests: by the end of the first week he had received ten balls and been out six times. The players spent the early weeks flirting with their female surfing instructors. Sadly, the captain's ambitions in this area were restrained by Mrs Chapman's beady eye. He consoled himself by chain-smoking cigars, and later he would attract much attention when he rode a miniature Basuto pony through Bloemfontein.

Maurice revelled in beach life and was impressive on the breakers but he was upstaged by Bob Wyatt who once appeared on his surf-board wearing a motorcycle crash helmet. Throughout the tour, the two Maurices dined off boiled eggs and champagne, Little Maurice standing the Moët. Despite attempts to stop him, he had won a fortune on a rank outsider at an up-country race meeting. Scanning the formbook, he had spotted a supposed cart-horse with the reassur-ingly Celtic name of Welsh Harp. His team-mates pleaded with him to examine the claims of the favourite but he slapped down a heavy bet on his fancy, whereupon it duly trotted up at 100–1.

The first Test began at Johannesburg on Christmas Eve. Maurice promised much in the first innings, but with his score on 28, he fell to the slow left-arm of Cyril Vincent. In the second innings he thumped 61 runs in 75 minutes. His performance threatened to win the match, but fine bowling from 'Buster' Nupen brought South Africa victory by 28 runs. Ian Peebles had been superb in the first innings with 4 for 43 but was used sparingly afterwards. On Christmas Day, he had incurred what is surely the most bizarre injury to a cricketer ever recorded. Showing characteristic exuberance, he strained a groin muscle while vaulting a flower-bed in an effort to avoid the attentions of his host's pet parrot.

The party returned to Cape Town for the second Test. Maurice batted at number five, and when he came in with the England score at 202, he appeared unusually nervous. Patsy Hendren was unable to calm him down and he was bowled round his legs for 7. England were responding to a total of 513, and their 350 produced a follow-on during which Maurice was clean-bowled by Quintin McMillan for 14. However, he soon hit form with an innings of 55 in even time against Natal.

He was still anxious to achieve some consistency and attended net sessions at Kingsmead. He recalls how one morning he noticed a 'funny little belt-wearing fellow' who was fielding the straight drives with extraordinary keenness. The stranger sidled up and asked if he could have a bowl. With a grin, Maurice agreed. The old boy's first delivery was laughably wide and Maurice shouldered arms. He was amazed when the ball broke a full yard and sent his leg stump cart-wheeling. Maurice was in the presence of greatness and had been bowled by the most vicious googly the game has known. His practice partner was Albert Vogler who, back in 1907, had been the best bowler in the world. (Sadly, by now Vogler was a chronic alcoholic who was mid-way through a 40-year assault on his liver.)

The session with Vogler was wasted. The Durban Test was ruined by rain and Maurice did not bat. The tourists spent the first part of February in Bloemfontein where their itinerary included a golf match. This was played as fourballs and Maurice was paired with Bill Voce. Going down the 18th, he and Voce were a dormy two points up. As the top ball, Maurice lost to a par, but Voce had five shots from 20 yards for a half and the match. He finally holed out for a nine, and Maurice (who always bet heavily on such matters) was inconsolable, Voce having destroyed much of the good work done by Welsh Harp.

In mid-February, the tourists returned to Johannesburg. Maurice had scored a brisk 25 when he was suddenly becalmed; he waltzed down the track to a McMillan googly and was stumped by a laugh-able margin. In the second innings he was held back to number nine and scored 0 not out. His dismal form continued with scores of 6 and 7 in the fourth draw of the series.

By the second week of March the tour was drawing to a close. During an up-country game against some fruit farmers, Ian Peebles was responsible for a choice entry in the scorebook: 'Peebles .... absent bathing'. In a festival match against a South African schools side, Maurice and Patsy Hendren treated the boys to a stunning display, flicking the ball to outlying sections of Grahamstown, Maurice's contribution being a rampant 89.

In the domestic season of 1931, Maurice scored two centuries but was unsuccessful by his own standards. He incurred the wrath of the MCC when, striving to engineer a win, he made several freak declarations. On one occasion at Cardiff, he and Percy Fender declared the Glamorgan and Surrey innings closed without scoring a run in order to ensure a finish during which Vivian Jenkins batted brilliantly to snatch victory for Glamorgan. At 86 years of age, Vivian Jenkins is warm, informed, and as sharp as a pin. Describing this match to the author, he side-stepped his own innings but supplied the following anecdote. We already know that Maurice fancied himself as a wine connoisseur. However, he had met his match in Percy Fender who had grown up in the trade. The amateurs stayed at the Angel Hotel and over dinner, a 19-year-old Jenkins sat sipping mineral water and observing the two captains. Maurice was desperate to impress Fender and he had spent hours in the cellar selecting a vintage claret. Fender drank it without comment, and by the time the coffee came round, Maurice was desperate for a reaction. He finally asked Fender what he thought. Old Percy George looked at the remnants of the bottle, sniffed them, threw them round his palate and delivered his verdict. 'Well Maurice, pretty good, but not quite a gentleman.'

The mandarins at Lord's were quick to issue a reproof over the declaration in this match which Maurice cheerfully ignored. He had a mind that was free from inherited wisdom and alive to what it saw, and he never lost sight of his duty to spectators. The MCC took the matter to heart and Maurice was out of favour for several years. In August 1932, he played the finest innings of his life when he pasted Larwood and Voce's prototype body-line all over Cardiff Arms Park to score a glorious 205. Jardine had hatched his plans for the forthcoming Ashes tour some weeks earlier and had told Larwood and Voce to experiment. Perhaps Maurice was extracting revenge for Voce's putting at Bloemfontein, perhaps he recognized body-line for the obscenity that it was. In a stunning display he creamed everything on the on-side for four or six. If the other counties had been able to respond in the same way, body-line would have been dropped and there would have been no rumpus in Australia.

It was not a vintage season and he did not sample the delights of the body-line tour. While Jardine was in Australia he supervised the administration of Glamorgan and pulled the club out of a financial mire. In the coming summer he would combine the rôles of secretary and captain, and over six years he turned the situation around. Maurice was also a superb after-dinner speaker. He flew around the valleys in his Riley sports car, and Tony Lewis has described how one of the pros remembered Maurice's supervision of fund-raising concerts: 'Dance our feet off, we would, and there would be the skipper at the door by midnight handing out the pay-packets.'

Maurice had been playing rugby for Cardiff since university but had been unable to break into the first XV, the scrum-half position being occupied by the club captain Howard Poole. Poole was dropped in the 1931–2 season. Maurice took his place and was in sparkling form against the touring Springboks. In the following winter, he had a superb season for Cardiff and on Boxing Day 1932, he was part of a team which destroyed London Irish 47–0.

In January 1933, Maurice became a treble international when he made his rugby début at scrum-half as part of the first Welsh team to defeat England at Twickenham. It was a scrappy match but Maurice put up a fine show and his passing to Cardiff club-mate Harry Bowcott was precise and assured. Wales exposed many English weaknesses to snatch a 7–3 victory. Winning their first caps that day were two other Glamorgan cricketers, Wilf Wooller and Vivian Jenkins.

Maurice was injured for the game against Scotland at Swansea but he returned for a humiliating 10–5 defeat by Ireland at Belfast in which his distribution from the scrum was inaccurate and unimaginative. The Welsh selectors discarded 11 players, and Maurice did not play international rugby again. Wilf Wooller believed that the authorities made a grave mistake in dropping Maurice. He was disheartened by his exclusion and his interest in the sport began to wane. He was not one of the great scrum-halves but he was widely remembered for quick thinking and resourcefulness. Vivian Jenkins remembers him as 'very fast and straight in his passing, with tons of guts at the base of the scrum and frightened of nothing'.

In July 1933, in front of an adoring crowd at Swansea, he was hit by Larwood who was still bowling body-line. There was uproar in the stands and several thousand miners would have strung up Larwood in Castle Street had they been allowed anywhere near the pavilion. It had been a useful practice session; at Lord's a fortnight later he had to negotiate more of the same in the Test against the West Indies. He had seen off a blitz from Martindale and looked well set on 28 when he drove carelessly at Ellis Achong. He did not play in the second Test at Old Trafford, and at the Oval he batted only once, scoring four before being beaten for pace by Martindale.

In the following season he took the county to seventh place in the Championship, a dizzy height for them at the time. In June he had made his highest first-class score against Worcestershire at Swansea. Glamorgan were responding to 123, Johnny Clay having taken 9 for

66. The home side lost its first wicket without scoring and Maurice came in with the total on 14 for 2. He settled quickly, and with support from George Lavis, he raced to 233 in under four hours.

By 1938, the brushes with Lord's over the phoney declarations were forgotten and Maurice became a Test selector. In May he flicked Constantine and Martindale around the Arms Park for a sparkling 60. He played his last innings in the following August at Grace Road where he hit 156. It was a grand way to go out; Germany invaded Poland six days later.

Since the previous year he had been courting Elizabeth Brook, the only daughter of William Brook of Scunthorpe. In a rush due to the war, they married in September 1939 and had a son, Simon, and two daughters, Sara and Georgina. In conversation with the author, Georgina Turnbull has recalled her mother's first words to Maurice: 'I hear you're a budding cricketer.' The response was electric: 'Madam, I have budded.'

As a county captain, Maurice had proved motivational without being demonstrative. He is said to have been worth his place on his captaincy alone. Given that he often topped the batting averages, his contribution was immense. Leslie Thomas has summarized the breadth of his impact: 'Turnbull, as captain and secretary, pulled Glamorgan up by the laces of its cricket boots. He organized both the bowling and the finances, he made centuries and friends, he was as articulate in the chair as he was in the field.' Wilf Wooller's views on his leadership include: 'Maurice was an adventurous but disciplined captain. He did have an autocratic manner and was something of a martinet, demanding a great deal from his team. He would brook no nonsense but he also drove himself hard on and off the field.'

Maurice took a generally tolerant stand on the antics of some of the younger players. At a game at Hinckley, Ted Glover and Vivian Jenkins were buying their morning papers when they saw a placard which read 'WANTED – A RESPECTABLE GIRL'. Glover filched the notice and gave it a border of sticking tape, after which the sign appeared on railway carriages and cars all over the country. Maurice finally stepped in at Scarborough, when the ageing umpire John Herbert King spent the best part of a session with the placard attached to his back.

Occasionally however, he would ride roughshod through dressing-room politics. He was a firm believer in the maxim that 'nice customs curtsy to great kings'. There are shades of Johnny Douglas here, and many have recalled a seeming aloofness. Like Douglas, he often expected colleagues to make contributions that were beyond their capabilities. He is also said to have insisted that the professionals made an appointment if they wanted to see him, and to have ensured that amateur and pro did not mix, even to the extent of booking separate railway carriages.

If all this seems feudal, it should be remembered that without Maurice's tireless work in the winter, his acceptance of the Glamorgan secretaryship on a nominal wage, and his private donations to the club, his professionals would soon have found themselves out of a job. Maurice not only stimulated interest in Welsh cricket, he won support for it. His devotion to an unfashionable county was limitless, and he often refused to play in glamorous festival matches in order to captain Glamorgan in low-key games against mining districts.

Many contemporaries believed that Maurice would have captained the England Test team after the war. The game would have been the richer for it, and would have benefited from his aggressive declarations. Maurice's fielding strengths were at short leg, but he was secure and tireless in the deep. His bowling changes were often inspired and he had what Richie Benaud has identified as the most important attribute for a cricket captain, the ability to convince your players that you are always about to pull something out of the hat.

His career at Test level is a catalogue of disappointments and unfulfilled promise. However, there can be little doubt about his class. For Glamorgan he scored over 14,000 runs, combining orthodox strokes with outrageous improvisations. His Achilles' heel was a vulnerability to high quality orthodox slow left-arm bowling. By contrast, he was superb against pace, showing both nerve and judgement. As a boy he employed an extraordinary grip with the top hand, his knuckles pointing to gully in the manner of Alan Knott. It was only after some intensive sessions at Aubrey Faulkner's indoor school in London that his grip changed and he became a proficient all-round player.

Despite having studied an arts subject at Cambridge, Maurice was logical and numerate. He was an accomplished and enthusiastic bridge player with an intolerance of the shortcomings of others. On the voyage out to South Africa in 1930–1, he had been part of a marathon match for sizeable stakes, the other players being Maurice Allom, 'Farmer' White and Mrs Chapman. By midnight, Maurice's vagaries had often driven his colleagues from the table. He would then roam the ship disconsolately in search of another four. The numeracy was demonstrated in the 1930s when he set up an insurance brokerage with fellow Glamorgan cricketer Ted Glover. (The pair became brothers-in-law when Glover married Maurice's sister,

Everilda, who was herself a hockey international). Without any training, Maurice did much of the actuarial work but he often neglected
the business to concentrate on fund-raising for Glamorgan.

Maurice's obsessions were for bridge, wine, horse racing and
poetry. At Cambridge, he had taken a paper on the Victorian novel
and his enthusiasms included Hardy and George Eliot. His own
writing can be beautifully figurative, the more inspired analogies
including the suggestion that Woolley's batting resembled Jean Barry
dancing a waltz. He was a considerable poet and was devoted to the
work and memory of Rupert Brooke. He would share Brooke's fate.

In November of 1939, Maurice joined the Welsh Guards. He spent
the winter with a training battalion in Colchester, transferring to
Dover in the following spring. More training followed at Scarborough
until his battalion moved to Eastbourne in May of 1944. Maurice must
have looked to the west across the Seven Sisters on the early evening
of 5 June. Some ten miles away he would have seen a glorious fleet of
landing-craft and fishing smacks streaming out of Newhaven: the
Canadians had left for Juno Beach. Further down the coast, British
and American forces were sailing for the Sword, Gold and Omaha
beach-heads. By midnight on the following day, the Allies had put
150,000 troops ashore and sustained 9,000 fatalities. By July, 850,000
troops were in Normandy.

Maurice went across on 16 June and landed at Arromanches. His
battalion assembled at Bretteville l'Orgueilleuse and moved to the
village of Cheux. Ahead of them, British and Canadian forces were
progressing towards Caen. The Americans had taken Cherbourg and
Maurice's battalion was co-opted into Operation Goodwood. On
17 July, he led an attack in the Caen Plain, after which he and his men
cleared the village of Le Poirier. They remained in the village until
23 July when they were ordered to move to the west and support the
Americans at Caumont. Over the next fortnight, the battalion
suffered heavy losses in the lush farmland of the Bocage region.
Matters improved in the first days of August; the village of St Denis
Maisoncelles was cleared and contact was made with the Americans.

On 4 August, the Guards took the village of Montchamp, but they
suffered heavy casualties from sniper fire. The *Wisden* obituary
(together with numerous writers who have copied it slavishly)
reports that Maurice was shot through the head by a sniper while
making a reconnaissance on the following morning. This is incorrect;
later on the morning of 5 August, Maurice led his No. 2 Company
along the Montchamp–Les Fieffes road. There was a bout of hand-to-
hand fighting near the village of Chênedollé after which a German

platoon retreated but not before using a field telephone to describe the enemy's location.

Major Ellis has described ensuing events in his *Welsh Guards at War*: '... a German counter-attack with tanks and infantry came in. No. 2 Company was lining a field when the first tank pushed its gun through the hedge and machine-gun fire opened from several directions. Major Turnbull, almost beside the tank, was killed and the company was cut in half.' Maurice's body lay prostrate in a ditch until it was discovered 20 minutes later by Sergeants Fred Llewelyn and Rex Fowles. In conversation with the author, Fred Llewelyn has described how he and his colleague ripped the door from a farmhouse and used it as a stretcher to carry Maurice to RHQ. He was buried a few weeks later near Bayeux.

It was 12 August when news of Maurice's death reached Cardiff. Glamorgan were playing the Fire Service at the Arms Park in front of a large crowd. A notice was posted on the scoreboard. A handful of spectators spotted it and word spread around the ground. Basil Easterbrook recalls the reaction: 'The crowd rose unbidden and stood there in the August sunshine in silence ... After a decent interval the people sat down and play restarted. Glamorgan were carrying on. Maurice would have wanted that above everything.'

10

John William Henry Tyler Douglas

b. 3 September 1882, d. 19 December 1930 at sea.

*'He was not a great captain, but he was most assuredly
a great man ...'*

Dudley Carew, *To the Wicket*, 1946

A little before midnight on Friday 19 December 1930, Ossi and Erik Hjelt prepared to exchange Christmas greetings. Their intentions were unremarkable but the manner in which they chose to communicate was spectacularly reckless. The brothers were in charge of the *Arcturus* and the *Oberon*, Finnish steamers serving the route between Helsinki and Hull. Their vessels were approaching each other in fog to the south-west of Gothenburg. The captains had gone on deck and were about to scream at each other through megaphones. Few can have been surprised at the outcome; the *Arcturus* stove in the side of the *Oberon* which listed immediately and sank in three minutes. Among the resulting death toll was Johnny Douglas, a treble international who had represented England at cricket and soccer, and Great Britain at boxing.

Contemporary accounts are contradictory, and the official enquiry was a cover-up which sought to conceal the shabby detail that while 36 of the *Oberon*'s crew were saved, only four passengers survived. Many of the passengers were employed in the timber trade and Johnny was returning from a buying mission for the family business which imported hardwood. It is likely that he could have saved himself; he was a competent swimmer and possessed extraordinary stamina. He almost certainly died while trying to save his ageing father. John Douglas Senior had been the Amateur middleweight champion for three consecutive years from 1875, a president of the ABA and among the most respected boxing referees in the country.

112

In May 1897, John Douglas Junior had arrived at Felsted School in Essex where he gained a reputation as a versatile athlete. In the previous year, Johnny's father had set up a gymnasium at his home in Wanstead and prominent boxers visited for sparring sessions. Felsted had been selected for its reputation at boxing, and in March 1899, the father was rewarded when Johnny won the Public Schools featherweight championship. The *Field* reports how at the Queen's Gymnasium in Aldershot, Johnny demonstrated superb footwork while outpointing F. L. Hansell of St Paul's.

He had begun to play cricket for the first XI in the previous year and by 1900 he was a key member of the side. In 1899 and 1900, Johnny played soccer in positions ranging from left-wing to full-back. In 1900, the *Felstedian* summarized his football: 'Douglas at outside-left plays a hard persevering game; though very slow, he centres and passes well.' By 1901, Johnny was boxing as a middleweight. In March, he won the Public Schools tournament again, putting A. W. Hansell on the canvas twice in the final. The *Field* commented: 'Hansell showed good defence but Douglas was too clever and active.'

Johnny played his early cricket for Wanstead, making his first appearance for the club in 1901. He also made his county début for Essex in this year, registering two ducks against Yorkshire at Leyton. He was bowled both times by George Hirst. Johnny made another duck in his one innings at Clifton against Gloucestershire, but avoided the infamous 'double pair' with a fine 61 against Derbyshire. This performance did not keep him in the Essex side.

He continued to box at the turn of the century. Between 1904 and 1908 he was among the best middleweights in the world, either amateur or professional. In the ring he demonstrated unbridled aggression and superb footwork which formed a marked contrast with his defensive attitude and leaden movements at cricket. In March 1904, he was beaten by E. Mann in the final of the ABA middleweight competition. In 1905, he again met Mann in the final, and *The Times* reported: 'Mr Douglas forced the fighting, and half-way through the third round he had his opponent beaten. Mr Douglas seems possessed of great strength and staying power, while added to a straight left, he uses his right effectively at close quarters.'

In the 1905 cricket season, Johnny found a rich vein of form with the ball and he appeared at the top of the Essex bowling averages. His most notable spell was against Yorkshire at Leyton where he took five wickets in eight balls. During this period Johnny was still combining cricket with boxing and March 1908 saw one of the most extraordinary events in his rich life. As part of a private entertainment at the *Blue Anchor* in Shoreditch, he got into the ring with the Canadian world heavyweight champion Tommy Burns. The incident has been dismissed as a 'folk tale' but there are numerous references to it. The most detailed appears in the *Sporting Times* and the article recalls that Johnny 'not only held his own, but proved himself superior, in the opinion of many judges, to the clever Yankee'. There is no question of it having been a full bout, the weight difference being enormous, but it was certainly a heavy sparring session. Nine months later in Sydney, and against a backdrop of horrendous racism, Tommy Burns was butchered by the American negro Jack Johnson in one of the most unpleasant boxing matches of all time.

In October 1908, Douglas boxed for Great Britain at the London Olympics. In his first bout, he outclassed the Frenchman R. Doudelle. In the semi-final against Rube Warnes, he used both hands effectively and floored his opponent with an upper-cut in the second round. The final against another multiple international, Snowy Baker, was slugged out toe-to-toe. When the judges indicated that they required an additional round in order to reach a decision, the strain proved too much for Johnny's father and he left the arena. Johnny was awarded the gold medal by the smallest of margins and the decision was disputed for years. On many unofficial cards Baker had won the bout, and the Australian may have smiled ruefully at the award ceremony. As president of the Amateur Boxing Association, it was Douglas Senior who put the medal around his son's neck. The enduring myth is that Johnny's father refereed the fight; it is demonstrably untrue. This victory marked the effective end of Johnny's boxing career.

Johnny played his first Test cricket on the 1911–12 Ashes tour. The tourists boarded the *Orvieto* in late September under the leadership of Pelham Warner. Italy was at war with Turkey and the vessel was escorted through the Gulf of Taranto by a torpedo boat. Johnny shared a 'stable' with Frank Foster with whom he struck up a close friendship. The pair allowed themselves to get drunk once a week and spent hours playing deck games with Warner's six-year-old daughter.

Warner soon succumbed to ulcer problems and there was no obvious candidate to replace him. After much discussion, Johnny took over the captaincy. Initially, he responded well to his duties, and in searing heat he played a fine innings of 101 against an Australian Select XI at Brisbane. However, at Melbourne he spent three hours making 33 runs. It was during this game that a wag in the stands saw potential in Johnny's initials of J. W. H. T., and he became 'Johnny

Won't Hit Today'. Johnny took the quip in good spirit and in later years he prided himself on the nickname. The innings must have been funereal and it prompted another barracker to yell, 'Fetch a constable and pinch him for loitering!'

There were already question marks over his captaincy. (Years later, a portrait in the *Cricketer* noted: 'He cannot be called a great tactician as he occasionally takes time to see the obvious.') At the most basic level, he exuded much authority but he was slow on the uptake and some of his bowling changes were bizarre. His field settings showed little imagination and the players found themselves making long journeys across the ground between overs. Johnny was also demonstrating an aloofness which quickly made him enemies in the Australian press. A notable feud was with the ex-Australian spinner Hugh Trumble whose match reports prompted Johnny to comment: 'Hugh Trumble has no place on a cricket ground. His proper place is up a tree in the bush.'

Despite skirmishes with journalists, he remained frank and approachable. Jack Hobbs underlines this in *My Life Story*, when he describes Johnny's speech at a welcoming banquet in Melbourne: 'He was a good boxer, but disliked public speaking, and his reply was somewhat as follows: "I hate speeches. As Bob Fitzsimmons once said: 'I ain't no blooming orator, but I'll fight any man in this blinking country'."'

Douglas's team took the field for the first Test in Sydney on 15 December 1911. The day before, a matter of some 53° of latitude away, Amundsen had reached the South Pole. Australia amassed 447. In England's first innings, Douglas was dismissed by 'Ranji' Hordern for a duck. The England total was 318, and in the second innings Douglas bowled well to take 4 for 50. In his second innings Johnny made a resolute 32 before falling to Hordern again as his side lost by 146 runs. Douglas's personal performance had been competent but he had committed a tactical error on the first day when he opened with himself in preference to the irascible Sydney Barnes. 'What does he think I am? Bloody change bowler?' was Barnes's question to Frank Woolley.

Jack Hobbs has described how reports of Johnny's tactical vagaries reached the ears of Pelham Warner who called a meeting in order to decide if the side needed a new captain. Johnny was not invited.

The second Test was at Melbourne and Barnes proved a pivotal figure, taking four wickets in five overs while conceding one run and bringing England victory by eight wickets. In the third Test at Adelaide, Australia collapsed to 133 all out. As his side arrived at its paltry total, the disappointment of Australian captain Clem Hill would not have been as great as that of Captain Robert Scott on the same afternoon. Scott had arrived at the South Pole and found a Norwegian flag there. The English batsmen went into over-drive and Jack Hobbs and Wilfred Rhodes put on 147 for the first wicket. The middle order added to the score in style and Douglas joined the spree with 35 runs in even time, after which his side coasted to victory.

> **Johnny Douglas has gone now, alas, so it can be said that some of us stood up for him at that sick-room meeting, and some did not. I have never regretted being on his side ... Not long afterwards did I learn that Douglas got wind of how the 'voting' went at the meeting.**
>
> **It happened that I wanted his support in a friendly argument, and said half-jokingly: 'Go on, stick up for me, Mr Douglas. I stuck up for you one time!' I was surprised to hear his quiet answer: 'Yes, Jack, and I know where.'**

> Jack Hobbs, *Playing For England!*, 1931

In the Melbourne Test, Australia were dismissed for 191 and the tourists responded with 589. Johnny was bowled by Armstrong for a duck but Hobbs and Rhodes brought England victory and the Ashes by an innings and 225 runs. At the close Johnny bowled superbly to take 5 for 46. As captain, he had proved largely competent both on and off the field. In Tests, he had failed with the bat, but his bowling warranted inclusion in one of the finest attacks of all time. He had also served Pelham Warner with more loyalty and fervour than that parsimonious and vacillating patrician could have expected.

Johnny had no time for Australian social mores, and initially his lordly bearing made him unpopular with journalists. He would not have given this a second thought and had he lived to see the film, he might have echoed Rhett Butler's advice to Scarlett O'Hara in *Gone With The Wind*: 'With enough courage, you can do without a reputation.' Unlike Jardine 20 years later, he did at least acknowledge the crowd. He would laugh heartily when the barracking manifested genuine wit and the Australians soon began to respect him for his integrity and appetite for a struggle.

Later in the year, a series of cricket matches was organized to raise money for victims of the *Titanic*. Johnny was marvellous with dogs, and at a game at Leyton, he formed a friendship with Joe, an ageing greyhound employed by the *Titanic* fund. Having been dismissed early on, Johnny loaded Joe with his collection boxes, and the pair spent the afternoon trotting round the boundary. Joe was buckling visibly under the weight of loose change when they returned to the pavilion.

Douglas Senior was not above a bit of shameless nepotism. The family timber firm proved successful and the company acquired the mortgage on the Leyton ground. In 1911 the club's finances took a turn for the worse, and it pleaded with the Douglas family for a reduction in the repayments. Old Man Douglas agreed but recommended that Johnny should be given the captaincy in place of Percy Perrin. He was put in charge for the forthcoming season and was to serve as captain until 1928.

In 1912, Australia and South Africa visited England to contest the Triangular Series. Despite competent performances, Johnny was omitted from the first five Tests. He was finally included for the deciding match against Australia at the Oval. He did not bowl but in the second innings he made a resolute 24. Several amateurs who were unable to make the 1911–12 Ashes tour had been recalled, but Johnny could have counted himself unlucky not to have taken a more prominent rôle in the series.

In 1913, Johnny became a treble international when he toured Eastern Europe with a party organized by the Amateur Football Alliance. On 1 March he played against Bohemia in Prague where the visitors won 4–0, the goals coming from E. J. Cotton and N. J. Cox, who scored a hat-trick. The standard of amateur international football at the time should not be underestimated but the credibility of teams between 1907 and 1913 is undercut by a schism between the FA and the AFA, both of whom were putting out international sides. The appearance is hardly one of Johnny's major sporting achievements but gives further evidence of his versatility. At Felsted, his soccer had been uninspired. As an adult he proved a resolute utility player with a healthy shoulder charge and a heavy if inaccurate shot. As might be expected, he was one-paced (slow), but he was respected for being fearless in the air.

In the winter of 1913–14, Johnny captained the England cricket tour of South Africa. Again, his strike force was Sydney Barnes. Barnes mesmerized the South African batsmen for most of the tour and took 49 wickets at an average of 10.93. As usual, the bowling changes left something to be desired. The match against Natal marked the one occasion on which Barnes was collared and Johnny kept him on too long. The legend is that in the middle of an over, Barnes stalked off the field, stretched out on the massage table and consumed several large whiskies. In the first Test in Durban, South Africa were dismissed for 182. Johnny made 119 as part of an England total of 450. It was his only Test century. South Africa's second innings of 111 resulted in England victory by an innings and 157 runs.

The second Test started in Johannesburg on Boxing Day. Rhodes scored 152 in England's only innings and Barnes produced match figures of 17 for 159 as England won by an innings. Johnny scored three runs and bowled six overs. The players remained in Johannesburg for the third Test. England's first innings total was 238 and the home side was dismissed for 151. In the second innings, Johnny contributed 77 to a total of 308. The South Africans rallied to 304 but were defeated by 91 runs. England had taken a 3–0 lead in the series. The rubber was now dead and Johnny failed with 0 and 7 in the fourth Test at Durban, which was drawn. A superb innings of 117 by Colin Mead in the final Test at Port Elizabeth ensured an England win by ten wickets. In the South Africans' first innings, the England captain had recorded figures of 4 for 14 from 5.4 overs. Johnny's Test aggregate of 266 runs from seven innings gave him a respectable average of 38, and his bowling performance at Port Elizabeth was inspired.

On the outbreak of war, Johnny obtained a commission in the Bedfordshire Regiment and, with no military experience, he commanded a battalion with distinction. He ended the war as a major but was commonly referred to as 'Colonel'. His service took him to Egypt and France, and in June 1918 we find him at Etaples. The Allies' progress had prompted some leisure activities and together with his Essex colleague Charles McGahey, Johnny played high-class cricket in front of astonished locals on a matting wicket.

In August 1920 he was offered the captaincy for the forthcoming Ashes tour. Later in the month, an article in *The Times* described him as 'precisely the sort of man the Australian understands' but concluded: 'Colonel Douglas's abilities as a captain, like his ability as a player are self-made and sound rather than brilliant.' The Tests were scheduled to be 'timeless', but only the third match at Adelaide went into a sixth day. The series was a nightmare 5–0 drubbing for the tourists who were competent as individuals but unbalanced as a unit. Johnny's personal performance was exceptional, and with 39.33, he was second in the English batting averages behind Hobbs. A loss by seven wickets to New South Wales was a significant prelude for what was to come. In the first Test at Sydney, Australia made a disappointing total of 267 but Johnny's men were bundled out for 190. Australia progressed to 581 in the second innings and then closed out the match by dismissing England for 281.

In the second Test at Melbourne, Australia opened proceedings with 499. England could only struggle to 251, with Douglas contributing 15. The tourists were obliged to follow-on and their total of 157 brought defeat by an innings and 91 runs. Armstrong won his third consecutive toss at Adelaide and his side scored 354. England responded with 447 of which the captain scored 60. There were three centuries in the Australian second innings and these scores formed the nucleus of a total of 582. A century from Hobbs together with 32 from Douglas brought the English total to a respectable 370 but it did not prevent Australia from winning the match and the Ashes.

At Melbourne on his fourth attempt, Douglas called correctly and Hobbs opened the batting wearing a bizarre grey felt hat. The England total was 284 but Australia replied with 389. The tourists' second innings was a triumph for Arthur Mailey who took 9 for 121. It did not however, descend into a rout. Rhodes, Makepeace, Douglas and Fender all made half centuries in a total of 315, but Australia knocked off the 211 required with ease. The Australians had taken a 4–0 lead in the series but the form of the touring captain remained excellent. He made 46 and 88 against New South Wales and also took 7 for 98 including a hat-trick. At Sydney, his team slumped to its fifth consecutive Test defeat, mainly as the result of a score of 170 by Charlie Macartney.

There were of course many mitigating circumstances for the catalogue of heavy defeats. The English authorities believed that the tour came too quickly after the ravages of the war and had agreed to the series against their better judgement. Mailey was superb throughout and Johnny proved to be his bunny. In ten Test innings, he fell to Mailey six times. He spent hours watching the diminutive leg-spinner through field glasses but seemed incapable of doing anything with his top-spinner other than lobbing it tamely back to the bowler.

As in 1911–12, Johnny's captaincy was widely criticized and there were suggestions that he should be replaced by Percy Fender. He fought these moves strenuously. Johnny was frequently abused for his slow batting though the Australian barracking could be both witty and erudite. During one of his more tortuous innings, the crowd started to sing 'The Dead March' from *Saul*. Johnny was unamused and sat down at the wicket until the concert was over.

Understandably, he proved testy on the field. He was impatient with mediocrity and was prone to occasional tactless acidities about his colleagues, though these were usually delivered in gentle tones. Richard Streeton notes that he was particularly unpleasant to Fender on the voyage out. With the professionals, Johnny remained a martinet and he tore strips off the Warwickshire pace-bowler Harry Howell when, as the self-elected postmaster, Howell began to address the Yorkshire amateur Evelyn Rockley Wilson in a familiar way while delivering the morning mail.

Despite the demoralizing nature of the defeats, Johnny remained convinced that his tactics were correct. He also over-bowled himself. At the time, the MCG boasted a scoreboard which gave a full bowling analysis. During one of his extended spells bowling with his back to the scoreboard, a wag shouted: 'Johnny, if you won't take yourself off, put yourself on at the other end where you can read your figures!' To his credit, he took this with good grace. Johnny had taken his parents on the tour. Uncharacteristically, he regularly absented himself during up-country games, thus breaking his usual rule of concerning himself at all times with the welfare of the players.

The 1921 domestic series followed almost immediately and both teams boarded the *Osterley* for the voyage to England. It is credibly reported that Warwick Armstrong used to pop down to the boiler room and stoke the ship for an hour a day, in an effort to stay at what for him was a positively svelte 21 stone.

In a fine summer, Australia won the first three Tests at a canter and England called on no less than 30 players during the series. Despite a mauling in the press, Johnny remained in charge for the first two matches. At Trent Bridge, he was unable to prevent an England collapse as the home side was bundled out for 112. A modest Australian total of 232 was followed by further England embarrassment as they faltered to 147 all out. This second collapse set up a ten-wicket victory for the tourists. The England performance was considered by many journalists to be the worst in living memory, the fielding being particularly inept. At Lord's, England were bowled out for 187. Johnny's 34 runs made him the second highest scorer after Frank Woolley who made 95. In reply, Australia scored 342. Woolley was again magnificent in England's second innings, this time stroking 93 runs. The England total of 283 left Australia needing 129 to win, which they achieved for the loss of two wickets.

Seven Ashes defeats on the trot were enough for the English authorities who decided to look elsewhere for a captain. C. B. Fry championed Lionel Tennyson who took over for the third Test. Australia raced to a score of 407. Johnny came in with the England score at 30 for 3, and immediately had his right thumb crushed to a pulp by a lifter from Gregory. In excruciating pain, he made a courageous 75 and his team-mates had to cut his glove away when he came back to the dressing room. At Old Trafford, England performed credibly for a draw but the game was curtailed by rain. Douglas did not bat and he bowled only five overs. At the Oval, Johnny contributed an undefeated 21 to England's first innings total of 403.

Johnny continued to serve as the Essex captain until the end of the 1928 season by which time he was 46 years old. By this time, he was losing not only his bowling action but the confidence of the Essex committee who suggested that he stand down in favour of H. M. Morris. Johnny had little respect for Morris who was significantly below first-class level as a player and was to prove an indifferent leader. There were many unpleasant scenes. Having carried Essex on his back for eighteen seasons, Johnny was deposed in a peculiarly ungracious manner.

As a bowler, he is remembered for the nervous mannerism of rubbing the ball across his forearm before every delivery. Reviewing his bowling, a *Daily Mail* obituarist concluded that he was 'a plodder rather than a strategist'. He certainly lacked subtlety, though he is remembered by Frank Chester as having made more use of the crease than any of his contemporaries, constantly changing his position and the angle of release. He could make the ball swing both ways and the movement normally came late. His action was hardly classical but was essentially sideways-on and he could produce a fine break-back at will.

Johnny's agony when the batsman played and missed was as Dudley Carew says 'something from which the sensitive spectator would veil his eyes'.

> **In Gentlemen vs Players, at Lord's in 1924, he bowled a wonderful opening over from the Pavilion end to Hobbs. I think Hobbs played at all six balls and only touched one. The very wicket seemed to shrink. Douglas was beyond speech, arms akimbo. Hobbs, tapping the wicket in his thoughtful way, said 'Well bowled, Colonel; well bowled.'**
>
> R. C. Robertson-Glasgow, *Cricket Prints*, 1943

Like Maurice Tate, Johnny appeared to gather pace off the wicket and in his *Manchester Guardian* obituary, Cardus recalled: 'His pace from the pitch was killing – the sort that knocks the bat out of your hands.' Pelham Warner notes that in England, he tended to bowl a foot or so short of an optimum length, but on the harder wickets of Australia this length was ideal.

As a batsman, Johnny was not helped by his career in the boxing ring, and he often appeared muscle-bound. He played with stiff wrists and scored predominantly in front of the wicket, though occasionally, and with much deliberation, he would glide the ball through fine leg. As with his bowling, his presence at the crease was characterized by many nervous mannerisms, the most notable being the habit of constantly tugging at his gloves with his teeth.

As a captain Johnny expected the best from his players and was usually able to extract it. He frequently struck outsiders as brusque, even stern. He was disarmingly frank and courageous to a fault, with a bluntness that was often misunderstood by those obsessed with niceties. Of recent England captains, he was nearest in spirit to Mike Gatting. Summations of his captaincy are as varied as they are colourful. In his autobiography, Arthur Mailey described Johnny as 'an ideal leader'. By contrast, C. B. Fry concludes in his own memoirs: '… in his captaincy no idea ever emerged.' In 1939, Home Gordon published his *Background of Cricket*. Having directed an inane diatribe at personal bugbears including the wireless, modern architecture and the 'two-eyed' batting stance, he devotes several pages to Johnny, and an undignified tirade includes: 'As skipper … he was not only bad but brutal, almost incredible in his ruthlessness.' Home Gordon did not play a single game of first-class cricket. Perhaps the debate should therefore be left to Mailey and Fry, if only because Dr Johnson once said something about sheep being the best judges of mutton.

Charles Bray ends his fine essay on Johnny with: 'You either liked and respected Douglas or you loathed him.' Bray notes that Johnny's consideration for his players was extraordinary. He would visit the pros in their lodgings, squat on their bed to check the mattress, and if things were not in order, the landlady would receive a stream of invective. A professional who found himself in financial difficulties could always rely on him for a discreet loan. At dances, he would even select girls for the younger players. His chiselled features had been unmarked by his years in the ring, and few women were able to resist his curious blend of diffidence and self-assurance.

Speaking during a memorial service at Leyton, Frank Gillingham mentioned that in the 25 years he had known Johnny, he had never made a single reference to his achievements as a boxer. Gillingham closed his address by noting that in a tight corner, he would rather have had Johnny Douglas on his side than anyone he had ever known. There was a rich vein of humour running through Johnny. A rare anecdote describes how in 1926, during one of his many witch-hunts of players not strictly entitled to play for their counties, Lord Harris had a famous argument with Lord Deerhurst. The protagonists could not understand why their argument had caused merriment in the Long Room until it was explained later that Johnny had been hovering behind the two men and mimicking the actions of a boxing referee.

Johnny Douglas sailed into oblivion in December 1930 at the hands of a pair of cretinous Finnish sea-captains. He remains one of England's most maligned Test captains and a character of the purest gold.

11
The Hon. Alfred Lyttelton

b. 7 February 1857, d. 5 July 1913

'July 5, 1913. To the Hon. Mrs Alfred Lyttelton:

My Dear DD

So Alfred has the start of us by a few years. He might have waited for you; but I suppose he couldn't help himself. We get our marching orders; and off we must go, leaving our wives and our luggage behind. Don't order any black things. Rejoice in his memory and be radiant; ... And come and close my eyes too, when I die; and see me with my mask off as I really am. I almost envy him.

Yours, dear DD, still marching on, G. B. S.'

Bernard Shaw, *Collected Letters* (ed. Max Reinhardt), 1965

When Baroness Lyttelton presented her husband with their eighth son, she was contributing a future cabinet minister and a double international at soccer and cricket to what has proved an extraordinary dynasty of achievers for over two centuries. Prolific as writers, politicians and divines, the Lytteltons' literary output gives the first hint of their diversity. Publications range from *The Place of Miracles in Religion* (Arthur Temple Lyttelton) to *The Handy Book on Pruning* (Charles Viscount Cobham). The Lytteltons were as prominent in politics as they were in literature. Alfred was a nephew of William Gladstone, his mother Mary Glynne and her sister Catherine having married George Lyttelton and the future premier on the same day. Noted for what Arlott would have called 'a pretty wit', Mary bore her husband twelve children and died six months after giving birth to Alfred.

The barony had been conferred on George Lyttelton in 1756 after his spells as Chancellor of the Exchequer and Leader of the

Opposition to Walpole. A generous patron of the arts, and an intimate of Pope and Fielding (*Tom Jones* is dedicated to him), George Lyttelton's own literary work was undistinguished and evoked a tart evaluation from Dr Johnson: '… nothing to be despised and little to be admired'. Alfred's father, George, was deeply religious but displayed a mercurial roguishness despite suffering from bouts of melancholia. He was prominent as a classical scholar, and in conjunction with Gladstone he translated extracts from Milton and Tennyson into Greek.

In April 1876, during a bout of depression, George committed suicide by throwing himself from a staircase. He is best remembered for some sonorous letters to his sons which often resemble those of Lord Chesterfield. His principal dictum was that all bowling should be played with feet rooted in the crease, advice which his offspring cheerfully ignored. He was frequently seen at Lord's for Eton vs Harrow fixtures where he would condescend to watch his sons while they were at the wicket but at all other times read a volume of Herodotus. Alfred's uncle, Spencer Lyttelton, is remembered by Home Gordon as a prodigious gossip and the only individual permitted to swear in front of Queen Victoria.

Never knowing his mother, Alfred became devoted to his step-mother, Sybella (née Clive). His first cricket lessons took place indoors. From the earliest days he employed an extended follow-through which began to inflict damage on the Chippendale furniture of Hagley Hall and he was soon taken into the nets. His preliminary schooling was at an indifferent prep school in Brighton where he appears to have known his own mind. Travelling down to Brighton from Hagley at the age of nine, and coached as to the exact fare between Paddington and Victoria, he advised an enterprising cab-driver: 'Kneel down on your box and thank your Maker you've got what you have.' In August 1867, we find a 10-year-old Alfred making up a Lyttelton family eleven which administered a ten-wicket pasting to Bromsgrove School. The team was composed of Alfred, his seven brothers, his father, and two uncles. *The Times* reports that Bromsgrove were bowled out for 150 and Alfred's father made an excellent tumbling catch. The family produced a total of 191 to which Alfred contributed 14.

In January 1868, Alfred was sent to Eton where he immediately rejected the classics but began to demonstrate massive gifts. Initially, he excelled at fives and Eton's wall and field games. Alfred soon made his mark as a cricketer; he gained a place in the first XI in 1872 and retained it for three seasons. In 1874, Alfred played his finest innings to date; a sparkling 104 against Winchester. As captain of the Eton XI in 1875, he scored 102 against Winchester and 59 against Harrow at Lord's. Alfred played regularly alongside his brothers Edward and Robert. Edward was a superb long-jumper, played cricket regularly for the Gentlemen, and like Alfred, also played soccer for England.

By no means wrapped up in athletics, Alfred took an active part in intellectual life at Eton. Many of his friends had no interest in sport. The range of his activity is extraordinary. In addition to editing the *Eton College Chronicle*, he was active in the debating society. Transcripts at Eton reveal some of the more choice subjects on which he spoke. They include: 'Does the reading of novels tend to improve the mind?' In this debate, Alfred comes down heavily in favour of the novel, citing Dickens and even George Eliot whose *Middlemarch* had appeared only the previous year. Alfred quickly became a moving force in 'Pop', Eton's athletic and debating society. He was already making money from writing. Dividing his time equally between master and boys without losing the trust of the latter, by 1875 he was enjoying 'an almost kingly position'. In March of this year, as editor of the *Chronicle*, Alfred flogs the old war-horse: 'Have athletes of the present in any way degenerated from those of the past?' Avoiding any sixth-form smartness, he concludes that the argument is pointless. He would have appreciated Don Bradman's final word on the subject, a century or so later: 'The swimmers are lucky, nobody can say the water's changed.'

Lyttelton remained, in the best sense, a public schoolboy for the rest of his life, with both the merits and potential excesses of such a type in appropriate balance. At school he had achieved everything that he or others could desire. Handing over his many positions at the end of his last term, he playfully observed: 'Only 48 hours between me and insignificance.' There is irony here; despite high political office, the rest of Alfred's life would be something of an anti-climax. Scott Fitzgerald deals with the theme in *The Great Gatsby* when he describes Tom Buchanan as '… one of the most powerful ends that ever played football at New Ham, a national figure in a way, one of those men who reach such an acute excellence at twenty-one that everything afterwards savours of anti-climax'.

Alfred went up to Cambridge in 1875 and immediately immersed himself in music. He was a fine pianist with a love of Brahms, and he sang in the Cambridge Musical Society. In later years, Alfred could be roused by music into 'a sort of ecstasy of vitality and enjoyment'. Although he was already destined for the Bar, Alfred read for the

History Tripos which had a significant legal content. He was attracted to real tennis and soon began to combine this with rackets. It was evident within days that he would become one of the best tennis players in the country. At tennis, Alfred played against Oxford between 1877 and 1879, while at rackets he gained blues in 1876 and 1877. In 1876 he also appeared in the Varsity athletics fixture and came second in the hammer.

Cultural life at Trinity was remarkably rich but Lyttelton shone among a set which included Hallam Tennyson, a son of the poet and father of Lionel, the English cricket captain. In a biography of his brother, Edward Lyttelton describes intellectual life at Cambridge as 'pronouncedly anti-Christian'. Darwinism was 16 years old but aggressive scepticism continued to make inroads into revealed religion. Alfred's magnetism and intellect placed him in an élite. His cricket blossomed and he appeared for Middlesex during the vacations. A good second-class degree was a major blow and Alfred left Cambridge with an inner sense of failure. His letters at the time are revealing: 'Intellectual self-confidence was never my weakness I think.'

At cricket Alfred appeared in all of the Varsity matches between 1876 and 1879. He could claim much credit for the three Cambridge victories in these years. As a 19-year-old freshman, he was among the best amateur wicket-keepers in the country, being picked for Gentlemen vs Players in 1876. He also confirmed his worth as a batsman, scoring 66. Alfred's one personal failure for the Light Blues occurred in 1877. It coincided with Cambridge's single defeat during his residence. In 1878, Cambridge played eight matches and won all of them outright. In addition to the defeat of Oxford, the wins included a victory over a party of Australians against whom Alfred hit a sparkling 113.

As an undergraduate, Alfred was already moving in exalted circles. In his second year he spent Christmas with Ruskin and Lord Acton. It was during this vacation that Ruskin took Alfred to see a by now infirm Carlyle who spent the whole interview quoting snatches of Burns, closing with the tremulous enquiry: 'Does the rising generation read me?' Coming down from Cambridge in 1879, Alfred spent several weeks in Paris where he immersed himself in Victor Hugo, worshipped Sarah Bernhardt, and improved his spoken French which would always display a Churchillian defiance of accent.

His soccer career was brief. He played in three Varsity fixtures, scoring a hat-trick in 1878 and laying on another goal as Cambridge won 5–1. On 11 March 1876, he and his brother Edward were part of

an Old Etonian side which played the Wanderers in the FA Cup final
at Kennington Oval. The match was drawn at a goal apiece. A report
in the *Field* describes the 'energetic rushes and excellent kicking of the
Hon. Alfred Lyttelton and the fine kicking of his brother at half-back'.
Exuding massive authority in the Eton goal was Quintin Hogg,
grandfather of the eponymous Lord Hailsham in our own day. The
replay took place the following week; after dominating the opening
minutes, the Etonians wilted and were defeated 3–1. Alfred was
superb throughout and the *Field* compliments him once more:
'Lyttelton was always a source of trouble, his dribbling being very
close and effective.'

In the following year, Alfred made his sole international appearance when he played for England against Scotland at the Oval.
Wretched weather produced a disjointed match in which a superb
Scottish defence swamped the English forwards. Alfred scored with
what the *Field* describes as 'a hard shot from a scrimmage', but a few
minutes later he handled the ball in front of his own goal and allowed
the Scots to equalize. The visitors then ran out to a comfortable 3–1
victory.

Alfred impressed opponents as a superb dribbler with a heavy shot
and shoulder charge. A contemporary press evaluation summarized
him as '… a very strong and fast forward and a splendid shot at goal'.
Edward Lyttelton noted that on the sports field his temper resembled
a tinder box and he played most of his games in a state of irascibility.

Alfred's Test début came in 1880. He had a quiet game with the bat,
scoring 11 and 13, and he did not effect any dismissals. His second
Test was at the Oval in 1882 where he caught fellow wicket-keeper
Blackham in fine style but failed with the bat. The most notable incident in his cricket career occurred at the Oval in 1884 when every
member of the English team had a bowl. With over 500 on the slate,
Lord Harris threw the ball to Alfred. W. G. donned the gloves and
positioned himself behind the sticks as Alfred proceeded to take 4 for
19 with underarm lobs. The legend is that Alfred did not bother to
remove his pads. Protected or not, Grace's shins were not in danger.
Contrary to popular accounts, the lobs were appalling, being delivered at snail-like pace and on occasion bouncing three times before
reaching the wicket.

As a county cricketer, Alfred appeared for Middlesex until 1884
after which he played in occasional first-class matches on public
holidays. His technique was classical and he made most of his runs in
front of the wicket. Here is A. G. Steel in *Wisden*: 'No first-class cricketer ever possessed the elegance of style that was his; no flourish, but

the maximum of power with the minimum of exertion.' The elegance was not restricted to his batting style. Egged on by W. G., Alfred once kept wicket for Middlesex vs Gloucestershire sporting a hard straw hat and an I Zingari neckerchief. He was blessed with immaculate timing, and using a bat that resembled a railway sleeper, he often found his forward defensive speeding to the boundary.

Lyttelton turned to wicket-keeping because there was a dearth of stumpers at Eton. A. A. Thomson has divided wicket-keepers into penny plain and tuppence coloured (with Godfrey Evans fourpence, Technicolored). Alfred was most certainly monochrome. He was too tall for the rôle, and in anything other than a Test match, he would plead with colleagues to take the gloves so that he could go into the outfield and indulge in 'a bit of scouting'. A catcher rather than a stumper, he would stand a pace back even to spinners. He was easily excited and given to outrageous and raucous appeals.

Alfred was called to the Bar in 1881. On his first day he took a case at half an hour's notice and successfully defended his client on a charge of manslaughter. Painstaking but rarely brilliant, he soon had more work than he could deal with. It was his name and the glamour of his personality which secured the briefs. Alfred studied under the renowned Marshall Hall. In turn, some years later, one of Lyttelton's less committed juniors would be Pelham Warner.

Despite a fiery temper on the sports field, the abiding impression of Lyttelton is one of restraint. Edward speaks of the 'singular sanity of his mind', developing the theme with: 'I cannot conceive of him entering into much that poets have described as the transports and ecstasy of love.' A chapter in E. T. Raymond's *Portraits of the New Century* (1928), constitutes the most perceptive treatment of Lyttelton to date. For Raymond, Alfred was '... a good, sound, humdrum lawyer ... standing for the straight life not less than for the straight bat'. (Raymond's piece is a superb, urbane summation. It is laced with affection, respect and a little gentle iconoclasm, but lacks any discussion of his sports career.)

In the summer of 1884, Alfred began to court Laura Tennant. Laura was in her early twenties; she was a daughter of Charles Tennant, the brewing mogul, and a sister of the future Mrs Asquith. She was sensitive and articulate with an exceptional intellect, and these attributes made her a guileless heartbreaker. She was also elfin, and soon wore down her small store of strength through charity work which included the foundation of a crèche in Wapping. (Her zeal for fundraising was such that Alfred spent much time in reclaiming his clothes from jumble sales.) Laura was quick to recognize the latent potential of her fiancé: 'It will be such a gorgeous Life if you live it to the top of its bent.' Even in the first days of her marriage, Laura seems aware of her impending fate. There are phrases in her letters which could be lifted straight out of *Wuthering Heights*: 'I always think the body is but a window from which the soul leans out.'

Alfred and Laura were married in May 1885. Alfred was a widower a year later when Laura died in childbirth. She had been close to Tennyson who described her as 'half child, half woman'. Laura could have been a fine poet herself. A devotee of Georges Sand, her letters stream with an innocence that leaps out at you over a century. It is not an over-statement to say that Laura Tennant was among the most remarkable women of her generation.

The child, Alfred Christopher, survived two years before succumbing to meningitis. By 1888, losing his wife and mother, a father to suicide and a two-year-old son, Alfred, as his brother notes in an unusually figurative moment, was 'old in grief'. The grief was tempered four years later by a happy marriage to Edith Balfour. A relative of Alfred's mentor, Arthur Balfour, the future Prime Minister, Edith was a prolific if impossibly mannered playwright and the biographer of an obscure painter, Florence Upton. She also wrote a biography of her husband immediately after his death. Constructed almost entirely from letters, it is a roseate encomium and offers little insight.

Alfred was always unhappy with Gladstone's policy on Home Rule, and he delayed the obvious step of standing for Parliament. After a final split with his uncle's party, it was as a Liberal Unionist that in 1895 he was first elected as the member for Warwick and Leamington. Never a fluent Parliamentary speaker, he was moderated and hesitant. In 1900 he was given his first major appointment when Joseph Chamberlain invited him to investigate fraudulent concessions made by President Krüger in the Transvaal. Alfred exposed a few of Krüger's more boyish pranks with slush funds and promptly returned home. He was unable or unwilling to expose labyrinthine layers of corruption. With no political pedigree, he was a surprise choice as Colonial Secretary in September 1903 when Chamberlain resigned.

After developing jaundice during a by-election in the same summer, Alfred was elected by a narrow majority, his wife having performed creditably in his place at the hustings. Years later she was capable of completing half-finished speeches when her husband's strength began to fail. Controversy raged as scarcity of labour in the Transvaal crippled the gold mines. Lord Milner began to support

South African calls for the importing of Chinese or 'Coolie' labour. Had he still been at the Colonial Office, Chamberlain would have shown Milner the back door, but the majority of Balfour's Cabinet supported the idea. The proposals must have violated many of Alfred's deepest beliefs but after some shabby apologetics, he defended the policy to the hilt. It does him little credit.

Alfred lost his seat during the General Election of 1906 which had been initiated by Balfour's resignation in the preceding December. On the issue of Free Trade versus Tariff Reform, Balfour had found open divisions in his ranks. On one notable occasion he retreated from the House and put up Lyttelton to speak for him. Alfred was unable to make himself heard for over an hour. Lyttelton adored Balfour as boys at Eton had once idolized him. He would no more have ignored an order from Balfour than he would have argued with Lord Harris when commanded to bowl at Lord's back in 1884. Having been deprived of political office, Alfred took on various directorships. He returned to Parliament as the opposition member for Hanover Square in June and immediately campaigned against sweated labour.

As a back-bencher, Alfred did much to fight the Parliament Bill of 1911 which sought to establish single-chamber government. Widely respected by Labour members, he also improved conditions of women at work. After being initially uncommitted on the issue, by 1913 Alfred was working tirelessly to give women the vote. In a January issue of *The Times*, he is reported as quoting Mrs Humphry Ward and pleading for female suffrage 'on a basis not of passion, prejudice, or instinct, but of love of fair play and reason'.

For many years after his retirement from first-class cricket, Lyttelton remained the best amateur real tennis player in the country, winning the national championship on numerous occasions and proving only fractionally inferior to the leading professionals. A late convert to golf, he could find his way round the Old Course in the low eighties. Bernard Darwin believed that Alfred absorbed too much golfing theory and allowed his natural ability to be stifled. In a charming article, Darwin notes that 'he did not begin to play golf in a sufficiently arrogant frame of mind. In the humble desire to learn he cultivated a swing of exaggerated length with an elaborate turning movement of the wrists.'

Alfred Lyttelton died on 5 July 1913 at the age of 56. His early death was precipitated by a cricket injury. In its obituary, the *Eton College Chronicle* quotes a letter to an old schoolmaster nine days before his death: 'Yesterday I was hauled out to play cricket! First time for ten years – poor wicket and professional bowling; saw it from first to last like a football and got 90. Think with sympathy of my condition to-day.' Alfred was complaining of stiffness; he had in fact received a blow in the groin which would cause an internal abscess that killed him a few days later.

The obituaries are largely unreflective and rhapsodist, but they all contain a note of acute grief. In the House, a trembling speech from Alfred's brother-in-law, Herbert Asquith, was prefaced with: 'It is a loss of which I hardly trust myself to speak.' A few days later, and roused from habitual narcosis, Balfour's summary at a memorial service was sensitive, perceptive, even uplifting. Taking time off from writing *The Thirty-Nine Steps* – it was published two years later – John Buchan contributed one of the more reflective tributes to the *Spectator*: 'He did all things well, many things brilliantly, but he was bigger than what he did.'

There is an old aphorism that the Lytteltons used to run both Eton and England. By the standards of the first part of the century, the family is now in the shade though Alfred's great-nephew is to a large extent running British jazz.

12

'Patsy' Hendren

b. 5 February 1889, d. 4 October 1962

'He was my first real hero. I think I made a good choice.'

Brian Johnston, *It's Been a Piece of Cake*, 1989

On 31 August 1937, a front-line Middlesex batsman returned to the pavilion without scoring. The reaction of the 17,000 spectators was unusual; to a man they broke into a chorus of *For He's a Jolly Good Fellow*. Patsy Hendren had played his last match at Lord's. In the first innings he had scored a glorious 103, and he was retiring from a game which he had adorned over four decades. He had made a duck in his début innings for Middlesex and a duck in his last. Patsy remains one of the best-loved players ever to have picked up a bat. He was prodigiously gifted at the country's two national sports but his whole bearing was characterized by a persisting wonder as to how he had come so far.

We are dealing with a cricketer of the highest stature. At the time of his death, he was second to Jack Hobbs as a maker of centuries and third to Sir Jack and Frank Woolley as a maker of runs. Small, rotund and often to be seen sweating like a racehorse, he was beloved of cartoonists ranging from Tom Webster to Arthur Mailey. Everything about Patsy was exaggerated, and a pug-like face was eclipsed only by a Cyrano of a backside. In the field, he resembled one of those bottom-heavy dolls which refuse to fall down. Middlesex through and through, Patsy makes a surprising appearance in Betjeman's 'Pot Pourri from a Surrey Garden'; a catalogue of Pam's bountiful body including: 'See the strength of her arm, as firm and hairy as Hendren's.'

Patsy was born within sight of the old Chiswick Empire during a period in which Mr Gladstone and Lord Salisbury alternately upheld the national dignity. He was destined to become an essential part of English and Middlesex cricket, and a prominent figure in football. He left St Mary's School, Chiswick, at the age of 14, having spent his early teens playing lamp-post cricket on a 'Street vs Street' basis.

As a boy, Patsy accentuated his lack of inches by wearing knicker-bockers. He narrates how an opposition captain in club cricket once complained that his stature was making the game a farce. Patsy was already electric in the covers and a few moments later he produced a stunning underarm throw which saw his critic run out by a matter of yards. His childhood was marred by the death of both parents, and a lifetime's clowning served only to disguise a trait of melancholy. He was a first-rate comic and mimic though not a wit. His clowning could be riotously funny but he was acutely aware of the thin line that separates the clown from the buffoon.

Patsy was apprenticed to a mechanic but was as likely to make an engineer as Cardus to make a typesetter or Arthur Mailey to continue as a plumber. In 1905, we find him on the Middlesex ground staff selling scorecards with no great enthusiasm. As teenagers, the Hendren brothers rarely went without a Sunday joint. In an unguarded moment, a Mr Court, the butcher at Turnham Green, offered a leg of lamb to anybody who could hit a ball from the pitch into his shop. The feat required a huge clearance across the busy Chiswick High Road but Patsy ensured that Mr Court made regular visits to his glazier.

Patsy made his début for Middlesex against Lancashire at Lord's in July 1907. It was a game ruined by rain. In these early seasons, his occasional appearances for the first eleven were due to the brilliance of his fielding. It was early in 1908 that he got to play a shot in anger when, in the home fixture against Gloucestershire, he hit the winning runs from the bowling of Gilbert Jessop. C. B. Fry was quick to recognize his talent, predicting that he would become the Johnny Tyldesley of Middlesex. It was not long before Fry's prediction was fulfilled; the maiden first-class century came against Sussex in his third season.

A happy but childless marriage to Minnie began early in 1914. As a devout but unobtrusive Catholic who was moderate in all things, though without a hint of prudery, Patsy was an easy husband. For 48 years Minnie coped with minor peccadilloes and a constant influx of surprise guests with a mixture of good-humoured tolerance and endless supplies of sherry. She also indulged Patsy in his passion for cats and the Hendren household teemed with strays. For the first four years, Minnie saw little of her husband. Straight after the honeymoon, he enlisted as a private with the 23rd Fusiliers where he had Andy Sandham for a colleague.

In 1919, Patsy began to blossom as a batsman and highlights included a century at a run a minute against Essex. It was in August 1920 that he became a household name. The climax of a glorious month was an innings of 232 against Nottinghamshire. Years later, he described it as his best ever innings: 'I never saw the ball so big, before or since.'

He made his first England appearance on Johnny Douglas's expedition to Australia in 1920–1. His Test début was at Sydney in which he scored 28 and 56. He remained competent but uninspired for the remaining Tests while scoring heavily in up-country games. He was one of the few players to emerge with credit, and in ten Test innings he scored 319 runs. Amid fielding that could mercifully be described as inadequate, Patsy's performance was several classes above that of anyone else as Douglas's men persistently shelled catches which, as the Robertson-Glasgow poem has it, 'a child would take at midnight with no moon'.

By this time he was a major attraction for Brentford FC at Griffin Park. Two-footed and with the acceleration of a whippet, he delighted crowds with in-swinging corners, taken from both flanks with alternate pegs. His status as a double international rests on the admittedly tenuous basis of an appearance for England against Wales in a 'Victory' International at Ninian Park in 1919. He performed credibly as England lost 2–1. Patsy received little service and was quiet in the first half. Early in the second, he beat the Welsh keeper from many yards out only to see his shot cannon against the cross-bar. In the last 15 minutes, it was a centre from Patsy which allowed Sydney Puddefoot to bring the scores level, but some five minutes later the Welsh took advantage of poor English defending to close out the match 2–1.

At 30, his best days as a footballer were behind him and increasing weight was robbing him of his pace. Had the First World War not cut a swath through his career as a soccer player, he would undoubtedly have made appearances at full international level. For several years, Patsy's Middlesex colleague Jack Durston played alongside him as the Brentford goalkeeper. Occasionally at the beginning of the cricket season, the pair's commitments at both sports resulted in near-impossible schedules. Thus, after a match against Surrey, the two men were seen getting into a cab at the Oval in cricket flannels and emerging at Griffin Park in football kit. Patsy played his last game for Brentford in 1927 when the club reached the fifth round of the FA Cup. Eleven thousand turned out at Griffin Park to salute him as the Bees drew with Newport.

A good start to the 1921 domestic cricket season seemed ideal preparation for the home Ashes series but Patsy failed miserably with 0 and 7 at Trent Bridge and 0 and 10 at Lord's. Despite massive support from an army of fans in the press-box, he was dropped for the

final three Tests. The supposed savants were already making insinu-
ations about a lack of Test temperament. He was never a good starter
and his nerves were often betrayed by a hesitancy in his backlift.

Returning to international cricket in 1924, Patsy scored his maiden
Test century (132) against South Africa at Leeds. The innings formed
the platform for a nine-wicket victory with Maurice Tate taking 6 for
42 in the tourists' first innings. Patsy's score of 142 at the Oval was
made in a rain-induced draw. His next Ashes tour was the 1924–5
expedition under Arthur Gilligan where he scored a Test aggregate of
314 runs at an average of 39. Gilligan and his men were unlucky to
lose the rubber 4–1.

In the Lord's Test against Australia in 1926, Patsy (now 37 years
old) made 127 not out in England's first innings. The match is significant for being the first occasion on which amateurs and professionals
shared the same dressing room, with Patsy well aware of the significance. This became a crowning moment for him, and remembering it
his autobiography, his writing becomes unusually expansive: 'Only
those who have run far ahead of their wildest dreams will be able to
appreciate what I felt that day.' The rubber was still live for the final
Test at the Oval where he failed with 8 and 15 as England regained
the Ashes.

He spent the winter of 1927–8 in Adelaide as coach to South
Australia. He proved competent and was offered a contract for the
following winter from which he was released to assist with the
successful and happy tour of Australia under Percy Chapman.
Highlights were innings of 169 at Brisbane and 95 at Melbourne as the
tourists achieved a 4–1 series victory. In the final Test at Melbourne,
Patsy showed his ability to nurse partners into form, consistently
shielding a nervous Maurice Leyland from Clarrie Grimmett. Patsy
made a fine 95 and Leyland's innings blossomed into a superb 137.

There had been an Australian débutant in the Test at Brisbane.
Batting at number seven, Don Bradman failed with 18 and 1 and was
dropped for the next game. The third Test was also at Melbourne and
was particularly fraught. In a vivid (and possibly fanciful) passage, A.
A. Thomson recalls how after the penultimate day's play, Patsy
sought to dispel the tension that had beset the England dressing
room. 'Pat waved his arms. Passing the gate of the grounds was a
brewer's dray and into this Pat bundled his disconsolate companions,
tall men, short men, professionals and amateurs alike. There they sat,
amid crates full and empty, first dazed, then relaxed and finally
uplifted. And there with Pat as conductor, they went bowling
through the streets singing anti-temperance songs.'

As usual, Patsy engaged Australian crowds in a stream of back-chat. On one occasion the abuse got out of hand when a more than usually aggressive inhabitant of the Sydney Hill capped a stream of invective by dismissing him as 'an ugly little bastard' and enquiring why nature had not equipped him with a tail. At the fall of the next wicket, Patsy began to climb the picket only to see the barracker make a hasty retreat from the stadium to general derision and tumultuous applause for his pursuer.

Patsy was fielding out in the deep just under the Hill. A batsman hit a steepling catch to him. Up and up it went and Patsy tried to position himself underneath. As he did so a voice from the Hill shouted; 'If you drop that catch, Patsy, you can sleep with my sister.' I asked him what happened. 'Oh dear, oh dear,' he said. 'As I hadn't seen his sister, I decided to make the catch.'

Brian Johnston, *It's Been a Piece of Cake*, 1989

In 1929, Patsy started well against the South Africans at Birmingham and Lord's, but failing at Headingley and Old Trafford, he was dropped for the final match at the Oval. In the following winter, he toured the West Indies under the Hon. F. S. Calthorpe. Both as a batsman and crowd-pleaser, it was to be one of his finest tours. He began with 80 and 36 not out in the first Test at Bridgetown which proved to be tasters for a superb 205 not out at Port of Spain and 123 at Georgetown.

The home Ashes series of 1930 saw an encounter between teams led by Bill Woodfull and Percy Chapman. At Lord's, Patsy contributed 48 to an England first innings total of 425. An early dismissal in the second innings cost Patsy his Test place as Henry Leveson-Gower presided over a cull of the Middlesex players. (Gubby Allen and Walter Robins were also dropped.)

Patsy was not overlooked for the 1930–1 tour of South Africa under the avuncular captaincy of Percy Chapman. He played in all five Tests, scoring 329 runs at an average of 47. As usual his abundant vitality was a mainstay of the social programme. His mime act in tandem with Maurice Allom included a mock wrestling bout that became a rage right across South Africa. At a fancy dress ball, he and Andy Sandham appeared as a pair of Gilbertian Pirate Kings after which Patsy spent the evening dancing with a Russian Mystic in the form of Allom. Developing tonsillitis in Johannesburg, he was left in the care of an enormous and predatory matron at the Carlton Hotel while the rest of the team set off for Rhodesia.

Back at Lord's in 1931, Patsy took a terrible blow on the skull from Larwood and was stretchered off. He returned a few weeks later sporting a Heath Robinson helmet, 'seemingly supplied from his own comic workshops'. It was composed of a sponge-lined cap with extra peaks resembling a deerstalker and had been knocked up by Minnie. The headgear produced as much ridicule as the towel with which Richard Daft used to swathe himself in the 1870s and Brearley's prototype protection in our own time. Patsy did not wear it for long.

At the age of 45, he was recalled for the first post-body-line Ashes series. Patsy made scores of 79 at Trent Bridge and 132 at Old Trafford. His hair-trigger reflexes were still allowing him to take blinding catches at silly-point. As the only professional selected for the MCC vs Australia fixture at Lord's this season, he found himself walking out to boundary alone until Chapman, with characteristic decency, invited him to walk through the centre gate with the amateurs. Later in the game, Patsy belted 135 and knocked the Australian chinaman bowler 'Chuck' Fleetwood-Smith out of the Test series.

As senior professional on the 1934–5 tour to the West Indies, Patsy played his last Test cricket. Against high-class pace bowling from Constantine and Martindale he accredited himself well. He was top of the Test averages with 28.85 as Bob Wyatt's tourists went down 2–1. In minor games he was prolific. Patsy became the subject of exuberant idolatry and countless children were named after him. Back in England for the domestic season, he proved overweight and frequently out of touch but was still fifth in the averages. In 1936 he scored an aggregate of 2,654 runs. His last season was in 1937 by which time he had become a totemic figure in a young and happy Middlesex outfit enjoying the enterprising leadership of Walter Robins.

At the age of 57, Patsy turned out for Old England versus Surrey, making 94 in front of George VI. His dismissal was through exhaustion and he had to take three hot baths in six hours to reduce the effects of a stiffness that threatened to become rigor mortis. He had made Alec Bedser look ordinary. The previous year, Patsy had moved to Hove where he proved a disaster as the Sussex coach. He was too good-natured to discipline the slackers and would wander aimlessly round the nets swapping anecdotes with his favourites. Fortunately, he was in charge of a highly talented squad which included the future Bishop of Liverpool. In correspondence with the author, the Rt. Rev. David Sheppard recalled: 'I think those of us who sat at his feet owed quite a bit to a great cricketer to whom the game was always meant to be fun and who brought a very generous spirit to it.'

Patsy was of course sympathetic and approachable, but seldom dispensed anything better than general encouragement. However, he formed a close friendship with the Sussex captain and secretary, Billy Griffith, and he proved a wily fund-raiser. He left Sussex to become the Middlesex scorer. His immaculate script and orderly habits were assets, but he was no mathematician. With Compton and Edrich piling on the runs and practical jokers of the calibre of Brian Johnston dropping into the box, he was often hard pressed to keep abreast of the play.

Patsy's stroke-play was largely orthodox. Equally at home on front or back foot, his drives owed much to a late push from the forearms. His favourite shot was the lofted on-drive. He was undoubtedly one of the greatest exponents of the hook shot which he played with short arms, frequently taking the ball from just off a pair of luxuriant eyebrows. Patsy was never a good judge of a run and his partnerships with the young Denis Compton must have been eventful. He proved an immense source of encouragement to Compton without being slow to lay down the law, on one occasion tearing strips off Denis when he failed to back up in the field against Somerset.

Mostly ingenuous, Patsy could at times be as sly as they make them. There is a chestnut of an anecdote concerning how at Lord's in 1929, he introduced himself to a young Alf Gover and asked Gover not to drop anything short since his eyes were no longer up to it. Of course he was still an exceptional hooker. Gover proceeded to feed Patsy a diet of bouncers, all of which found their way to the ropes. It was only when Jack Hobbs interrogated Gover and discovered the deception that Alf was persuaded to bowl a full length. On the county circuit, Patsy's closest friends were his Surrey neighbours Jack Hobbs and little Bobby Abel. He would officiate at their fiercely contested table-tennis matches and when Abel lost his sight, Patsy was often seen shepherding him around the ground before going out to bat.

Soon after retiring from his position as Middlesex scorer in 1960, Patsy suffered a stroke. Despite the professional attentions of his wife, his mind dulled and the puckish face lost its mobility. The stroke also marked the onset of Parkinson's disease. Patsy Hendren's life ended on 4 October 1962 in the Whitington Hospital, Highgate. He was 73. A final excursion had been to watch the Cross Arrows at Lord's with

Billy Griffith – now MCC secretary – neglecting his duties to be at his side throughout.

An article by Jack Hobbs in the 1935 *Wisden* provides a good indication of Patsy's status. 'Pat Hendren is my ideal batsman, for I think he has every stroke for all sorts of wicket against all types of bowling.' There is little to add; in 83 Test innings Patsy scored 3,525 runs at an average of 47.63. Few people have denied his supreme talent and fewer still have ever said a mean thing about him.

13
Reginald Spooner

b. 21 October 1880, d. 2 October 1961

*'Why do we deny the art of a cricketer, and rank it lower than a
vocalist's or a fiddler's? If anybody tells me that R. H. Spooner did
not compel a pleasure as æsthetic as any compelled by the most
cultivated Italian tenor that ever lived I will write him down a purist
and an ass.'*

Neville Cardus, *Good Days*, 1949

In the late afternoon of Wednesday, 3 August 1904, a 15-year-old
insurance clerk and aspiring music critic stood outside the *Manchester
Evening News* office in Cross Street. He was waiting for another
urchin to rush out with a Reuters wire, and he occupied himself by
spitting into the gutter. The night before, he had offered up a small
prayer: 'Please, Lord, don't let Reggie get out; let him score a
century.' Doubting that this would be enough, he had convinced
himself that if he could spit between the bars of a drain, Lancashire
would have a successful innings. The batsman was Reginald
Spooner, the fixture was a Roses match at Leeds, and of course the
youth was Neville Cardus. The prayer went unanswered. Many of Sir
Neville's anecdotes have been exposed for what Benny Green has
called 'a tincture of white lies', and this is no exception. Even a quick
glance at the match report shows that Sir Neville's description makes
little sense. No doubt a pedant will soon prove that he spent the afternoon delivering laundry for his mother or devouring Dickens in the
Manchester Free Library.

It was Sir Neville himself who told us that it is more important that
history should be romantic than it should be precisely true. If his
memory is at fault or his imagination is in over-drive, the essence of
the story is that the frail loveliness of Spooner's batting had captivated a budding aesthete. Cardus created the legend but he also
obscured the man. This analysis of Spooner's cricket will descend
shamelessly into a Cardusian patchwork but the discussion of his

extraordinary sporting versatility has more merit. It has been ignored since his death, and Sir Neville's interest in his rugby exploits would have been as extensive as Reggie's views on tempo in *Die Meistersinger*.

Reggie was born on the outskirts of Liverpool to the Venerable George Spooner, Vicar of Litherland and later Archdeacon of Liverpool, and Edith Spooner, née Boult. Reggie's father served in the diocese of Liverpool for 59 years. As a scholar at Oxford, he was prominent in cricket and rowing, and as a young curate he did invaluable work in slum areas. He was a cousin of Rev. W. A. Spooner who gave his name to the 'Spoonerism'. A *Times* obituary includes: 'He sought peace not by ignoring differences, but by taking ground above them. His fine presence was matched by a still finer courtesy.' These qualities were passed on in no small manner to his second son.

In 1893, Reggie was sent to Marlborough College. 'Thank God / I'll never have to go through those again' is Betjeman's verdict on his own five years at Marlborough in *Summoned By Bells*. Reggie's time at the college was far happier. However, he was certainly subjected to a Spartan régime and one which gave rise to the old story of a new internee on the Burma railway being greeted with 'Cheer up old man, it's not half as bad as Marlborough.'

Reggie made his début for the college cricket XI in 1897. At the time he was excelling as a wicket-keeper, and against Cheltenham he not only played a sparkling innings of 82 but also took three catches and a stumping. In the winter of 1897–8, he was prominent in the college rugby XV as a three-quarter, and the *Marlburian* notes: 'He has a thorough knowledge of his duties, and the skill to perform them. He has a difficult swerve and keeps his head, a quality invaluable for a centre.'

In the 1898 cricket season he gave up wicket-keeping but complemented his batting with heavily spun underarm lobs. The big game of the year was against Rugby at Lord's. Reggie scored a flawless 139 during which he hit a towering six clean through the reading-room window. In October 1898, Marlborough were trounced 26–6 at rugby by Nomads with Reggie scoring the college's solitary try. He made few contributions to cultural life at the school. This was hardly due to lack of talent but stemmed from acute shyness. He did, however, win regular prizes for his charcoal drawings, and at the Christmas concert of 1898 he was persuaded to read extracts from W. S. Gilbert's *Bab Ballads*.

During the Easter term of 1899, he captained the college hockey XI as a centre-forward. Match reports in the *Marlburian* stress that as a hockey player, his stickwork was often inspired and that he had a fearsome shot. In the 1899 season he was prominent in several games against Oxford colleges, scoring a hat-trick against Balliol. His finest game was against Old Rossalians during which he scored seven goals.

At the end of the Easter term, Reggie performed superbly at the school athletics day, winning the 100 yards in 10.8 seconds. (It is worth noting that as a schoolboy, Eric Liddell was clocking the same time.) Despite his light frame, we find him contesting the shot put and the hammer; he won both events with 26' 10³/₄" and 59' 8¹/₄". He then sprinted to the other side of the college where he came third in a bicycle race. Earlier in the term he had performed creditably for the unbroken voices section of the Glee Club. He had also won the college Rugby fives competition with Harold Jonas.

In July he made 98 impish runs against Clifton. He was also inspired with the ball, taking 6 for 60. His schedule was hectic and on the following day he made 103 against Wiltshire Club and Ground. Reggie captained his school against Rugby at Lord's where in the first innings he hit some ferocious off-drives to score 69 in even time. This was merely the taster for a stunning 198 which *The Times* described as 'one of the finest innings played by a schoolboy at Lord's'. Later in the match he gave further notice of his versatility by taking 3 for 47 with his lobs which had a deceptive loop. However, as a lob merchant, Reggie was already a dinosaur and his bowling in first-class cricket was negligible.

He was being hailed as the finest schoolboy batsman since A. G. Steel. A few weeks later, he made his début for Lancashire against Middlesex at Lord's. In 80 minutes he scored 44 runs against Albert Trott and 'Old' Jack Hearne. ''E'll do' was Trott's verdict as he stepped into his bath. The fairytale continued: in the second innings Reggie made 83 in two hours, playing regal cover drives. He was hitting the headlines but was also demonstrating the modesty and reticence for which thousands would adore him. A week later, he made creditable scores of 46 and 31 not out against the touring Australians.

At rugby, Reggie was a stylish three-quarter in an era when players were allowed a good deal of time and space. He is remembered as having an excellent eye for an interception and being fearless when charging down. In March 1900, he played for Lancashire against Durham at Blackburn where his side was beaten 13–5. Reggie had a quiet game which disappointed his close friend and fellow double international Albert Hornby. At the age of 53, Hornby was haring about as a touch-judge.

A month later Reggie joined the militia and in April he was posted to Ireland. In October he entered the Manchester Regiment as a Second Lieutenant, leaving for the Boer War shortly afterwards. He spent 18 months in action during which he demonstrated exceptional gallantry which earned him the Queen's Medal with four clasps. He was wounded at Heidelberg but remained at the front line, returning home in May 1902 with a bad bout of enteric fever.

He threw off the fever during the summer and in November 1902 he turned out for the Lancashire rugby team and scored the opening try as his side defeated Cheshire 6–5. In late December the Roses rugby match was played at Aigburth. It resulted in a draw at one try apiece. Reggie impressed with his handling and pace, and this performance brought him a place in the North vs South fixture in the following month. In poor light, the North won a disjointed match 11–10, Reggie providing the final pass for the North's two tries.

On 3 January 1903, he played for the Rest of England against Durham. Reggie contributed significantly to his side's victory by three goals to a try, and he was selected for the match against Wales at Swansea on the following Saturday. Many years later, he recalled that it was 'a terrible game' and that his own form was woeful. A strong England XV was disappointing amid rain and hail. Reggie's handling was poor and for once he showed a lack of tactical awareness. He and his team-mates received a roasting in the press and *The Times* report is particularly damning: 'Spooner, who clearly was not accustomed to the Welsh methods, was frequently at fault and upset the combination.'

Reggie was dropped for the next game against Ireland. This was disappointing but on reflection he may have been delighted. Frank Keating notes that three of the England players contracted typhoid in Dublin. Two of them recovered but Reggie's replacement, the Blackheath three-quarter Reginald Forrest, was dead by 11 April at the age of 26. Reggie's rugby career was ended by a knee injury shortly after his international appearance.

In July 1903 he emerged from a drought to hit 247 against Nottinghamshire. The *Nottingham Daily Express* enthused: 'It would be difficult to find a prettier batsman ... His success will be gratifying to the friends of an exemplary young fellow both on and off the field.' At close of play, John Dixon, the Nottinghamshire captain, was led off the field gibbering. A crowd of miners had cheered every run and Dixon had found it impossible to set a meaningful field. Later in the same month, Reggie opened with Archie MacLaren against Gloucestershire at Aigburth. MacLaren raced to 204 before being bowled by Harry Huggins. Reggie had moved effortlessly to 164 but was bowled by Huggins a few minutes later. The stand was worth 368 and remains a record for Lancashire's first wicket.

Reggie was always happier among the elegant lawns of Aigburth than against the grim back-drop of Old Trafford, and he played many of his finest innings at Liverpool. George Hirst saw him at Aigburth in 1903 and remarked: 'That lad will have to have some bad luck if he does not play for England shortly.' He was selected for Pelham Warner's tour of Australia in the winter of 1903–4, and an evaluation in C. B. Fry's memoirs includes: 'My belief is that if he had been able to go to Australia he would have proved one of the biggest scorers in the annals of Test Match cricket.' Sadly, Reggie had no private income. In Denzil Batchelor's glorious phrase, he was 'an amateur with his living to earn' and he could not take time away from work. He was disappointed but professionalism was unthinkable and 'shamateurism' would have been alien to his monumental integrity. On his return from South Africa he had resigned his commission. He took some time to find his feet in business and a succession of jobs included a spell at the wine merchants Hatch and Mansfield, after which he studied estate management at Wye College in Kent.

Reviewing the 1904 season, *Wisden* selected him as one of its five cricketers of the year. His aggregate had been 1,889 runs at an average of 43 which he achieved despite three consecutive ducks. Cardus has recalled his reaction as a 16-year-old:

> **One evening I read in the stop-press. 'R. H. Spooner b Wilson 0'. R. H. Spooner was my favourite cricketer, and whenever he failed much of the savour went out of my life. But next evening, or the evening after, a worse blow befell me. Again I turned to the 'close of play' score and there, in cold print, was this announcement: 'R. H. Spooner b Wilson 0', – a 'pair of spectacles' for him. I hadn't the heart, that summer evening, to play cricket with my schoolmates. I wandered the streets blighted.**

> Neville Cardus, *Wisden*, 1951

Reggie soon put these failures behind him and discerning judges began to realize that he was destined for the Pantheon. Here is William Bettesworth writing at the end of the season: 'Mr Spooner is very young, and as time goes on he may develop powers which will place him on a level with the giants of all time.' A high point of this season had been an innings of 215 on a shirt-front at Leyton. Reggie gave a sitter to Johnny Douglas early on which Douglas obligingly shelled and he went on to display some dazzling strokes.

Reggie made his Test début at Old Trafford in the 1905 Ashes series. He appeared nervous in his early overs when beaten repeatedly in the air by Warwick Armstrong. After a few comforting words from Stanley Jackson, Reggie pulled Armstrong for a towering six into the railway booking office. He was on his way and settled down to make a characteristically graceful 52 during which he repeatedly flicked Monty Noble through the covers.

In his first innings at the Oval Test, Reggie was bowled for a duck when he shouldered arms to a massive break-back from 'Tibby' Cotter: 'I hardly saw the ball in a bad light against the pavilion. It was terribly fast.' In the second innings he soon found a rich vein of form. In partnership with Johnny Tyldesley, he put on 137 in 80 minutes. Reggie's contribution was 79 runs. In Australia's second innings, he underlined his versatility by putting on the gloves as a substitute for Dick Lilley. He had not kept wicket since Marlborough but he performed creditably and caught Victor Trumper off Walter Brearley.

The 1906 season was poor by his own standards. The highlight came in June with an innings of 240 against Somerset during which he made a century before lunch. In the following month, he scored 114 for Gentlemen vs Players at Lord's. Reggie worshipped Archie MacLaren, and in 1906 he was instrumental in organizing a public testimonial for his skipper. Archie was hopeless with money and he spent the proceeds on a luxury car in which he and Reggie would hare around Lancashire, prompting the following in a local newspaper:

'To Archie MacLaren quoth Spooner:
"I'm thinking of buying a schooner."
Said Archie: "What rot!
When a motor I've got
We can get to the cricket ground sooner."'

In June of this year, Reggie made a press statement to the effect that he would soon stop playing full-time cricket. After going on a world tour, he would be 'taking up a job which would occupy all of his time'. The tour began in the autumn of 1906. The best clues as to his movements are in his game diary which details his travel in India, Ceylon and Japan. In December we find him at Dhola where he went on several shoots with Ranji, agonizing when his party wounded some blackbuck.

Work prevented him from playing much cricket at the end of the decade. In 1908, he was taken on as assistant land manager at Apthorpe, the Northamptonshire home of Leonard Brassey. He excelled at the work and in October 1910 he was given control of Lord Londesborough's estate at Blankney near Woodhall Spa. He would spend 30 years at Blankney, occasionally turning out for the village cricket team to the delight of the locals. C. B. Fry was a regular hunting guest and often turned up without a mount. Reggie adored C. B. and ensured that Fry was given the best horse in the stable.

In July 1909 he was selected for the fourth Test against Australia at Old Trafford. An army of fans assembled, only to see him caught and bowled by Cotter for 25. His score of 58 in the second innings had the *Morning Post* correspondent rifling through his thesaurus: 'The charm of his batting lay not in the number of his runs but in the sinuous grace, the almost negligent ease, the abundant variety of strokes with which he made them.' At the Oval he failed with 13 and 3.

Reggie played little cricket in 1910. However, the Lancashire Committee had no problem in persuading him to turn out for Jack Sharp's benefit against Yorkshire. Reggie was conscious that a massive Bank Holiday crowd was expecting much from him. He had shown woeful form in the nets and as he walked out, he remarked to William Howard of the Old Trafford ground staff: 'I don't feel like making many runs today.' Howard gave his idol a shilling on the condition that Reggie would pay him a penny for every run he made. Reggie scratched around for several overs and he was dropped on 9. However, when Albert Hornby Jnr declared the Lancashire innings closed, Howard had made a profit of 15s. 8d., Reggie having breezed his way to 200 not out. Contemporary newspapers are dominated by the Crippen case (he had been arrested in Quebec on the previous day) but a short report in the *Manchester Evening News* includes: 'Spooner charmed our eyes with a cut as sweet as a filbert.'

The 1911 season was an uninterrupted success. In late July at the Oval, he was rampant when making 224 for Lancashire against Surrey. *Cricket* enquired: 'Is there any more brilliant off-side player now before the public?' During this innings he was also prolific through square leg and mid-wicket. Several Surrey fieldsmen returned to the pavilion with blackened hands and there is an oft-quoted legend which describes how Bill Hitch jumped into the air rather than field one particularly ferocious drive.

Again he was considered as an England captain when South Africa and Australia came over for the Triangular Series of 1912. However, the eventual skipper for the series, C. B. Fry, notes that 'Spooner disliked the responsibility of captaincy.' At Lord's on the first morning of the game against South Africa, there was a long delay after overnight rain. Warner was returning to Test cricket after his ulcer problems in Australia during the previous winter, and as the England players eventually took the field he received a rapturous welcome. Reggie was in a frisky mood, and with the cheers for Warner growing, he playfully doffed Warner's cap for him and made off with it around the boundary.

The South Africans were bundled out for 58 and Reggie came in at number three. After a characteristically uncertain start he moved smoothly to 67 overnight. Warner and Fry were content to play the sheet-anchor, but in the morning, Frank Woolley matched Reggie for speed of scoring. Reggie is often described as the 'right-handed Woolley', and the morning session must have been a cricketing aesthete's delight as these two consummately gifted batsmen played with total abandon. Woolley made a vintage 73 and Reggie played flawlessly until he was caught off 'Dave' Nourse for 119.

Against South Africa at Leeds, Reggie grafted to 82 in three hours, a funereal rate by his own standards. However, the innings formed the cornerstone of an English victory by 174 runs. His form tailed off in the final games. On his home ground he was bowled by the Australian opener William Whitty for 1, and at the Oval against South Africa he scored 26. In the final game against Australia he failed with 1 and 0. It was a sad to go way out; he would play no more Test cricket. There had been a moment of high comedy in the Australians' first innings when Claude Jennings made a towering hit. Before taking the catch himself, only inches off the ground, C. B. Fry nominated 'Tiger' Smith, Reggie and Wilfred Rhodes. (The legend is that he also called upon George Hirst, who was in Huddersfield at the time.)

Reggie entered the Lincolnshire Regiment as a captain in the first week of August 1914. He was soon mobilized and sent to Le Havre. Nine days later the Germans took Brussels. In company with the Royal Scots Fusiliers, Reggie and his men marched to Frameries. The period saw the first use of aerial reconnaissance. Sadly, this was often inaccurate and cost many lives. On 23 August the Lincolnshires constructed barricades in the outskirts of Mons. At 14.00 hours Reggie and his men began tending to the remnants of the Middlesex Regiment which had been beaten back from St Symphorien. German infantry swarmed round a street corner a few minutes later and there was some vicious hand-to-hand fighting. Reggie demonstrated exceptional gallantry and he was awarded the Mons Star. The area had become a demented slaughterhouse; over 48 hours, 4,533 Allied personnel were killed or wounded.

The battle of the Marne began on 7 September, by which time Reggie and his men had marched to Soissons. Nearly 200 members of his regiment were killed or wounded as the Lincolnshires relieved the Royal Fusiliers at Vailly. In the following weeks, he performed wonders during artillery bombardments. His work at the Blankney estate had given him a wonderful rapport with animals; to the horror of his men, he would often go above ground at night and attempt to quieten horses. In late September, the company travelled by motorbus to the outskirts of Lille. On 20 October, Reggie was briefing junior officers when a shell burst over Battalion HQ. His sergeant was killed and eight others were wounded. Reggie received serious leg injuries and he was immediately taken to a dressing station. He was sent home a few days later.

His private letters reveal that by March 1915 he was regaining his mobility and he returned to his regiment in the spring of 1915. On 13 June, we find him at an infantry depot outside Ypres. Later that day he was ordered to the front, and his battalion marched down the Menin Road, passing the infamous Hell Fire Corner. On 16 June, Reggie's group was involved in prolonged close-quarter fighting at the Birr Cross Roads. His battalion suffered 101 fatalities on this single afternoon. The regimental history quotes a letter home from one of his men: 'Captain Spooner stood out in that day's battle as an evening star stands out against an ever darkening sky.' Again, Reggie received serious leg injuries. By now he had been wounded twice, had a bad case of trench foot and was suffering from the after-effects of mustard gas. A medical officer took a brief look at him and sent him home. His war was over.

At the end of the decade, Reggie set about reviving the estate at Blankney. In May 1920, he married Lucy Marjorie Lowthorpe-Lutwidge. His bride was from Cumberland and her family had strong army connections. They had two sons, Edward and John. Edward has retired to Andover after a career in the City. He has been unfailingly kind to the author during the research for this chapter. Sadly, the marriage was not a lasting success and by the time they were teenagers, Reggie's boys were being brought up by their father alone. Despite having played little cricket in the previous season, at the age of 40, Reggie was asked to captain the Ashes tour in the winter of 1920–1. Initially he accepted, but niggling injuries were taking a long time to heal. His son notes that Reggie's real need was a cartilage operation on the knee that had been injured during the war. The technology did not exist, and in August 1920 he told the MCC that he considered himself unfit.

Reggie played his last county championship matches for Lancashire in 1921. He remained active within Lancashire CC and attended the major functions. At a dinner in 1927, Home Gordon reviewed the decade and started paying extravagant and heartfelt tributes to him. These were met with exuberant approval from the audience, and it was suggested that Reggie should complete the speech. Poor Reggie nearly choked on his port and came close to leaving the room: 'Oh, Home, I could not, so don't ask me.'

Reggie spent much of his life at Manor House in Metheringham, Lincolnshire, on the Blankney estate. In the 1930s, he combined his work with the task of bringing up his two sons. He regularly took them to Test and county matches at Trent Bridge and the trio would chug sedately to the ground in an old Crossley. On arrival, the spectacle of Larwood and Voce limbering up at either end with the new ball was a sight for any eyes.

In 1940, to the immense joy of his sons, Reggie married for the second time, his wife being Bertha Ellerbeck who was always known as 'Anne'. Three years later, his eldest son, John, was killed on active service with the Royal Fusiliers in North Africa. He had been recommended for the VC a fortnight earlier and had won the DSO. In a letter that could bring tears to a glass eye, Sir Neville commiserated with Reggie on his loss: 'We have had better luck than the present generation. We have seen the times of spaciousness, and dignity and gentleness.'

As a batsman, Reggie was characterized by his extraordinary wristwork. Don Davies speaks of 'the elegant proprieties of Mr Spooner whose wrists shed grace and breeding all over England'. Gilbert Jessop twins Reggie with another true immortal: 'Woolley was to left-handed batsmen what Reggie Spooner was to right at this period ... There are *centuries*, and centuries, just as there are different brands of champagne, and a "Spooner" century was the last word in charm and grace.'

Despite the seemingly fragile qualities of his play, Reggie had a solid frame and much sinewy strength. Like David Gower, he hit the ball extremely hard but with little apparent effort. He rarely lofted his drives but this was hardly from an urge to play the percentages. Reggie is often stereotyped as a mannered stylist whose forte was statuesque cover-drives. He was in fact extremely strong all round the wicket, and his driving off the back foot could be ferocious.

I watched Spooner rippling the sunlit grass with strokes that were without solidity or earthly momentum, and he leaned gracefully forward and flicked his wrists and the whole of the June day and the setting of sky and white tents and the trees of Canterbury were as though the created element of this lovely player's every motion and breath of being.

Neville Cardus, *Second Innings*, 1950

Reggie was congenitally incapable of playing a graceless shot. Describing his cover-drive, Cardus is more than usually inspired: 'It really does seem that he makes the stroke even as an artistic house-maid uses a feather duster.'

In a first-class career spanning from 1899–1923 but repeatedly disrupted by military service and business, Reggie scored 13,681 runs at an average of 36.28. Like many, Sir Neville was entranced by Reggie's fielding in the covers: 'As a cover-point he was the acme of grace, as swift and accurate as he was lovely to see.' The great Lancashire cover-points include Vernon Royle, Cyril Washbrook and Clive Lloyd. By any criterion, Reggie remains near the top of the pile. Reggie's lobs had brought him some success at Marlborough but he always fancied himself as a substitute wicket-keeper and he appears to have been competent with a neat and unfussy style.

In *My Life Story*, Jack Hobbs narrates how at Lord's in June 1912, Charlie Macartney was caught off Frank Foster for 99. As Macartney strode off, Reggie ran the length of the ground to pat him on the back in genuine sympathy. Sir Jack finishes the narrative with: 'Reggie's personality was as delightful as his cricket.' There are many similar anecdotes: they would become saccharine on repetition but the stories underline the spontaneity and warmth of this inordinately modest man. Reggie was unassuming to a fault. In conversation with the author, his daughter-in-law recalled that prompting him for reminiscences was like getting blood out of a stone. On the few occasions that he opened up, he would narrate a Test match century as if it had been net practice. Naturally, he never uttered a word about his superb war record, a fact which hardly assisted this research.

Reggie was not a great reader and unlike many of his contemporaries, he had no ambition as a sports writer. He did, however, knock out pieces of nonsense verse for his boys. Essentially, he lived for the outdoors; his passions were hunting, shooting and fishing. He was an excellent marksman and rode superbly to hounds. To Cardus's horror, he was not musical but he had a fondness for Offenbach's *The Tales of Hoffmann*. Despite his massive sporting gifts, he was a poor golfer. He dabbled with the game but found that the legacy of his flicked cover drives was an appalling slice. When the course was quiet, he would occasionally hack round Woodhall Spa accompanied by his terriers Tiger and Tim.

Blankney Hall was damaged by fire during the Second World War and the surrounding estate was sold. It was a fitting time for Reggie to retire. He made regular visits to his native Lancashire but remained in Woodhall Spa where he took a suite at the Golf Hotel. His passion for cricket remained with him and he attended Lancashire county games until two years before his death. Reggie would hunt down a few old friends and lurk anonymously in the bar. Occasionally he was announced to the crowd over the public address system, and the resulting attention embarrassed him enormously.

Reggie died peacefully on 2 October 1961. The obituaries do him little justice. He had outlived his contemporaries by two, even three decades. A painful loss had come in 1958 when his Lancashire colleague Don Davies perished amid the slush of an aeroplane runway in Munich. Here is Davies remembering his hero, only two years before his own death: 'There is no one whom we would rather see moving to the middle than Reginald Spooner, the Marlborough boy who walked straight from school into the Lancashire and England XIs and who, above all others, if Trumper be excluded, led us through the wicket of fancy into Heaven's meadow and set us gathering stars.'

14

Kenneth Cecil
Gandar-Dower

b. 31 August 1908, d. 12 February 1944 at sea

'When, in that hurried moment, out of sight
Of friends, when waves rush up to meet the air,
I find I do not wake a child at night –
That will be death. I think I shall not care.

I shall not see the glory fade,
The vision pass away,
Of mind and muscle shrink dismayed
Beneath a slow decay.
Ere cracked and tuneless rings the bell,
Ere clouds obscure the sun,
Ere broken be the golden spell
And summer days be done,
At least I shall have died right well
When I was twenty-one.'

Kenneth Gandar-Dower, *Granta*, 1929

Few men write their own epitaph and fewer still do it in decent verse. Replace 'twenty-one' with 'thirty-five' and you have an accurate summation of a short but remarkable life that was terminated by the Japanese Navy, fifteen years after this poem was written.

At 2.39 p.m. on 12 February 1944, the SS *Khedive Ishmael*, a troopship bound for Colombo out of Mombasa, was 60 miles from Addu Atoll in the Maldives when, after a massive explosion, the ship began to list. Rent apart by a torpedo from a Japanese submarine, it went down in 90 seconds with a death toll of 1,297. The incident remains the third highest loss of life sustained by Allied naval forces in a single action. As the vessel sank in the manner of a corkscrew disappearing into a bottle, 260 people were picked out of a shark-infested stretch of the Indian Ocean. With frantic survivors thrashing in the water, the captains of other ships in the convoy made the excruciating decision to attack the submarine with depth charges, and it was destroyed some minutes later. Among the lives lost was that of Kenneth Gandar-Dower. An enigmatic poet, explorer and journalist, he had been a double international for England at lawn tennis and squash.

Born at Regent's Park to a family of politicians and writers, he was sent to Harrow School in 1922. Recollections of Kenneth stress that while his ball-sense was prodigious, he had the wrong technique for every game he tried. At racket sports, his victories stemmed from his court sense and games eye rather than his strokes. He is described (somewhat ungrammatically) in the *Harrovian* as 'the worst ever good player of fives, squash rackets, tennis and lawn tennis'. The awkwardness can be traced to a childhood nurse who, appalled at his tendency to left-handedness, forced him to become a right-hander. The ambidexterity did mean that Kenneth was well placed to play fives and he became the strongest player in the school, captaining Harrow in his final year. He proved light on his feet and remarkably agile despite being of above average height.

A competent bowler and middle order batsman, Kenneth hovered on the fringe of the Harrow first XI. He turned out for the school in 1927 against Winchester but was not selected against Eton. For several seasons he was prodigious for the second XI and for his house. Playing soccer on the left wing, he was occasionally criticized for following the ball, but was noted for flighted corners and a heavy shot. In the winter term of 1927 we find him scoring twice with his left foot as Harrow defeated Charterhouse 3–0. (The childhood nurse does not appear to have supervised his football.)

He had been writing since the age of eight, and soon began to bombard the *Harrovian* with an extraordinary range of material. Most notable is a piece of mock operetta which features a chorus from the 'Tottenham Hapsburgs'. Even at this period there are hints that he would evolve into an urbane essayist and a significant poet. Later he would confess: 'I have a child-like conception of romance ... To me poetry is preferably the language of escape'. Early literary obsessions were with Masefield and Lewis Carroll while later enthusiasms included Rider Haggard. He was not the only budding man of letters at Harrow in this period. Again, the *Harrovian* reports how in his final year, Kenneth won the Handicap Rackets Competition. A lower school boy had been scheduled to play with a handicap of five but scratched before the first round. We can only speculate as to the youngster's reasons for defaulting. Perhaps he had a deadline for some dialogue; his name was Rattigan.

By the summer of 1927, Kenneth had won the prestigious Rothschild Scholarship for the best all-rounder of the year and an open scholarship to read history at Trinity, Cambridge. Before going up to university, he played in a national schoolboy lawn tennis tournament where he reached the quarter-finals, attracting the attention of the *Evening Standard* correspondent as 'a most determined retriever with a capable defence'. Later that summer, accompanied by his housemaster and close friend, the Rev. Digby Kittermaster, Kenneth went on holiday in the Tyrol where he found the scenery indistinguishable from a matinée of *Autumn Crocus*. In a preface to one of Kenneth's subsequent travel books, Kittermaster remembers his pupil as initially shy and awkward, going on to note that by no means a prodigy, he achieved extraordinary success at Harrow through 'limitless perseverance and a superb memory'.

Kenneth arrived at Trinity in October 1927. Intimate friends at the college included fellow Harrovian, Michael Warriner, who would win Olympic gold for the coxless fours in the following year. Living on the same staircase, Maurice Turnbull was no more than a nodding acquaintance. In the first week of the summer term, Kenneth was selected for Turnbull's XI in the freshmen's cricket match. Turnbull won the toss and elected to bat on a shirt-front. With the openers looking set, Kenneth disappeared to play in the freshmen's lawn tennis tournament. At the change-overs, friends who were commuting from the two venues on bicycles advised him as to the progress of the innings. While Bryan Valentine amassed 114 runs, he won two matches after which he leapt on to the back of a tandem which sprinted back to Fenners. Naturally, Kenneth followed the script; at number nine he stroked 54 not out. The antics did not impress Turnbull and Kenneth was unlucky to find himself carrying the drinks as twelfth man in the 1928 Cambridge cricket side.

There was little time for tennis in 1928. His attempt to make the Varsity XI had been a distraction, and he was always a keen student. However, he played much squash and became the leading player at Queen's. Abandoning cricket in 1929, he won the university lawn tennis tournament and gained singles victories against Oxford. In June of this year he played in his first Wimbledon, where, in the second round, he took a set from the eventual winner, Henri Cochet. Commenting on the game, a critic noted that with his wristy style, Kenneth's strengths were his half-volley and superbly disguised backhand pass. His serve and volley proved consistent weaknesses.

In June 1930, he was undefeated in the Varsity tennis contest. It had been a busy academic year in which he had been prominent in the Trinity debating society, spoken at the Cambridge Union and edited the main university magazine, *Granta*. He had also represented the university at Eton and Rugby fives. At Wimbledon in the second round, Kenneth came through a tough four-set match against John Olliff. In the subsequent round, playing outrageous half-volleys from near the baseline, he troubled Jean Borotra, eventually going down 4–6, 7–9, 8–10, having missed several set points.

By December 1930, Kenneth was giving notice that he was truly versatile. As an inexperienced squash player, he entered the Amateur Championship at the Bath Club. Playing off one leg after his opponent had stood on his foot, he won his fourth-round match with some brilliant drop shots. He then sailed through his semi-final and found himself playing the holder, Victor Cazalet. Kenneth lost a marathon five-game match in which many rallies exceeded 50 strokes. Again his unorthodox approach was noted, the *Manchester Guardian* correspondent commenting: 'His style is not pretty, but his foot-work is so controlled that he gets up with obvious ease, returns which the ordinary player would not get near.'

Kenneth crashed out of the 1931 Wimbledon in the first round but he recovered his form to win singles and doubles matches when Oxford and Cambridge took on Harvard and Yale at Eastbourne. He played much tournament tennis during this season, his most notable victory being over Frank Shields at Queen's. (Shields's granddaughter now appears regularly in the players' box on Centre Court; her name is Brooke.)

Kenneth had left Cambridge the week before Wimbledon having represented the university at a staggering seven sports: lawn tennis, real tennis, rackets, squash rackets, billiards, Eton fives and Rugby fives. He was bitterly disappointed at missing out narrowly on a first-class degree. His range of sports remained phenomenal and he was now one of the top squash players in the country, though a surprise defeat occurred in the quarter finals of the 1931 championship where his stamina was criticized.

By early 1932, with his Cambridge triumphs behind him, Kenneth was bored. Victory in the Eton fives championship in January provided only a passing diversion. He spent much of his time lounging about at Queen's Club. Roy McKelvie recalls that Kenneth and his cronies would often challenge each other to play every game available at the club in the course of a day. (Subject to the season, these might be lawn tennis, squash, rackets, ping-pong, real tennis, a quarter-mile, single wicket cricket, throwing the cricket ball, bowls and billiards.)

It was hardly a constructive existence; at 23 he was in danger of becoming what Scott Fitzgerald describes as 'that most limited of all specialists, the "well-rounded man".' A trip to New York in April during which he achieved the odd ambition of driving down Fifth Avenue in a taxicab did little to stimulate him. He returned to England and rescued a decrepit and foul-smelling Puss Moth which he suspected had been used by a previous owner to transport dead cats. He passed his flying examinations in the following month and in June he entered for the King's Cup Air Race with Angus Irwin. A veteran of sniper fire in the Dublin Revolution, Irwin was a grizzled aviator who, against his better judgement, allowed his co-pilot to thrash the 135 horse-power Moth as they took fourth place. Later, Kenneth did much solo flying. He often nourished his own myth, and there is a legend that having been forced down in the Indian Ocean he was picked up by a recovery plane which found him teasing the sharks with his toes.

In the spring of 1932 Kenneth played some of the best lawn tennis of his life to be runner-up at Queen's. In the semi-final he employed a mixture of top-spin drives and backhand drop shots to grind down D. H. Williams in three sets on a sodden shale court. In the final, his passing shots proved wayward. He took a set from John Olliff but went down 3–6 in the third. A few weeks later, Kenneth took his most notable scalp when he defeated the great Australian Harry Hopman in the quarter-final of the London Championship. Hopman was unable to live with Kenneth's bizarre gamut of pace and spin, and Kenneth came through 7–5, 3–6, 6–3. *The Times* commented: 'Gandar-Dower is a master of every stroke in an unorthodox manner and does nearly all the things that he should not, with complete success.' His opponent in the semi-final was H. Timmer who crowded the net after heavy serves and breezed to a 6–2, 6–4 victory.

In July, Kenneth made his first international tennis appearance for England against Scotland at Peebles, where he won his singles against J. T. Hill for the loss of only five games. He then partnered Dickie Ritchie in a five-set doubles which the Englishmen lost 14–12 in the fifth. On the second day he saved three match points before going down in four sets to I. G. Collins, but gathered himself to combine with Ritchie and take another five-set doubles. In his late eighties, Dickie Ritchie is alive and well, having come through the horrors of the Burma-Siam Railway. He remembers Kenneth as being fearless on crucial points, tolerant of a partner's shortcomings, a fine tactician and an even finer man. In a letter to the author, he summarizes Kenneth with: 'His volleying was not always successful but he learned to improve it, at the same time acquiring a decent service. However, it was Gandar's footwork and activity which were his strongest points.'

Aviation was by now an obsession and in October Kenneth decided that he and Irwin would fly their Moth from London to Madras. At the time, his mother was living in Brighton. Kenneth and Irwin were driven from Brighton to London by Hazelgrove the family chauffeur, and the pair took off from Heston on 26 October. Kenneth had persuaded his mother that he was taking a motoring trip in Yorkshire and somehow he managed to keep the flight out of the newspapers. The ruse worked and Mrs Gandar-Dower was still in a state of ignorance when her son was well past Cairo.

The press had been out in force at Heston in order to follow a trip to Cape Town in another Moth, planned by two engaging, Betjemanic girls, Audrey Sale-Barker and Joan Page. After a quick slug of champagne and with Hazelgrove 'weeping tears of enthusiasm and loyalty', Kenneth and Irwin took off in style, reaching Dungeness in 35 minutes. Even in Europe their navigation proved inaccurate and they would often drop down to read the names of railway stations. Safety equipment was similarly Heath Robinson, consisting of a pair of antiquated parachutes and some Dunlop inner tubes.

As he flew over Monte Carlo, Kenneth remembered a previous visit. 'I had been to Monte once before, and had not been able to get into the casino, being too young. Today I was again unable to get into the casino, being too high.' With even less navigational skill than the men, the girls followed in close convoy until they folded their Moth around a pylon outside Cairo. They emerged unscathed and went immediately to a ball where Joan Page spent the night dancing with Kenneth. As Irwin took off from the Jordanian town of Amman, his navigator had difficulty in locating an aerodrome at Rutba Wells in Western Iraq, consigning the following couplet to his diary: 'Where the hell's / Rutba Wells?' In total, he and Irwin flew 7,000 miles and landed 60 times. Kenneth describes the trip as 'supremely insignificant'. It was certainly modest. Amelia Earhart had made a solo flight across the Atlantic five months earlier, but two previous attempts to fly from England to India had resulted in a fatality in the south of France, and a forced landing in the Persian Gulf.

In August 1934 we find Kenneth on an expedition to Mount Kenya. It is the subject of his superb *The Spotted Lion*. The dedication is monumental: 'I dedicate this book to those ferocious quadrupeds of Africa

by whose clemency I have lived to write it.' Intending to fly solo as far
as Egypt and travel by sea to Nairobi, Kenneth was forced to land in
the Rhine Valley when the Moth's oil system failed. A bizarre journey
to Innsbruck saw him molested by Alpine cattle. He finally arrived in
Nairobi via the Suez Canal, and was horrified by what he refers to as
'the Bognorization' of Africa, noting: 'Kenya was a greater blessing to
the world when she produced imaginings and wonder rather than
sisal and coffee.'

Barely able to handle a rifle, speaking no Swahili, and with riding
experience limited to two outings on a donkey along Brighton beach,
he needed expatriate help. It came in the wildly eccentric form of
Raymond Hook, a white hunter and dilettante who has been described
as 'a happy compound of James Robertson Justice and Buffalo Bill'. On
his farm he had trained a wild buffalo to run with his cattle, while his
nightly cocktail of sherry and aspirin induced pronouncements on
subjects including God, athleticism, positivism, Pythagoras and the
Russian errors at the battle of Tannenberg. In Hook, Kenneth had not
found his Allan Quatermaine but a bizarre variant on Evelyn Waugh's
Captain Grimes. In earlier and more temperate years he had discovered a race of antelope which still bears his name as Hook's duiker,
and his wilder eccentricities included milking deadly puff-adders for
their poison.

Initially, Kenneth had intended to investigate the legend of the
Nandi bear, a fabled creature which was alleged to have driven
several beholders mad. However, his interest switched to a half-
mythical race of miniature, spotted lion which was said to inhabit the
Aberdares. The whole undertaking was a disaster and the party
found no trace of its quarry. Much of the blame lay with a team of
dogs that 'seemed more ready to face euthanasia than a mountain',
and a group of inexperienced and incompetent bearers. For Kenneth,
progress was slow on Jifu, a spirited Somali pony who looked 'exactly
like an A. E. Housman character retiring hurt from a rugger match.'

Kenneth was more successful as a photographer and the book is
superbly illustrated. Against his better judgement, he shot his first
and only lion, for which he felt nothing but shame. As he rushed back
to his tent in tears, he recorded in his diary: 'I felt as if I had been
cheating at school or pinching points at tennis.' John Pollard describes
Kenneth's subsequent actions: 'The slaying had a strange effect on his
sensitive soul, and he offered penance in an original way. Stripping
naked, he ran out on to the veld to learn at first hand just how it felt
to be a buck or a zebra when a lion was on its trail.'

I remembered that I had come from England vaguely, greenly, determined to drink of the intoxicating wine of Africa before her chalice had been drained of wonder.

K. C. Gandar-Dower, *The Spotted Lion*, 1937

As lack of food and sleep took their toll, Kenneth's fevered imagination envisaged himself and Hook as heroes in a mock Masefield novel. The expedition came to a creaking halt when two of the bearers contracted chicken-pox. In marked contrast with the shabby standards of the time, he abandoned the most important stage of the project to obtain medical attention. He had treated the boys superbly throughout. The only hint of discord occurred when two potential mutineers demanded a pay rise. By now possessing a smattering of Swahili, and knowing the words for 'want', 'come' and 'camp', his advice was as follows: 'Want baksheesh, come camp. Don't want baksheesh then bloody well hop it!'

Newspaper coverage of the expedition was unflattering. Sub-headlines included 'Dour Dower Spots Spotted Lion', and Kenneth's own articles in the *Field* produced sceptical correspondence. The book achieved modest sales and was neglected by the British press, though the *New York Times* gave it an enthusiastic review: 'The author's youth is ardent but not cock-sure, his self-visualization is humorous. He is not only open-eyed but sensitive and he has an awareness of beauty which he expresses in beautiful English; he really can write.'

Kenneth went back to Africa in 1935. Initially he trekked through the Belgian Congo and scaled several volcanoes. Preening himself on being the first to capture a giant forest hog, he returned to the Aberdares. By now he was intent on capturing a spotted lion, and he was willing to throw a small fortune at the exercise. Kenneth and Hook established camps a mile or so apart and communicated through bugles, with Hook playing the odd voluntary when bored. A team of bearers constructed traps using football nets. The nets ensnared dogs and hyenas but no spotted lions. After several weeks they left the traps in the care of assistants and produced the definitive map of the Sattima mountain. As usual, Kenneth was molested by angry elephants, while Hook was pestered one evening by a rhino. Buoyed up by his regular intake of sherry, he turned on the animal and chased it out of the camp.

Kenneth remained in Kenya until December 1936. In the final months, he captured a dozen cheetahs. He travelled back to England with the animals and left them in quarantine. In the spring, he and Hook spent a month canoeing in Herefordshire, after which Kenneth constructed elaborate quarters for the cheetahs in Croydon. His intention was to race the animals at greyhound tracks against themselves and whippets.

There were immediate problems. Cheetahs are more shrewd than greyhounds, and they will not chase an inanimate object. Unlike lions, they do not hunt in a group, and when one of their number gets ahead it is allowed to pursue the quarry alone. Thus, the moment an interesting race emerged, all but the leader would drop out. The pair overcame these problems and in August, a demonstration was given at White City during which the cheetahs disgraced themselves by cutting off corners. Kenneth had a favourite, a two-year-old male. On one famous occasion, with no announcement, he brought the animal into the bar at Queen's Club on a lead. (The writer shudders to think how many pink gins were spilt that evening.)

He was allowed to have practice sessions at the Harringay track where he rushed around in an MCC blazer and a Helen Wills eye-shade. He was now confident that the cheetahs would not bite lumps out of the handlers or the greyhounds, but another stumbling block was their inability to cope with tight curves. A fully grown cheetah can weigh up to ten stone and within seconds it can reach a speed of 70 miles an hour. The cheetahs were normally brought on as a novelty after normal racing, and when an oblivious punter, quietly marking his card on the rails, was knocked over by one of the cats which had missed a bend, the authorities at White City decided that the circus was no longer welcome.

Reluctantly, Kenneth shipped the animals back to Nairobi and turned his attention to journalism and squash. He was given top seeding for the 1938 Championship at the Bath Club. In the semi-final against E. Snell, he dominated from the T in a marathon of an hour and a quarter, and impressed with his volleying and the length of his ground strokes. The final was another epic against the army cham-pion, Douglas Burnett. At four points all in the third game, Kenneth astounded the crowd when, having fallen at the back of the court, he played a shot while kneeling and went on to win the rally. With the players trading exquisite drop shots, Kenneth won a superb match 2–9, 10–8, 9–6, 10–8 in an hour and 17 minutes.

Later in 1938, two volumes of light satire appeared under the joint authorship of Kenneth and his Harrow contemporary, James Riddell. *Inside Britain* and *Outside Britain* are now sadly neglected; the volumes have a gentle, ironic tone and are occasionally clairvoyant in their political speculations. In 1936, Riddell had captained the British

Olympic ski team at Garmisch. He decided to teach his friend how to ski, and spent many months in the Alps with Kenneth who proved fearless but incompetent.

On 17 March 1939, Kenneth became a double international when he played squash for England against Scotland in Edinburgh. He played first string and was matched against the Scottish captain, Roy McKelvie. Kenneth took the first two games 9–6, 9–6, before winning the third 9–0. The *Sports Despatch* reports: 'McKelvie put up a very good fight against Britain's best amateur, but after offering some resistance to Gandar-Dower he faded somewhat in the third game. Gandar-Dower played extremely well, and McKelvie could make nothing of him.'

He had spent a protracted time in England, and in the spring he left for Africa. At the outbreak of war, he was in the Belgian Congo photographing gorillas and working on a book. In some reflections on the pre-war antics of Mussolini, Kenneth had noted: 'By temperament I am pacifist and internationalist.' This stance did not prevent him from spending the middle years of the war as a front-line journalist. At the onset of hostilities, he made immediately for Nairobi where he acted as a liaison officer between the press and the military. He returned home in 1940, and worked on the Mass Observation project with Tom Harrisson. A kindred spirit, Harrisson had travelled in Borneo and the New Hebrides in the 1930s, spending time with a tribe of cannibals.

By June 1942, the UN had resolved that Madagascar should remain French, and in September of the same year, Kenneth was posted there as an observer for the East Africa Command. In his *Into Madagascar*, he describes the Allied operations as 'much less than a war and rather more than an obstacle race', while the backdrop is remembered as 'sadly lacking in lions or cannibals, and correspondingly full of malaria and missionaries'. He proved nerveless when grenades exploded only yards away from him, his main concern being to expose his pictures properly. He describes disembarking with the East Lancashires from the first landing craft to attack Tamatave, and wading ashore wearing a battered bowler hat with a camera in one hand and a typewriter in the other.

Whenever you sat down, a picture of dear old gaga Marshal Pétain, dressed in his ticket collector's hat, brought you to your feet, not so much out of respect as for fear that he might charge you twopence.

K. C. Gandar-Dower, *Into Madagascar*, 1943

The fighting in Africa was completed by the end of 1943, and in the following January he wrote to Rev. Digby Kittermaster for the last time: 'I can't stand this. I must do something dangerous.' For Kittermaster, Kenneth was '... a complicated, contradictory, versatile character. A professed agnostic, he believed with all his heart in the Christian doctrine of love. He was of a pacifist turn of mind, he hated the idea of bloodshed, he was determined to survive the war if he could. He loved life, indeed he clung greedily to the idea of life; yet he would not have safety on any terms.' That a middle-aged clergyman-turned-schoolmaster and his agnostic pupil should have formed a sufficiently close friendship that they chose to spend a summer holiday together and thereafter corresponded regularly until the end of the latter's life, reveals much about both men.

A month after writing to Kittermaster, Kenneth left for Colombo and a passage to oblivion at the hands of the Japanese Navy. There was a news blackout on the circumstances of his death and there are few obituaries. (*Wisden* is colourful but inaccurate.) In a short paragraph, the *Daily Telegraph* noted: 'It was not his record-breaking that made him friends. They loved him for his humour, his modesty and his high spirits.' There is searing irony in the concluding paragraph of *Into Madagascar*: 'So far in this war, the campaigns I have covered have been carried out either against Italians, who did not want to fight at all, or Frenchmen, who did not want to fight us. Sooner or later I shall come up against the Germans or the Japanese, and then I can see I am going to get a shock.'

15

Frank Mitchell

b. 13 August 1872, d. 11 October 1935

'I shall never forget the coons who were named conductors ... I have
had dealings with negroes in several parts of the world, but those
whom I encountered in American trains should have a twelve month
stay on a Boer farm. They would learn something there which might
mend their ways.'

Frank Mitchell, *My Innings*, 1935

The subject is a farrago: a racist and bigot, a sportsman of rare talent
if not genius, an army officer of outstanding bravery, and an individual of unfailing modesty. This mass of contradictions was brought up
in Yorkshire where at the age of six, he was taken to see Dave
Gregory's Australian tourists. In his memoirs he recalls having been
entranced by the bowling of Fred Spofforth who became a life-long
hero. He had played in his first cricket match earlier in the season,
trotting on to the field as a substitute fieldsman for his father's club
side at Birdsall.

At the age of 11, he was sent to St Peter's School, York, where he
would become captain of rugby, cricket and rowing. The versatility
soon surfaced and he also excelled at swimming and athletics. He did
not neglect his books, and the *Peterite* lists him as a prize-winner in
classics and divinity. In the summer terms, F. M. could often be found
sculling on the Ouse. The rowing may have been responsible for
developing his massive frame, and by his final year he was six foot
tall and weighed a shade over 15 stone. Photographs suggest that he
carried a good deal of superfluous flesh for much of his life, his most
notable feature being a pair of deep-set eyes which stare vacantly out
of a moonish face.

The range of skills displayed at school is impressive. In 1886 he
played Antonio in *Much Ado About Nothing* and Baptista in *The
Taming of the Shrew*. The school magazine is critical of the first
performance ('suffered from youthful voice ...') but glowing about

the second: '... good; his painstaking rendering of senile foibles praise-worthy'. He appears to have been less painstaking at the crease, and a summary of his cricket ends with: 'Useful bat but in too big a hurry to make runs and often throws away his wicket.'

In 1889 he captained the rugby team and the verdict on his play at centre is: 'Though not fast, might run a little more before passing, and try to get the ball out to the wing on the full pitch.' A hint of his future reactionary outlook emerges at the debating society where he vigorously supported the motion: 'The Irish are unfit to govern themselves.' His first sporting achievements of note were two centuries for the school in the same match against the Gentlemen of Yorkshire in 1889.

F. M. left St Peter's at the end of the summer term of 1890 and moved to Brighton where he spent three years as a master at Greyfriars Preparatory School. He recalls that 'cricket and both codes of football filled up my spare time'. He had no experience of soccer but found the game attractive and decided to become a goalkeeper. Many of his pupils moved on to Brighton College and he would hang around the playing-fields in the hope of being invited to join pick-up games. Within weeks, he became a superb keeper and in the winters of 1891 and 1892 he played both soccer and rugby for Sussex.

In 1891, he joined Blackheath RFC, and in the middle of the decade he played many games for the club, heading the list of points scorers for the 1894–5 season. In his summer vacations he played cricket for the Sussex Gentlemen, and in August 1892, he made a fine half-century against London County. In 1893, he headed the batting averages at the Brighton CC, scoring 594 in nine innings.

It was during this summer that he made a belated decision to try for a university career, and after some hasty cramming he was offered a place to read classics at Gonville and Caius, Cambridge. He walked into the university rugby team and won his first blue in the following December. Although their scrummaging was effective, Cambridge were outclassed in the loose and lost by a try to nothing. *Pastime* produced some player profiles and its treatment of F. M. includes: '... a hard worker. Uses his feet well and knows the game thoroughly'. His activities were not restricted to the sports field and in his first year he acted as vice-president of the college literary and historical discussion group.

In the early summer he was prolific in college cricket matches. In the course of seven days he scored 143 against Emmanuel, an undefeated 203 against Peterhouse and 136 against Selwyn. More significant was his 67 in mid-May against a side which approximated to a full-strength England amateur XI. *The Times* described how F. M. 'met the bowling with a vigour and precision that created a very favourable impression'.

He became a certainty for the Varsity fixture where he failed with 1 and 28. The Cambridge bowling was weak and by now F. M. had made himself into a useful trundler. He was brought on as second change and took 4 for 44. This excellent spell did not prevent an Oxford victory by eight wickets. F. M.'s batting form had deserted him and his début for Yorkshire during the vacation was a disaster. He made a 'pair' against Derbyshire at Sheffield and dropped a sitter in front of the pavilion which was greeted with a hail of ginger-beer bottles. He notes: 'Then I could have done with an underground tunnel to the pavilion.' *Wisden* is scathing about his performances and Mitchell has the grace to quote the notice in his memoirs: 'On the few occasions he played for Yorkshire ... he displayed no skill sufficient to contend against the difficulties which presented themselves.'

Mitchell's schedule became hectic on his return to Cambridge in September. He was elected secretary of the university cricket and rugby clubs, condescended to attend a few lectures and wrote some fatuous pieces for *Granta*. As a classicist, he knew what he liked and liked what he knew. His journalism suffers from the familiar under-graduate habit of trying to make every remark an epigram, and such Latin and Greek as had been forced on him laces everything he writes.

Ranji had gone up to Cambridge in the autumn of 1894. F. M.'s racism did not extend to Indians and the pair became close. He was a regular guest on the Prince's shooting parties and in later years he spent summer holidays fishing for salmon at Ranji's country retreat at Ballynahinch Castle. Wearing three overcoats, Ranji was at Queen's in the following December to watch his friend in the Varsity rugby match. F. M. was successful with a conversion in an uninspired game which ended at a goal apiece. The game is notable in that the referee, a Colonel Lawrence, blew up ten minutes early. (F. M. and Lawrence both spent their retirement in Blackheath and Mitchell would always greet the Colonel by asking him for the time.)

In the following January, he made his international début for England against Wales under the captaincy of Sammy Woods. In the opening minutes he missed a simple penalty kick and immediately lost his nerve. When England scored their first try, he was faced with an easy conversion, and *The Times* reported: '... the chances were all against the missing of the goal; but Mitchell failed'. His side was fortunate to win by a goal and three tries to two tries, the victory owing much to a brilliant performance from Woods who took over as the place-kicker.

Mitchell was fortunate to retain his place for the fixture against Ireland in the following month. England won by two tries to one in appalling conditions, the *Field* noting: 'It was a mudlark from beginning to end.' He failed to convert England's try and sustained a knee injury which did not prevent him from doing some fine work in the scrum. F. M. arrived back in Cambridge in a dreadful condition; his knee had swollen to the size of a balloon and he was succumbing to 'flu. By March he was fit for the Calcutta Cup and his dribbling was a rare high-spot in a depressing game which England lost by a goal and a try to a solitary goal.

At university level, the 1895 cricket season was another series of triumphs. In May he pasted a Somerset attack all over Fenners and was particularly severe on Sammy Woods. *Cricket* notes that the innings included 'some of the most powerful off-driving ever seen on the ground'. Against Oxford he looked well set on 28 in his first innings when he was dismissed by Leveson-Gower. In the second innings, F. M. made a fine 43, *Cricket* reporting that 'his batting was characterized by great freedom, and he puts more powder into his strokes than any player on either side'.

In the autumn he captained a mediocre team of Varsity players on a tour of North America. The party played five matches, recording two victories, two losses and a draw. F. M.'s form was poor, his highest score being 58 against Pennsylvania University. The tourists were trounced at Haverford where the Gentlemen of Philadelphia defeated them by an innings. The defeat in Philadelphia did not go down well with the city's expatriate population, and the captain received some rancid hate-mail. At the same time, Lord Dunraven had brought his *Valkyrie* to the States in an attempt on the America's Cup but had withdrawn at the last moment. One of F. M.'s correspondents expressed himself as follows: 'Dear Sir, —You are a lot of stiffs; go home in the *Valkyrie*.'

In December 1895, he captained the Cambridge rugby side to victory over Oxford by a goal to nothing. His side scored early on and his forwards had complete control of the match, though many of their tactics were negative. There are few concrete details since the fog at Queen's was so bad that few people in the press-box could see anything. In the following January, a strong England pack destroyed the Welsh at Blackheath. The home side won by five goals and five tries to nothing, F. M. scoring the third try. In March he won his greatest sporting honour, when, as an undergraduate, he captained

England in the Calcutta Cup at Glasgow. It was not a successful day
for the visitors who went down by a goal and two tries to nothing.
The Scots were superior in every department. Gregor MacGregor, the
English Test wicketkeeper, was superb for Scotland in the loose and
the weakness of the English three-quarters was consistently exposed.
It was F. M.'s last rugby international.

In July 1896 he was involved in much controversy when, as the
Cambridge captain in the Varsity cricket match, he instructed his
bowlers to deliver deliberate wides in order to avoid imposing a
follow-on which at the time was compulsory. His players were jostled
as they returned to the pavilion and an elderly clergyman emerged
from the Old Blues' Stand, threw a pair of field-glasses at him and
used some language which would not be found in the litany.

F. M.'s action proved both misguided and controversial. Many of
his team were upset by the fracas and they lost several wickets early
on, allowing Oxford to snatch a brilliant victory. Mitchell's personal
contribution to the game was minimal; he scored 26 and 4 and bowled
two overs. Earlier in the year, he had won his third blue as a shot
putter. It was not an event for which he trained regularly, and he
turned up on the day to fill a last minute gap. With a crude technique
he achieved 34' 10" to take third place.

Mitchell was disappointing in the 1897 Varsity cricket match,
scoring 6 and 1. He had a quiet season for the university but came
good in July with scores of 133 and 58 for MCC against the Gentlemen
of Philadelphia. He left Cambridge in 1897 with a dismal third in the
classical tripos. There is little doubt that he was the best soccer goalkeeper at the university throughout his residence, but to his credit, he
refused the chance of additional blues so that 'a regular soccer man'
should not be deprived.

After a brief stint as a master at the Abbey School in Beckenham,
F. M. spent 1898 in attempts to establish himself as a journalist. He
played little first-class cricket though his rare appearances were
successful and included an innings of 161 for MCC against his old
university. In the autumn he toured North America under Pelham
Warner. The party had a horrendous crossing on a dilapidated liner
whose engine malfunctioned only three hours out of Liverpool. F. M.
had grown attached to the ship's cat and was distraught when it was
decapitated by a swinging door during rough weather. Warner's team
was undefeated in eight matches and F. M. enjoyed a rich vein of form.
Wisden reports: 'Among the batsmen, Frank Mitchell was the most brilliant, and the most dependable, fully earning his place at the top of the
averages.' Mitchell's finest innings was at Ontario where he scored 128.

At Montreal the opposition included W. R. Gilbert, a cousin of W. G. Grace who after one of cricket's most depressing incidents, had been packed off to the Dominions in 1886 when he was found stealing loose change from the coat pockets of his Gloucestershire team-mates. F. M. had by now developed a keen interest in wine, and he visited many vineyards. (He was said to be a better judge of claret than of a run, and in later years his cellar became legendary.) Other excursions were to Armour's slaughterhouse in Chicago and New York's Central Park. At Armour's, F. M. vomited, and while striding through Central Park his progress was impeded by 70,000 Knights Templars who were holding a jamboree: 'I never want to see such a horde again. Beer and tobacco to chew seemed to be their hobbies.'

Within a matter of weeks he was sailing to South Africa under Lord Hawke with a team which played two matches which have subsequently been given a dubious status as Tests. F. M. was included on the recommendation of W. G. who, having seen him bat for the first time, pronounced him to be 'good enough for any team'. He took an immediate liking to matting wickets and played superbly for 162 against the Transvaal and 81 against Cape Colony. His performances in the Tests were uninspiring. He scored 28 and 1 at Johannesburg and 18 and 41 at Cape Town, but in all games his aggregate of 857 runs was the highest in a party which included Johnny Tyldesley and Albert Trott.

F. M.'s vitality proved a mainspring of the social tour. At Cecil Rhodes's farm he took charge of a team of six mules, causing much amusement when he became hopelessly stuck in a drift. On the voyage home, the passengers included the George Edwardes Gaiety Company who took much pleasure in dressing the cricketers for a fancy dress ball. Warner went as a girl and was so convincing that he was obliged to fend off amorous advances from his team-mate Willis Cuttell. F. M. was equally impressive as W. G., and he cut a dashing figure on the dance floor with Albert Trott who came as a Russian orthodox priest.

In the 1899 season, F. M. established himself as a Yorkshire regular, making 1,502 runs. A rare lapse was against Kent at Tonbridge where he was clean bowled by Colin Blythe's first delivery in county cricket. Blythe had been unprepossessing in his approach to the wicket: 'I did not take much stock of him; he looked weedy and as if a square meal would do him no harm.' F. M.'s greatest triumph in 1899 was a blistering innings of 194 against Leicestershire. He also played much country house cricket at the turn of the century, and he recalls an encounter with his boyhood hero Fred Spofforth. The match took place at Castle Howard where the pitch was unsafe and the players were guests of the Countess of Carlisle who was well-known as a teetotaller: 'Fancy that wicket with old Spoff bowling and only lemonade if you get hit!'

F. M. spent 1900 serving in the Boer War. It will be apparent by now that the writer finds him unsympathetic; the uncompromising and gratuitous racism is repellent. It needs to be stressed, however, that in two conflicts he demonstrated exceptional courage. At Cambridge, he had been a captain of the University Volunteers and within weeks of the outbreak of war he was clamouring to enlist. After several rejections he joined the Yorkshire Dragoons. Again, it is to his credit that he joined as a private. On the voyage out, he was promoted to quartermaster, and he later served as a lieutenant. His regiment was ludicrously ill-equipped and it arrived to face a Cape Province winter with no overcoats and lacking items as basic as mess-tins. Food was scarce and the Dragoons resorted to eating mules as well as horses. The regiment saw action in Boshof Free State where casualties included Patrick Campbell, husband of the actress. On 13 August F. M. reports in his memoirs that he celebrated his 28th birthday by leading his men through artillery barrages on the Magaliesberg Hills where he is said to have proved nerveless under fire.

Mitchell could sleep on a meat hook and he was happy camping in the open. However, a year of eating horse flesh and dry biscuit finally wore down his constitution, and after several bouts of malaria he was ordered home. Whatever his courage during the Boer War, he remained crass and insensitive when reflecting on the campaigns: 'It may seem small beer after Armageddon, but it did our regular Army a lot of good.' It is difficult to reconcile this verdict with the statistics: British casualties exceeded 21,000, and 26,000 women and children died in Kitchener's concentration camps. If Mitchell was unable to get his modest intellect around these figures, he might have spared a thought for his Yorkshire team-mate Frank Milligan, who died at Mafeking.

F. M. recovered his strength quickly, and in 1901 he topped the Yorkshire batting averages with 46.17. He scored 1,801 runs for the county including seven centuries. Four of these came in succession within the space of two weeks, the most notable being an undefeated 162 at Edgbaston. He was chosen as one of *Wisden*'s cricketers of the year, and in his autobiography, he describes this season as phenomenally happy, the Yorkshire side revelling in the eccentricities of David Hunter and Schofield Haigh. F. M. had a great love of domestic animals, and took a keen interest in Hunter's prize-winning canaries. He would visit the birds regularly and feed them with Hunter's secret concoction of cayenne pepper which produced a distinctive red plumage. Similarly, at Cambridge, when Ranji bought a couple of puppies (Mascara and Flighty), it was F. M. who lavished much affection on the dogs and took them to coursing events at Plumpton.

His attempts at journalism in 1901 had been unprofitable, and towards the end of the season he told Lord Hawke that he needed a job. Hawke immediately thought of Abe Bailey, the South African diamond millionaire, who offered F. M. a position as his secretary. He sailed for South Africa at the beginning of 1902 and was able to combine his duties with a successful career as a stock-broker. He also extended his journalistic experience by spending seven years as the financial columnist for the *Transvaal Leader*.

He had little time for cricket but he played for Transvaal in the 1902–3 Currie Cup, making a superb 102 against Griqualand West. At the beginning of 1904, F. M. became Bailey's campaign manager in the infamous Cape Election and he trekked in an open cart to every corner of the Province. In the aftermath of the election, Bailey decided to direct some of his personal fortune at an attempt to foster relations between England and South Africa through the medium of cricket, and in the summer of 1904 he financed a tour of England by a strong party of South Africans.

Mitchell was elected as captain of a side which batted all the way down to number ten and featured the exceptional wrist-spin of Reggie Schwarz, another double international who, like Mitchell, had played rugby for England. F. M. started well with 102 against Cambridge University but his form tailed off in the middle part of the tour. However, he rallied with a fine 75 at Lord's as his team achieved a brilliant victory by 189 runs over a near full-strength England XI. The tourists' schedule was crowded but not heavy enough for F. M.'s boundless energy and he squeezed in several games for Yorkshire in the middle of the programme. In 1906, Mitchell married Theresa Kelly of Barkly West. Over the next few years he suffered several setbacks on the stock exchange. He was obliged to work all hours in scraping a living as a journalist and had no time for Test or Currie Cup cricket. He was able to play a small amount of club cricket and in 1911 we find him scoring 226 for the Wanderers against the Pirates.

In 1912, South Africa were invited to contest the Triangular Series. The initial choice as captain was Percy Sherwell – yet another double international (cricket and lawn tennis) – but when Sherwell refused, F. M. was touted as a candidate for the captaincy which, at the age of

39, he accepted with reservations. The South African bowling proved inept, and Schwarz, who had also been reluctant to tour, was a ghost of his former self. F. M.'s form was appalling; he scored 11 and 0 in the first Test against Australia at Old Trafford, and two runs from as many innings against England at Lord's. He dropped himself for the second match against England at Headingley and when he returned against Australia at Lord's the awful run continued with scores of 12 and 3, failures which prompted him to stand down for South Africa's remaining matches.

F. M. settled in England in 1913 after failing on the South African stock exchange. His last cricket match of consequence was for MCC versus Cambridge University in 1914 when he bludgeoned his way to 66 runs in a little over an hour. Predictably, he was clamouring to be in colours when the Great War broke out a few months later. At the age of 41, he was unsure as to what contribution he could make. His old Yorkshire team-mate Stanley Jackson was assembling a battalion of the West Yorkshires. He spent a few days acting as an unofficial adjutant for 'Jacker' and together they got up a fine group of men. The pair took their battalion to Matlock which he describes as 'not a very nice place for infantry, though it might be alright for goats'. Later, he transferred to the Divisional Ammunition Column, serving with the West Riding Royal Field Artillery at Mons where he was promoted to Lieutenant-Colonel and mentioned in despatches.

By 1919, F. M. was resurrecting his career as a journalist and he began writing for the *Cricketer* soon after its establishment in 1921. His varied literary output is uniformly feeble, but it is revealing and warrants consideration. When not slapping himself on the back over his modest level of erudition, he demonstrates crass Blimpery and excruciating levels of royalist sycophancy. Trading on his name, he wrote for many quality national papers and his stylistic vagaries must have kept an army of sub-editors working through the night. In the snobbery stakes, he leaves Evelyn Waugh and Lytton Strachey for dead; a notable gem occurring in a chapter on physical fitness which he contributed to the Badminton Library: 'It is to the City man that training is a necessity. He lives, perhaps, in a humble lodging in Bloomsbury – the most hateful of all fates.'

In 1935, Mitchell's memoirs were serialized in the *Cricketer*. It should be emphasized that in describing his own exploits on both sports and battle fields, F. M. is uniformly self-effacing. However, it is in his treatment of body-line in the *Cricketer* that he finally establishes his credentials as an idiot with: 'When we won the fifth match at Sydney our captain had every reason to be proud of the work he had done ...' E. W. Swanton speculates as to what sort of reception the piece might have received from Jack Fingleton, a recipient of body-line and an infinitely finer batsman, journalist and man. F. M.'s sentence structure can be Byzantine in its complexity and when his sentiments are unsound, the combined effect is peculiarly offensive. Frank Mitchell writes with a limp.

At rugby, he was a brilliant if erratic place-kicker. In the loose, he was surprisingly nimble given his bulk and he had a happy knack of making crucial tackles. At cricket, he made 4,090 runs for Yorkshire with an average of 34.35. As a bowler he was of medium pace with a high action but few additional attributes. Apart from a competent spell in the 1894 Varsity game, he did little else with the ball. He is remembered as being a poor fielder; a naturally heavy frame combined with the rowing at St Peter's had made him muscle-bound and his catching was far from safe. Despite his massive bulk, he fancied himself as a wicket-keeper and as a treat, Lord Hawke would occasionally allow him to stand-in for David Hunter behind the sticks.

As a batsman he had a relaxed stance and a false backlift, a rarity at the time. For A. A. Thomson, he was 'one of those rare ones who had both glorious hitting powers and a rock-like defence'. He scored predominantly in front of the wicket and loved to drive on the up. As a captain, F. M. was competent if uninspired; he was unobservant in the field but exercised much authority through a military brand of discipline. He had excellent technical knowledge but needed to lead from the front, and if his own form was poor, he was unable to inspire his team-mates.

When not assisting Pelham Warner, F. M. spent much of his retirement pottering around Rectory Field and building up a superb wine cellar. He remained active and served on the Barbarians committee. He also maintained his fanatical quest for physical fitness and would jog round Lewisham at a sedate pace right up until his final years. He was also remembered with affection for his enthusiastic coaching of junior rugby sides. The strength as well as the stamina stayed with him to the last, and residents of Blackheath fondly recalled how he would act as a human scrummage machine for his colts.

F. M. died peacefully on 11 October 1935, with his autobiography unfinished. Warner was moved to write an unusually graceful obituary in which he describes him as 'what Nyren would have called "a good face-to-face man"'. However unsympathetic he may be as an individual, his performances in an England rugby jersey and the 1901 cricket season for Yorkshire guarantee him a pew towards the rear of the Pantheon.

16

Andrew Ernest Stoddart

b. 11 March 1863, d. 3 April 1915

'My heart goes out to my Creator in love
Who gave me Death, as end and remedy.'

Stevie Smith, 'My Heart Goes Out', 1969

The *Daily Telegraph* for 6 April 1915 narrates proceedings at Marylebone Coroner's Court on the previous day. They are undistinguished if grim. P. C. Corrie of the Paddington division described how on 3 April he had visited 115 Clifton Hill, Maida Vale. In an upper bedroom he found a man slumped in bed with blood running from a head wound. The court had already heard that he was 52 and a sometime secretary of Neasden Golf Club who had been suffering from depression arising from financial losses. The deceased's widow, Ethel, told how her husband had produced a duelling pistol. A brief struggle ensued. Finding the barrel empty, she had hidden a box of cartridges. The jury returned a verdict of 'suicide while of unsound mind' and the court dispersed. Spectacularly mundane, the case would have warranted half a column inch, save that the victim was 'Stoddie', Andrew Ernest Stoddart, a former captain of the England cricket and rugby teams, and a sportsman touched with genius.

He had spent his early boyhood in South Shields where his father was a prominent local cricketer. When he was 12 the family relocated to London where he entered the Rev. Oliver's school in St John's Wood. Rugby at the school was exceptionally physical and Stoddart soon received an injury to his side which he never threw off; he was often found writhing in agony on the dressing-room floor only minutes before games. At the Blenheim Cricket Club he was outstanding with bat and ball, and he made his first century in 1880.

In his youth, Stoddart had shown a gift for drawing which resulted in an apprenticeship to an architect and a brief course of study at the Royal Academy School. As a young man he would play club cricket of any standard at a moment's notice. On holiday in Bournemouth in

174

1884, he scored two centuries for the town but spent much of his time fishing from the pier with twine attached to his cane. A hint of decadence emerges in early manhood during which he appears to have been poised and immaculately dressed. By the late 1880s he had evolved into a mixture of Regency buck and late-Victorian fop. Alan Gibson uses the word 'masher' to suggest a lady-killing aesthete. In a superb biography, David Frith has described how Stoddart kept a scrapbook of society ladies. He was adored by women, keeping the gossip columnists busy for much of his life. The lustre that accompanied his achievements on the sports field was enhanced by a jaunty, crooning voice and a talent for the banjo.

Years later, the *Morning Post* recalled that in his teens, Stoddart played hockey for Hampstead as a wing forward. He was also proficient at rackets, billiards and hurdling and was a competent boxer. His hand-to-eye co-ordination was prodigious and he once made an undefeated 110 while batting with a broomstick. He would turn out in a variety of events at the Hampstead athletics meeting, lining up cheerfully for the egg-and-spoon race at which he was undefeated for several years. He combined rugby and cricket from the earliest days, playing much of his rugby for Blackheath after a spell with Harlequins.

Stoddart played 114 games for Blackheath between 1883 and 1896. He captained the club between 1889 and 1891 and was prolific as a scorer of tries and drop goals. In his first year as captain, when faced with an impending combined tackle and a massed defence, he had the imagination and nerve to turn on his heel and retreat many yards before stroking an exquisite drop goal. It requires only a slight suspension of disbelief to imagine Stoddart turning out for Blackheath with an enduring figure in English literature. In 'The Sussex Vampire', Robert Ferguson enlists the help of Sherlock Holmes by letter, adding as a postscript: 'I believe your friend Watson played rugby for Blackheath when I was three-quarter for Richmond.' As a Blackheath player in the 1880s, Dr Watson must have been near to international standard and he would have lined up alongside Stoddie at Rectory Field.

In the winter of 1887–8, Stoddie formed part of a cricket tour to Australia under George Vernon, which will be discussed later. At the conclusion of the trip he remained in Sydney. A rival cricket tour organized by Alfred Shaw and Arthur Shrewsbury was running concurrently. The pair had grown in confidence as promoters and had made arrangements for a tour of Australia and New Zealand by a group of English rugby players. Stoddie was invited to join the party. Composed largely of working men from the north, the tourists were captained by Robert Seddon. The members who were still playing seven years later at the time of the Great Divide would certainly have defected to rugby league. The tourists played a sophisticated game built around heeling from the scrummage which contrasted with the basic, mauling style of the Australasians.

The visitors played their first game against Dunedin on 28 April. Seddon scored the opening try as his side won 8–3. The tourists also proved superior to Canterbury, winning by four goals and two tries to two goals. One of the most important games came in the third week of May against Auckland where a massive crowd saw the locals achieve a 4–0 victory. Stoddie had a quiet match but Seddon was superb throughout and the Lancashire batsman Arthur Paul did invaluable work in the loose.

In early June, the tourists sailed for Australia where, against their better judgement, they were persuaded to play a few games under Australian Rules. Many of the players found the local code awkward but Stoddart made the transformation effortlessly. On 9 June they played New South Wales at union, and the Reuters report notes: 'The visitors obtained an easy victory, defeating the home team by two goals and six tries to a goal and a try. Mr A. E. Stoddart, for England, made some splendid runs.' A week later, the party was at Melbourne where it played the Carlton Club under Australian Rules in front of an intrigued crowd of 25,000. The visitors were defeated by 13 goals and 17 behinds to 3 goals and 11 behinds. They showed much enthusiasm and a fair degree of tactical awareness but the *Melbourne Leader* was realistic: 'To say that they were able to make anything like a good fight against the premier club of the colony would be foolish and fulsome flattery.' A few expatriates who were familiar with Australian Rules approached Seddon. His men were encouraged to jump properly for marks and after some intensive coaching they defeated teams from Ballarat and Kyneton in late July.

Stoddie was on excellent terms with Seddon, and on the morning of 15 August we find them at the Maitland Rowing Club on the Hunter River. After the pair had spent a few hours messing about in a skiff, Stoddie went bathing while Seddon took an outrigger on to the river. Ten minutes later, Seddon was dead at the age of 25. Staff at the club had been disturbed by his seeming inexperience as he left the landing-stage and they were hardly surprised when he capsized the craft a few minutes later. Concern turned to horror when Seddon swam a few strokes and sank like a stone. The *Newcastle Morning Herald* carried a report on the inquest which noted that he was a strong swimmer and had probably been suffering from cramp.

The loss cast a gloom over the rest of the tour, though Stoddie performed wonders in lifting morale. He assumed the captaincy and in his first game as skipper, he steered the tourists to a comfortable victory against Queensland. In early September, the party returned to New Zealand where it was lucky to defeat a spirited and physical Auckland team by a single try. Stoddie and his men sailed for England at the end of the month and the tour was widely hailed as a resounding success.

In the following year, a New Zealand team visited Great Britain. Predominantly composed of Maori natives, it was captained by Joe Warbrick. The Maoris took on England in February at Blackheath where they lost by a goal and four tries to nil. Several of the tourists claimed that the refereeing by Rowland Hill of the RFU had been incompetent and biased. At half-back, Stoddie impressed all with some bewildering runs. Early in the second half, his shorts were so badly ripped that he required a new pair. Accounts of the ensuing events vary widely but they all have the trappings of farce. It appears that as the players huddled around him while he changed, Frank Evershed picked up the ball and claimed a try. At first it was refused while players and referee argued. Incredibly, Evershed repeated the performance and this time Rowland Hill awarded the score, where-upon three of the visitors walked off the field.

In the aftermath of much political bickering, England played her first home international for four years against Wales in February 1890. Stoddart distinguished himself with some imaginative kicking as his side went down by a try to nothing. He was injured for the Scotland match but reappeared as the England captain against Ireland at Blackheath, scoring a try from just under the posts during a home victory by three tries to nothing. It was two failures in 1893, combined with increasing susceptibility to concussion, which brought his rugby career to an end. In January, England played Wales at Cardiff and both Stoddart and Sammy Woods proved ineffective as England lost 12–11. In March, the Calcutta Cup was contested at Headingley where the home side lost 8–0 amid appalling handling from Stoddart. *The Times* describes how a promising England move broke down: 'Stoddart blundered in failing to take a pass from Wells', later noting that 'Stoddart again failed at a critical time'. It was his last international.

From assimilated knowledge, Arlott summarizes the finished rugby player as 'an agile and originative wing three-quarter'. A portrait in the 1886 *Football Annual* concludes with: 'He is the prettiest and most graceful three-quarter of the day.' He certainly possessed superb balance and incorporated extravagant swerves into his running without losing a yard of pace. Naturally, a safe pair of hands on the cricket field ensured that until the very last season, his handling was superb.

Back in 1885, the form of a 22-year-old Stoddart for Hampstead CC had been widely noted and in August he made his début for Middlesex against Yorkshire at Lord's. He failed in the first innings with 3 but promised much with 21 in the second. A few days later he travelled up to Trent Bridge where he scored a sparkling 79.

Earlier in the month, Stoddart had produced an extraordinary innings of 485 for Hampstead vs Stoics. At the time it was the highest innings in any kind of organized cricket. Various contemporaries record that on the morning of a match, Stoddart would conserve his energy by staying in bed until half an hour before start of play. On this occasion he never went home. He spent the night dancing and playing poker, and at seven in the morning he was clocking up a few lengths at a pool on Hampstead Heath. David Frith relates how Stoddie detailed his activity in the evening. When asked if he was tired, he answered: 'Well, perhaps I was, but we had a lawn tennis match, a four, on that evening, so I had to play that. Then I had another tub, and had to hurry too, because we had a box at the theatre and a supper party afterward. But after that I got to bed alright, and it wasn't nearly three!' There is no record of what Stoddie saw that evening but his options included Henry Irving and Ellen Terry in *Faust* at the Lyceum, and Kate Vaughan in *The School for Scandal* at the Haymarket.

The maiden first-class century came nine days later against Kent at Gravesend where he raced to 116. In the winter of 1887–8, two cricket teams visited Australia. Stoddie formed part of a tour captained by Lord Hawke. The trip has already been touched upon in the discussion of his rugby. At exactly the same time, Shaw and Shrewsbury sent a team under Aubrey Smith. This odd situation was the result of rivalry between the Sydney and Melbourne Cricket Clubs. There was no ill-feeling between the teams and Hawke recalls how, travelling out together on the *Iberia*, the players put on a production of an obscure farce *Old Soldiers*. In February, a composite side took on a full Australian XI. In his first Test, Stoddart was England's second highest scorer in both innings, making 16 and 17 on a difficult wicket.

In the winter of 1890–1, he toured Australia under W. G. In the opening Test at Melbourne he scored 0 and 35, while at Sydney he captivated the crowd with a fluent 27 in the first innings. In the second innings he played quite brilliantly for 69. His play in provincial games was glorious, a highlight being 45 in half an hour at Ballarat. In the third Test at Adelaide, he gave two chances early on but rallied to move a little unsteadily to 134 before he was lbw to George Giffen. The *Sporting Life* reports: 'While it can scarcely be termed a remarkably brilliant innings it was an attractive display, in which sound defence was combined with powerful hitting.' The highlight of the social programme was a kangaroo hunt in which the Doctor nearly broke the back of his diminutive mount and spent much of his time encouraging Stoddie and little Bobby Peel.

At Lord's in May 1892 we find Stoddart playing for Single vs Married and scoring 42 and 53. The selection criterion appears eccentric but was mundane compared with other fixtures of the period. These included: Slow Bowlers vs Fast Bowlers; Over Thirty vs Under Thirty; Left Handers vs Right Handers; Whiskers vs Clean Shaven (usually won by the hirsutes); Teetotallers vs Whisky Drinkers (invariably won by the topers); Smokers vs Non Smokers and, perhaps the most charming of all, Classicists vs Modernists.

In the 1893 season, Stoddart produced some vintage performances, most notably at the Scarborough Festival where he and Stanley Jackson put on 176 for C. I. Thornton's XI against the Australians. At Lord's in the fixture against Nottingham, he scored 195 in the first innings, following it with 124 in the second. Despite these triumphs, he had a moderate Ashes series. At Lord's, he deputized as captain for W. G. Having received a blow on the elbow from Charlie Turner, he failed with 24 and 13 in a drawn match. His 83 in England's single innings at Lord's was the second highest score in the match by an Englishman but was hardly authoritative. At Old Trafford, having been slow to back up, he was run out by W. G. for a duck in the first innings but made 42 in the second.

In this period, Stoddart was sharing bachelor digs in Hampstead with fellow double international, Gregor MacGregor. MacGregor had been the England wicket-keeper during the 1893 series, and as a full-back for Scotland he had opposed Stoddart in the previous winter. Regular guests at their lavish dinner parties included W. G. and Sammy Woods, and the evenings would always end with a marathon whist session.

In the winter of 1894–5, he captained the England Ashes tour. Stoddie took two wicket-keepers in Hylton 'Punch' Philipson and Leslie Gay. In winning his single Test cap at Sydney, Gay also became a double international; he had kept goal for England at soccer in the previous year. The side's early form was sketchy and the Australians were quick to note that amateurs and professionals stayed at different hotels. However, Stoddie proved amenable and co-operative with local journalists who appreciated his democratic manner and his delight in good play from either side.

The first Test at Sydney remains one of only two instances in international cricket of a team winning after following on, the other occasion being Botham's and Willis's epic performance against Australia at Headingley in 1981. Stoddart registered scores of 12 and 36. The match was won for the tourists by the thrilling margin of ten runs thanks to the slow left arm of Bobby Peel. On the final day, Peel had arrived at the ground hung-over if not still drunk. A patient Stoddart put him under a shower. As he towelled himself down, Peel surveyed the ground and realized what had been apparent to his captain from midnight. In his cups, he had slept through a thunderstorm which had transformed the wicket into a spinner's paradise. He was soon clamouring for the ball and Stoddart allowed him to open the attack.

Peel took 6 for 67 and England won by 10 runs. Leslie Gay had a hand in three of the dismissals but he had dropped George Giffen three times in the first innings and never played Test cricket again. Unemployed, he compiled a fascinating diary. It includes a list of the 245 species of wildlife he slaughtered on shooting expeditions and a catalogue of the ladies he danced with (fewer than 245 but evaluated in a similarly zoological tone).

The fever-pitch intensified in the second Test at Melbourne when England were dismissed for 75. Stoddart found himself at the wicket for the second ball of the day when Archie MacLaren registered a golden duck. He was soon bowled for 10 by Turner. In the second innings he scored a fluent 173, later describing it as '*the* century of my career'. As a score by an England captain in a Test match in Australia it was only overhauled in 1975 by Mike Denness on the same ground. Stoddart's innings was interrupted by a thunderstorm during which Johnny Briggs spent an hour reciting speeches from *Macbeth*. Poor Johnny was always on the verge of hysteria, and four years later he would be bowling fantasy overs in the Cheadle Lunatic Asylum. After fine bowling by Peel and Brockwell, England won by 94 runs.

Played amid temperatures of 105° in the shade, the Adelaide game saw England chasing an Australian first innings total of 238. Most of the tourists were out of sorts having taken up to three cold showers during the night and they replied with 124. Feeling wretched, Stoddart relegated himself to number five and was bowled by Giffen for 1. Australia amassed 411 and England collapsed to 143 and a defeat by 382 runs with Stoddart stranded on 34 not out.

The tourists returned to Sydney for the fourth Test. The home side made 284 and the England captain made 7 and 0 as his side was dismissed twice on the third day. George Giffen has recalled the prelude to the deciding game of the series: 'Thousands of people had poured into Melbourne from all parts of the Colonies. Special trams brought human freight in hundreds ... I know that when Stoddart and I went into the ring to toss, he was as white as a sheet. I won it ... Poor Stoddart gave me a despairing look, which said as plainly as words, "I'm afraid it's all over George".' He was being unduly pessimistic. On a shirt-front, Australia amassed 414. In reply, Stoddart began to master a rampant Giffen before being stumped off Harry Trott for 68 as part of an England total of 385. Richardson bowled superbly to limit the Australian total to 267 and England needed 297 to win. Stoddart was bowled for 11 by Harry Trott but England cantered to a 3–2 series victory.

Despite the achievements in Australia, Stoddart was replaced by W. G. as captain for the 1896 domestic Ashes series. At Lord's, he was bowled for 17 in the first innings, while in the second he made 30 not out. In the second Test he hung around gamely while making 15 and 41 against some exquisite leg-spin from Harry Trott. Stoddie withdrew from the third Test at the Oval. Explanations for this are legion. He certainly had a cold, and in the light of threatened strike action from the professionals, a large squad of players had assembled. However, the most likely cause of his sudden unavailability was pique at an attack in the *Morning Leader* which had carried a large caricature and copy which included 'one amateur is to receive a larger sum in the shape of expenses than all the professionals put together'. There was much debate at the time over W. G.'s expense account but it is probable that this article is a gibe at Stoddart. His replacement was another amateur, Archie MacLaren. Alfred Gibson narrates how he was once told that when pressed about why he had stood down, Stoddart had snarled 'Archie needed the money'.

In the mid-1890s Stoddart took up golf and partnered Billy Murdoch regularly in foursomes against Sammy Woods and W. G. It's not a bad quartet; three double internationals and the first man to score a double century in Test cricket. All four would cheat outrageously, often repositioning the ball in the bunkers, with Murdoch and Stoddart not above throwing their ball out. In the winter of 1896–7, Stoddie performed superbly on a tour of the West Indies under Arthur Priestley. In twenty completed innings he amassed 1,079 runs.

In the winter of 1897–8, Stoddart was the English captain for another tour to Australia. It proved an unhappy expedition. In the run-up to the first Test, he was told that his mother had died. He spent the rest of the tour disoriented and distressed by Australian barracking. He was in no state to play in the first two Tests and the side was captained by MacLaren who skippered the tourists to a massive victory by nine wickets at Sydney and defeat by an innings at Melbourne. David Frith notes that during the Melbourne game, Stoddart's chiselled features and luxuriant moustache were seen peering forlornly from the dressing-room window, prompting local papers to suggest he was looking for a wife. 'Whose wife?' was the response of one wag.

The atmosphere soured when Ernest Jones, the Australian fast bowler, was no-balled for throwing by umpire Jim Phillips. Universally known as 'Jonah', Jones was a tearaway pace merchant and the fastest bowler in the world. The incident gave rise to the mother of Australian cricketing anecdotes. The legend concerns a Sunday school teacher in Sydney who, some years later, decided to test her children's knowledge of the Old Testament. She enquired of them: 'What was the most surprising episode in the life of Jonah?', and was staggered when one of her pupils piped up with: 'The day he was no-balled by Jim Phillips.'

By mid-January, Stoddie was beginning to surface from intense grief and he returned to the Test team at Adelaide. As Australia piled on 573, he called on eight bowlers including wicket-keeper Bill Storer. He held himself back to number seven and was caught by Jonah off Howell for 15 as England were dismissed for 278. In the follow-on, MacLaren and Ranji put on 142 for the second wicket. Stoddart contributed 24 before driving uppishly at Charles McLeod. His side eventually lost by an innings and 13 runs. Problems on and off the field escalated and Stoddart remained unduly sensitive to crowd hostility.

At Melbourne in the fourth Test, Australia began with 323. Again batting way down the order, Stoddart came in with the tourists floundering on 103 for 6. He was caught by Joe Darling off Jones for 17 and the visitors were dismissed for 174. In appalling light, England followed on and Ranji made a half-century. At number six, Stoddart was greeted by a scoreboard showing 4 for 147. He was well set on 25 when he played on. It was his last Test innings.

In an interview with the *Sydney Referee*, Stoddart described how at Brisbane, he had engaged a barracker in reasoned debate. He claimed to have made a convert: 'I talked to him quietly and seriously for ten minutes, during which he gazed at me and seemed to wonder what sort of person I was. At the end of that time he said "he was damned if he would ever hoot them again".' In the same interview, Stoddie described how persistent jeering had made Tom Richardson lose his head and his bowling, finally leaving the field in tears.

Summations of Stoddart the cricketer abound. For Grace he was 'graceful, spirited and finished' while C. B. Fry was impressed by his fluid movements: 'All Stoddart's hitting is distinguished by a fascinating elasticity, indeed, this quality is what makes his style when at his best so charming.' He was a prolific driver, normally keeping the ball on the ground. He used a light bat and was never known to slog. Many contemporaries comment on the speed of his scoring; in the 1890 North vs South match, he made a half-century while Grace was scratching around for 3. Stoddie was a competent hooker and he relished duels with pace bowlers. However, he remained mindful of the overall state of a game and could apply himself to a defensive innings when required. As a captain, he coaxed rather than drove, and he always set an example by covering acres in the field.

One's difficulty is that Mr Stoddart became great in what may be called the transition stage of batsmanship. He led a host of followers as far as the very banks of the Jordan and then he declined himself to enter the promised land.

Philip Trevor, *The Lighter Side of Cricket*, 1901

In 1903 he was employed as secretary of the Neasden Golf Club where he played off scratch, having made much progress since the early hacking with Billy Murdoch. In October 1906 came a late and unhappy marriage to a vivacious young Australian in Mrs Ethel Luckham. Earlier in the month, he had become secretary of Queen's Club. He took up real tennis and was confused by his first lesson since it undercut all that he had been taught about cricket and golf: 'I don't understand the game. The fellow kept on saying "Keep your head up, Sir" till I was looking at the skylight and couldn't see the blessed ball at all. All I've got is a crick in the neck.' At Queen's he was well liked by the members and competent at his job.

In 1910 the club became concerned by suffragette activity. Queen's had been portrayed as a bastion of chauvinism and the committee decided to hire three watchmen and a dog. The watchmen were retained for many months but the dog was sacked early one morning when it bit a steak out of Stoddie's leg. At the time, Queen's hosted a variety of sports fixtures including the Varsity rugby match, and the secretary's status as a rugby player was valued on these occasions. Severe tennis elbow forced him to give up golf for which he had developed a passion though he would occasionally play bowls. A serious bout of influenza coincided with severe financial losses and the realization that his marriage had been misguided and offered little hope of happiness.

By the beginning of 1914, his nerves and constitution were wrecked and he was in no state to work at Queen's. The end was approaching quickly. Around this time Stoddie also gave testimony at the inquest of a young coach at the club who had shot himself, and he appears to have been greatly upset by the incident. Stoddart's own obituary appeared in *Wisden* alongside tributes to Victor Trumper and W. G. (Pages 140 to 222 – at about four entries per page – are a catalogue of the slaughter in France and Belgium.)

For his *Times* obituarist, Stoddart was '... the only man who has captained England in a Test Match and a "Rugger" International'. (Reading this over breakfast in Cheshire, A. N. Hornby must have spluttered over his kedgeree and reached for pen and paper fairly quickly.) The summation can be left to an opponent. Even when reflecting on the bad-tempered Ashes tour of 1897–8, Frank Iredale had this to say: 'We looked upon him as the beau ideal of a skipper, and as fine a sportsman as ever went into a field.'

17

Reginald Erskine Foster

b. 16 April 1878, d. 13 May 1914

'My whole life was but a schoolboy's dream. Today my life begins.'

Oscar Wilde, *De Profundis*, 1905

'Tip' Foster was the third son of a family of seven boys and three girls. His father, Henry, was educated at Winchester and Clare College, Cambridge, where he emerged as a strong cricketer who was unable to afford the substantial match fees, a detail which hardly does the university credit. At Winchester he had played cricket against Eton in 1862 and 1863. He played much high-class club cricket and was a prominent member of the Worcestershire committee. After graduating in 1867, he attended theological college and began teaching at Malvern College. Over a career of 48 years, Henry Foster evolved into an engaging pedagogue and amiable eccentric whose vitality and candour touched thousands of pupils.

In August 1871, Rev. Foster had married Sophia Harper, the daughter of a well known club cricketer. Tip's mother was a fine games player who excelled at hockey. The legend is that she would fling down lobs at a lively medium pace while her sons acquired the basics of batting, after which they were handed over to their father for fine-tuning. On Boxing Day mornings, the ten siblings and assorted uncles and aunts played the rest of the county at the Worcestershire Golf Club, usually giving their opponents many strokes and a beating.

Tip arrived at Malvern in 1890. He broke into the cricket XI in June 1893 when, at the age of 15, he held up an end for an hour while the future England soccer player 'Pinky' Burnup savaged the Sherborne attack and gave the college a narrow victory. Tip played indifferently in the following season but came good with a precocious 69 against Repton. He was by no means obsessed with sport and he made significant contributions to cultural activities, appearing in Molière's *Le Malade Imaginaire*.

In October 1895, the editor of the *Malvernian* was expecting much from him on the soccer field: 'Foster at centre-half is the most promising; he spoils his play by selfishness, but works hard and is an undeniably good shot.' He became a regular member of the soccer XI during this term and in the following month he played superbly as the college went down 2–1 to a strong Corinthian team. Throughout his short life, Tip was able to produce something on the big occasion and he was quite dazzling as his team defeated Repton 6–2.

In March 1896, Malvern lost to Rugby in the semi-finals of the Public Schools Rackets Cup. However, Tip was proclaimed the finest schoolboy player in the country and the *Malvernian* enthused with: 'We cannot speak too highly of the brilliance of Foster who was acknowledged to be the best player up. His service was magnificent …' He had little interest in track and field but excelled at many other sports, his speciality in the gymnasium being the horizontal bar.

In June, the college put on a lavish open day which included a production of *A Midsummer Night's Dream* in which Tip played the combined rôle of Snug and the lion. In the afternoon, the grounds had been littered with stalls and amusements, most of them manned by the Foster family. Tip's sister, Jessie, performed Grieg piano sonatas while his father took charge of the captive golf ball.

Foster entered University College, Oxford, in October 1896. He declared an intention of reading modern history but was focused on sport. He is described by an obituarist as 'a stout man at an oar', but cricket, soccer and rackets allowed him little time for rowing. However, he was an enthusiastic follower of the college boat. At Eights Week he turned up in full fig – Authentics Blazer and immaculate white ducks – and become unusually animated when the University boat triumphed in a close finish. Breaking away from his friends, he jumped into the river and swam 100 yards to embrace the crew. *Isis* reports that he appeared a little peaky on his return but was revived with a gooseberry ice-cream.

A portrait in *Isis* stresses his popularity with women: 'There is a rumour that at a leap year dance he had thirty-three applications.' The article continues by listing a few of his achievements and ends: 'It is rumoured that a short biography in six volumes is about to issue from the Clarendon Press.' Tip won his first blue in March 1897 in the Varsity golf match at Royal St George's. On the front nine he took an early lead against Harold Marriott. The pair were all square at the turn but Tip missed several fairways on the back nine and went down by two holes. Cambridge won the match by 16 holes to 11 under the captaincy of Bernard Darwin, a grandson of the naturalist and perhaps the greatest ever golf writer.

Another blue followed a fortnight later. In the Varsity rackets match, Tip was defeated 3–0 by Edward Garnett. The transition from schoolboy rackets would take several years, and the *Times* attributed his defeat to tactical naïveté: 'On occasions he made splendid strokes off the side walls, but he did himself no good by keeping the ball low.' The previous day he had gone down in a marathon doubles match in partnership with Raymond De Montmorency (father-in-law of E. W. Swanton) who was also a notable all-rounder. He had been part of the Oxford golf team at Sandwich, and he would later score a fine 62 in the Varsity cricket match.

As a freshman, Tip did not break into the Oxford soccer team, but he won a cricket blue at Lord's in June 1897. He failed with 27 and 6. It was a busy term, and at college level he performed creditably in the hammer and shot put. In February 1898, he gained a soccer blue against a strong Cambridge side. Tip's form was poor and the *Isis* report is damning: 'Foster did not come up to expectations: he dribbled well but showed little judgement.' Yet another blue followed a few weeks later when he gained revenge over Edward Garnett at rackets. In June, he scored 57 in his only innings as Oxford gained an unexpected victory over Cambridge. At Queen's Club in February 1899, he was competent but uninspired during an unremarkable Varsity soccer match which Cambridge won 3–1.

He began playing soccer for the Corinthians at this time and would represent them sporadically over the next three years. Team-mates included Charles Wreford-Brown, a double international himself who displayed wide-ranging talents; his second sport was chess. In early July, Tip was again unsuccessful in the Varsity cricket match (21 and 18), but three weeks later he scored 134 and 101 not out for Worcestershire against Hampshire. His brother Bill also made scores of 140 not out and 172 not out in this match, and *Cricket* noted: '... the wearied bowlers could do nothing with them in either innings'. As a feat in first-class cricket, Tip and Bill's performances were unequalled until March 1974 when Ian and Greg Chappell both scored two centuries for Australia against New Zealand at Wellington.

In March 1900, Tip made his international soccer début as an inside-forward against Wales in a game which was drawn at a goal apiece. He was tightly marked by the Welsh captain Dai Jones who knocked him into a bog within a few minutes of the kick-off. When roused, Tip could muster a massive shoulder-charge; he cheerfully returned the compliment and immediately helped Jones out of the mud. A few

seconds earlier, Geoffrey Plumpton Wilson had put England ahead
and the visitors retained their lead until midway through the second
half when Wales equalized with a spectacular volley from Billy
Meredith. The *Liverpool Sporting Express* commented: 'Foster can if he
chooses make his way through most places and it is no pleasant task
to try conclusions with him. The one fault he has is doing too much on
his own account.'

His performance in the 1900 cricket season was awesome. He began
in May with scores of 128 and an undefeated 100 for Oxford against
A. J. Webbe's XI. A few weeks later, W. G. took his London County
side to The Parks. Tip made his third consecutive century when he
raced to 169. In a single over he hit the Doctor for four sixes, the only
occasion on which Grace suffered such an indignity. For once W. G.
took a hammering gracefully: '"Not very respectful to an old man,
was it, Tip?" said the Champion, "but it was worth seeing".'

In July of the same year, he finally came off against Cambridge when
as captain, he scored 171 and 42. A report in the *Star* is ecstatic: 'The
Dark Blues' captain stands out head and shoulders above the twenty-
one other players.' An even more spectacular performance came in the
following week when he scored 102 not out and 136 for Gentlemen vs
Players at Lord's. He was imperious throughout and during one spell
he scored 72 while C. B. Fry scratched around for 9. He had made three
centuries at Lord's in ten days. Soon after the game, *Cricket* featured
Tip on its front page and the profile includes: 'He has the world of
cricket at his feet.' He had averaged 77 for Oxford during this term and
the *Sporting Gazette* pronounced: 'It is not improbable that in Foster we
have one of the greatest batsmen that cricket has yet produced.' There
had been little time to attend lectures and in July he graduated with a
dismal fourth which is hardly a reflection on his intellect.

On 9 March 1901, England beat Ireland 3–0 at the Dell and Tip was
superb throughout, the *Manchester Guardian* evaluation being: 'Foster,
whose individual play was brilliant, shot whenever he got a chance,
which was not infrequently.' Tom Crawshaw of Sheffield Wednesday
put the home side into the lead in the first half during which Tip had
tested the Irish keeper with several rasping volleys. With ten minutes
remaining, George Hedley increased the English lead to two goals
and Tip scored a third in the closing seconds. Both the English full-
backs in this game were also double internationals. At right-back,
William Oakley had coped admirably with a barrage of Irish crosses.
Oakley was a world-class long jumper who had represented England
against the USA in 1895. Playing a jaunty if inconsistent game alongside him had been one C. B. Fry.

In mid-March, the Welsh side travelled to St James's Park for a 6–0 drubbing. The scoreline was unflattering, and for half an hour the visitors remained on level terms. Five minutes into the second half, Tip made a fine run and was brought down near the Welsh goal. 'Nudger' Needham, the Derbyshire cricketer, made no mistake with the penalty and a few minutes later England were awarded a free kick from just outside the box. Tip stretched the Welsh keeper with a thunderous shot and Steve Bloomer pounced on the rebound to put England two goals ahead. The home side scored four more, one of these being a solo effort from Tip from his own half-way line.

Twelve days later came England's biggest test of the season, the fixture against Scotland at Crystal Palace. The turf resembled a bog but Tip coped with the conditions adequately and after half an hour he supplied a pass which put England ahead. Scotland equalized early in the second half. The visitors then went 2–1 up, but with ten minutes to go, Steve Bloomer ran 20 yards to score a fine goal and secure a draw which owed much to the brilliance of the English goalkeeper John Sutcliffe. The chapter is degenerating into a celebration of contemporary sporting all-rounders, but it is worth noting that Sutcliffe was yet another double international. Back in 1889, he had played rugby for England against the Maoris. Tip's performance tailed off badly in the second half and *The Times* report includes: 'Foster, with his clever dribbling, was prominent, but his fondness for keeping the ball close did not succeed on the sodden ground, and after change of ends his methods quite failed.'

In 1901, he played his last full season of county cricket. In July he engineered a spectacular win against Surrey, scoring 135 after Worcestershire had collapsed to 17 for 3. In August, he made 111 against Derbyshire in just over an hour, and against Gloucestershire he trounced an attack including Gilbert Jessop for a robust 136. In first-class cricket his average was 50.66.

There were still manifold calls on his time and in September he was chosen to play soccer for an England amateur side against Germany at White Hart Lane. The scoreline will be an eye-opener for many: England won 12–0 at a canter. It should be noted that this was Germany's first international and the *Manchester Guardian* concludes: '... the English side discovered that it had a giant's superiority and proceeded to demonstrate the fact in a rather determined fashion.' Tip scored six goals and his tally would have been greater had the German keeper Lüdecke not played superbly.

He played his last soccer international in March of 1902, captaining ten professionals against Wales at Wrexham racecourse. There was much controversy over the state of the pitch, and the *Football Field* correspondent was at a loss: 'A racecourse is – well, a racecourse, not a football pitch.' The first half was even but the Welsh dominated much of the second. A Reuters wire describes how Tip scored a goal that was disallowed on the grounds that the Welsh goalkeeper was unsighted! In the second half the game petered out into a scoreless draw.

In August 1903, he married Diana Cammell. Diana was a granddaughter of Charles Cammell, a Sheffield steel magnate whose company, Cammell-Laird, had done much to introduce the first steel ships. They had one daughter, Joyce, who is now living in France. In correspondence with the author, Tip's granddaughter has recalled that Diana was petite, amusing and fashionable. The couple launched themselves into a hectic social programme. When not on the country house circuit, they entertained in style at their London home in Ovington Square with Tip singing regularly after dinner.

Tip had played little cricket during the season but was a surprise choice for Pelham Warner's tour to Australia in the winter of 1903–4. The voyage was a riot, much of the merriment emanating from Diana who travelled with the team as part of her honeymoon. Tip's young wife was an inveterate practical joker and in cahoots with Warner's fiancée, Agnes Blyth, she played good-natured tricks on the professionals, her favourite stooges being the diminutive Herbert Strudwick and her husband's county colleague, Ted Arnold. There were endless games of deck cricket during which the ladies would argue vociferously with the umpire, the hapless Bishop Welldon whose lbw decisions met with little approval. At a deck-sports day, George Hirst (variously impeded by Diana) won the obstacle race while Tip made up much ground to come third in the egg-and-spoon.

The social programme on board was hectic; at the fancy dress ball Warner took the honours as the Rajah of Bong while Tip and Diana won second prize as a pair of gondoliers. (Special commendation went to Herbert Strudwick who, with uncharacteristic daring, had filched Bishop Wheldon's cassock and gaiters.) When not playing games, Tip spent many hours looking for whales and preparing a ledger in which he detailed expenses and projected gate receipts. He had been trading successfully on the Stock Exchange for much of 1903 with the prominent brokers Cazenove, and Warner, who recognized his financial astuteness and gave him financial control of the tour.

There were various stop-overs and old George Hirst attracted many female admirers while charging round Colombo in a rickshaw. The tour itself is chronicled in Tip's personal diary, a battered exercise book now kept in the MCC Museum. It will be used here on the occasions that the author has been able to decipher his subject's appalling handwriting; unattributed quotations come from this journal. Tip was no Evelyn or Pepys; the diary is hardly confessional and his bride receives only cursory mentions. The tourists arrived in Melbourne on 12 November and the diary entry includes a revealing touch: 'This I hope will be the last time we stay in different hotels.' He is referring to Warner's insistence on separate accommodation for the amateurs and the professionals, a policy which Tip resented on general grounds but particularly since it meant separation from Ted Arnold.

By mid-November he was growing accustomed to Australian conditions, and against Victoria he scored 71. On the day after this match, R. E. and Bernard Bosanquet played golf at Sandringham where they threatened the course record and drove several of the par fours. At Newcastle he opened with Tom Hayward and raced to 105 in a shade over an hour. It was an ideal loosener; his greatest hour was upon him.

Warner and his team had much to prove as they lined up for the first Test at Sydney. MacLaren and Fry had been prevented from touring by financial constraints and were venting their frustration by knocking out some graceless articles in which they made gloomy predictions about the forthcoming series. These pieces were syndicated with much relish by the Australian nationals and the atmosphere was distinctly sour as the game got underway.

The home side made 285 and the England reply stuttered when Warner went for a duck and Hayward followed him shortly afterwards. However, at number three, Johnny Tyldesley played superbly to steady the innings. Tip came in when Tyldesley was bowled by Noble for 53. He was in woeful form for the rest of the day: 'I kept at it very slowly ... the ball was always doing something.' He gave several chances including a sitter to Syd Gregory when on 49, and Frank Iredale commented: 'I don't think I ever saw so large an innings start so badly.' At stumps on Saturday the England score was 243 for 4, Tip having accumulated 73 with much caution and not a little good fortune.

The wicket had eased by Monday and Tip reached his century with a cut off Frank Laver. He then raced to 175, beating Ranji's record score for England against Australia. He passed Syd Gregory's landmark of 201 off Gregory's own bowling and then overhauled Billy Murdoch's 211 at Kennington Oval in 1884. *Wisden* takes up the story: 'The third day was marked by the most brilliant and sensational cricket ... Foster, with a magnificent innings of 287, beating all records in Test matches. He was batting for seven hours, among his hits being 38 fours. The latter part of his innings was described as something never surpassed.'

Some extraordinary stands included 192 for the eighth wicket with Len Braund. More crucially, he and Wilfred Rhodes put on 130 for the tenth wicket in under an hour. At the time of writing, this remains an English Test record against all countries. The diary description includes: 'We both had our eyes in, and began to paste them properly.' The tourists' innings finally ended on 577 when Tip, who was visibly wilting, skied a drive off Jack Saunders. He had demonstrated maturity and patience and, towards the end, a massive contempt for the finest bowlers in the world. To date, the innings not only remains the highest score on Test début but it is also the highest score by an Englishman in a Test on Australian soil.

As a reply, Victor Trumper glided to the wicket and stroked an ethereal 185. Initially, he struggled against Rhodes and his discomfort prompted the prettiest compliment ever paid on a cricket field: 'For Heaven's sake, Wilfred, give me a moment's peace!' Trumper's score formed the nucleus of an Australian total of 485. In his second innings, having scored 19, Tip waltzed down the wicket to a Warwick Armstrong googly and was stumped by yards. There was another tremor when Braund went for a duck, but Hayward and Hirst steered the tourists to a comfortable victory by five wickets.

It had been the most extraordinary Test début of all time. Only six men have made centuries against Australia in their first Test match. They include W. G., Ranji, George Gunn and the Nawab of Pataudi. In July 1993, a Surrey player flicked Merv Hughes, Brendon Julian and Shane Warne around Trent Bridge to make 114 on international début. He is also a double international, having played schoolboy football for England against Holland, Wales and Scotland in 1987. Every indication is that he comes from the same drawer as his predecessors; his name is Graham Thorpe.

In late December, Tip and Ted Arnold missed the game against the Melbourne Juniors and spent several days fishing on the Yarra. Tip had assumed responsibility for Arnold's cultural development, and one evening he dragged him along to a production of *The Mikado*, taking much pleasure in Ted's obvious approval. He enthused about Gilbert and Sullivan and had a happy knack of embroidering his conversation with patter from the operas. Wreaths at Tip's funeral would include a tribute from the D'Oyly Carte.

The Melbourne Test started on New Year's Day 1904. Tip had picked up a chill in the nets. He came in at number four, and played a polished innings of 49 before retiring ill. His diary includes: 'Our fielding was disgraceful and seven catches were missed.' His chill worsened in the closing stages of the match and he was ordered to spend a week in a sanatorium. He spent three days there. On the second evening he enraged his nurses and captivated a large crowd when he escaped from the ward and went for a long walk with Diana around the Royal Botanical Gardens clad in his pyjamas and a fedora.

Tip rejoined the party for the third Test at Adelaide where he failed with 21 and 16 as Australia achieved a comfortable victory. However, he recovered his vitality and on the evening of his return to Melbourne we find him playing in a pick-up game of cricket with the hotel grooms. In Tasmania he scored 43 and 23 during a bad-tempered match in which he was quite scathing about a declaration decision by Warner. Tip was losing money on his expenses allowance and his humour was not improved when he and the rest of the side dropped a fortune on Harkaway, the favourite for the Hobart Cup. The head porter at the Imperial Hotel had sent the side off to Risdon Park full of enthusiasm and Dick Lilley and Len Braund who fancied themselves as judges of horseflesh were dispatched to the parade ring. They returned pronouncing themselves satisfied and the team waded in only to see Harkaway beaten by a head. Nobody spoke to Lilley and Braund for the rest of the week.

The tourists returned to Melbourne in early February and the move marked the beginning of a poor run for Tip. Against Victoria he fell for 7 to the pace of Frank Laver during a game in which he was enraged by Warner's poor man management: 'I have never seen a side captained worse than we were ... Warner has not kept the team together as he should.' Tip's innings of 19 and 27 on an awkward pitch in the fourth Test at Sydney did little to restore his confidence in another ill-tempered game during which spectators bombarded the outfield with watermelons.

By now he was debilitated by the humidity and his running between the wickets was processional. In the final Test at Adelaide, the tourists were skittled out in their first innings for 61. With 18 runs, Tip was England's highest scorer. The tourists were responding to a total of 247 and when the home side was dismissed for 133, Tip achieved a fair measure of success against Trumble who was turning the ball square. With 30, he was once more the top-scorer, falling to a one-handed catch by Trumper from the bowling of Noble. It was a futile gesture; England collapsed to 101 all out and defeat by 218 runs. In the final match of the tour, Tip came good with an exquisite 73 against South Australia. A soccer match was arranged for the day after, allowing a local promoter to bill-board Tip as 'the celebrated international'. He scored a languid goal with a thundering shot from near the half-way line and Warner recorded in his diary: 'Foster, of course, was a tower of strength, and carried everything before him.'

The team returned in triumph, though Tip left the main party in Paris to pursue business on the Bourse. By late April, he was back in London for a celebration banquet during which several guests quietly voiced the opinion that the tour would have been happier and more successful had Tip been captain. He had stood-in for Warner as both skipper and speech-maker, and though no orator, his candour and enthusiasm on the rostrum had contrasted with the fatuity of Warner's leaden clichés. He had also done much work to keep the professionals integrated with the amateurs and would often leave the top table in order to relax over a beer with Arnold, Hirst and Rhodes.

Tip had no private income, and the need to support Diana prevented him from playing first-class cricket in 1904. Nevertheless, *Cricket* describes how in May, he made 129 out of 175 for Butterflies against Eton College, complementing this performance with 6 wickets for 54 runs from his occasional (and very ordinary) fast medium. Like his contemporaries, Reggie Spooner and Stanley Jackson, Tip could pick up a bat after a long absence from the game and make runs at the highest level. He played no first-class cricket in 1905 until August when Worcestershire played Kent at New Road on an old-fashioned 'sticky-dog'. Tip ambled to the crease as third wicket down and proceeded to cane Colin Blythe and Edward 'Punter' Humphreys while making an awesome 246 not out.

On 1 July 1907, he became the only man to captain the full England cricket and soccer sides when he led England against South Africa at Lord's. As an occasional county captain, Tip had been prone to point-less declarations and while he had a sound technical knowledge, he was hardly a motivator. However, in a three-match series in which he won every toss, he led the side with authority and a fair measure of insight. In the first Test England scored 428 in her only innings. Sadly, the England captain had scored 8 when he was stumped by the South African captain Percy Sherwell from the bowling of Albert Vogler. (Sherwell was himself a double international and is a rare bird; he is one of few men to have played Test cricket and international tennis.) Tip was able to motivate his old friend Ted Arnold superbly, and Arnold took 5 for 37 as South Africa crumbled to 140 all out. Having been obliged to follow-on, Sherwell scored 115 and his side was placed on 185 for 3 when rain washed out the final day.

In Albert Vogler, Reggie Schwarz, Gordon White and Aubrey

Faulkner, the South Africans had an unusual side-show, a quartet of wrist-spinners. They fascinated Tip who contributed a technical evaluation of each bowler to the 1908 *Wisden*. The article is literate and sprightly but is the kind of piece which Arlott would have dismissed as 'filthily technical'. As characters, Tip's subjects warrant some digression. Two of them were double internationals: Schwarz played rugby for England and White played quasi-official soccer for South Africa. They were all eccentrics and they were all doomed. Vogler degenerated into a hopeless drunk, White died of his wounds on the Western Front two weeks before the Armistice, and Schwarz died a week after it of pneumonia contracted on active service. Having come through the war with a DSO, Faulkner set up an indoor cricket academy in London. The school became insolvent in 1930 and its director placed his head in a gas oven, his suicide note reading: 'I am off to a better world, via the bat room.'

Headingley was the venue for the second Test at the end of July, a game which C. B. Fry recalls as 'the tautest cricket match in which I ever played'. Having elected to bat, Tip was bowled by James Sinclair for a duck and Faulkner took 6 for 17 to dismiss the home side for 76. Rain had turned the wicket into a spinner's paradise and Colin Blythe bowled out the tourists for 110. Tip fell to Faulkner once more in the second innings for 22. Blythe took seven wickets in the second innings to give England victory by 53 runs and himself a match haul of 15 for 99. Ten years later, Blythe lay dead on the Somme.

Tip rushed from Headingley to Worcester, and on the following day he made a chanceless 174 against Kent. He played his last Test at the Oval in August where he finally hit form by making 51 and 35, the second innings being his side's top score in a total of 138. England were on the winning end of a draw, C. B. Fry having found unusual fluency to make 129 in the first innings.

After a three-year absence from the first-class game, he returned to county cricket in August 1910. At New Road against Yorkshire, he stroked an effortless 133. In three and a quarter hours he steered Worcestershire to a total of 205. On the August bank holiday of 1912, he played his last major innings, scoring 127 in style for MCC against a Public Schools XI at Lord's. It was a grand way to go out; less than two years later he was dead at the age of 36.

In his eight Test matches, Tip scored 602 runs at an average of 46.13. A 1903 profile in *Cricket* catalogues his gifts: 'Mr Foster has all the qualities which go to make up a great cricketer: quickness, suppleness of wrist, strength, great skill in placing, and a keen appreciation of the right ball to hit.' He was remarkably quick on his feet and his cover driving was often dazzling. The *Daily Chronicle* obituary includes: 'Without being at all like Ranji in his general method, he was not far behind that incomparable player in ease and rapidity of execution.'

Because he never grew old, Foster remains an unblemished symbol of the Edwardian ideal, a carefree virtuoso whose life appears to have been one long romp under the sun ... he embodies all the pathos of a young man mercifully ignorant of his own impending fate.

Benny Green (ed.), *The Wisden Papers 1888–1946*, 1989

Tip had a short backlift but an extravagant follow-through. Here is Cardus's summary: 'To give contemporary cricket lovers some idea of Foster I might do worse than describe him as a more flexible and sounder E. R. Dexter. Dexter's equal, even superior as a driver and a much finer cutter.' Tip used a light bat which was not much heavier than a Harrow, noting 'I can waggle it quicker.' He was unselfish in his running, and his pace between the wickets allowed journalists to pun on 'Tip and run'.

C. B. Fry notes: 'He is one of those cricketers who have all the faculties required for a batsman, and a graceful manner of using them.' As a fourth change bowler he had a fair turn of speed but few additional attributes though on his day he could beat anybody for pace. As a slip fielder he ranks with Wally Hammond and Bobby Simpson. In a 1942 radio broadcast, Pelham Warner, who played with and against Tip for 16 years, insisted that he could not remember him missing a catch.

C. B. Fry has also summarized Tip the soccer player: "Foster was tall and long-limbed and quick without being fast. He had fine dexterity of foot, and controlled the ball, caressed and persuaded it with an almost manual cunning. His feet had, as it were, the Oxford accent.' His favourite position was centre-half but he was adept as a wing forward and made several creditable performances as an emergency goalkeeper. He was an exceptionally speedy dribbler and as elusive as a dog at a fair.

In 1913, Tip's constitution was ravaged by insulin-dependent diabetes. In the spring he travelled to South Africa to convalesce and *The Times* for 10 May reports that 'the latest accounts of him are very encouraging'. This was idle fancy; he returned to his home in Knightsbridge shortly after showing no improvement. Diabetic keto acidosis was resulting in frequent comas. Banting and Best would begin injecting their patients with insulin only seven years later, but at the time there was little understanding of diabetes and still less in the way of treatment. Tip's condition worsened in the second week of May 1914 when he was weakened by a chill. At 11 a.m. on 13 May he was gone.

He had always been adored by the professionals. While Lord Hawke and Lord Harris were trotting out cloying verbiage in the broadsheets, an *Evening News* correspondent had the sense to go and see Jack Hobbs who was visibly shaken: '... the finest batsman ever seen in county and international cricket; a thousand pities'.

Many photographs of Tip suggest a Regency quality. He was certainly a resourceful, innovative, and at times outlandish dresser. While the rest of the team on the 1903–4 tour to Australia are usually seen in regulation blazer and slacks, Tip is conspicuous in a bizarre flannel suit and extravagant felt hat.

By 1947, the Somerset leg-spinner Len Braund was a double amputee. In his dotage, few visitors left his bedside without being told of his proudest moment. It had occurred in Sydney 44 years earlier and was of course the afternoon when he had put on 192 for England's eighth wicket at Sydney with R. E. Foster. Here is a similar detail that could bring tears to a glass eye. In August of 1938, Len Hutton made 364 runs against Australia at the Oval to shatter Tip's record score for England in Ashes matches. When Sir Len returned home he found his house littered with telegrams of congratulation from the great and the good. Towards the bottom of the pile was a short but heartfelt message from a parson's widow in Malvern. Sir Len made some enquiries about the sender. It was of course Tip's mother; her son had been dead for 24 years.

At the time of writing, Tip Foster holds two records; his 287 at Sydney is still the highest score by an English batsman in a Test in Australia, and he remains the only man to have captained the full England cricket and soccer teams. The first record will go; the second distinction will be Tip's for all time.